PM48

PORT MANAGEMENT AND OPERATIONS

LLOYD'S PRACTICAL SHIPPING GUIDES

Other titles in this series are:

Chartering Documents
4th edition
by Harvey Williams

The Hague and Hague-Visby Rules
4th edition
by John Richardson

*ISM Code: A Practical Guide
to the Legal and Insurance Implications*
by Philip Anderson

Laytime and Demurrage in the Oil Industry
by Malcolm Edkins and Ray Dunkley

Marine Claims
2nd edition
by Christof Luddeke

Maritime Law
6th edition
by Chris Hill

Neil Cockett on Bunkers
by Neil Cockett

Principles of Maritime Law
by Susan Hodges and Chris Hill

The Handbook of Maritime Economics and Business
by Costas Th. Grammenos

*Combined Transport Documents:
A Handbook of Contracts for the
Combined Transport Industry*
by John Richardson

PORT MANAGEMENT AND OPERATIONS

BY

PROFESSOR PATRICK M. ALDERTON

M.Phil., Extra Master, Dip.Maths, M.C.I.T.

SECOND EDITION

LLP

LONDON HONG KONG

2005

Informa Professional
(a trading division of T & F Informa UK Ltd)
Informa House
30–32 Mortimer Street
London W1W 7RE
professional.enquiries@informa.com

FAR EAST
Informa Professional Asia
No 1 Grange Road
#08–02 Orchard Building
Singapore
professional.asia@informa.com

First edition 1999
Second edition 2005

British Library Cataloguing in Publication Data
A catalogue record for this book
is available from the
British Library

ISBN 1-84311-422-4

Text set in 10/12pt Postscript Plantin by Tony Lansbury, Tonbridge, Kent
Printed in Great Britain by MPG Books, Bodmin, Cornwall

PREFACE

The aim of this book is to give a universal presentation of the essential elements of ports, covering their administration, management, economics and operation. As ports are among the oldest forms of transport infrastructure which have remained in continuous use, and have been a vital part in the social and economic growth of regions, it is necessary to consider, at least briefly, the historic development of ports in order to understand many of their facets.

The purpose of this book is to give a complete picture of the ports industry so that those involved with ports can see their own specific field of interest in perspective and understand how the basic model of the port operates within Maritime Transport Industry. Maritime Transport is a rapidly changing industry and, since the Second World War, it is not sufficient to learn one's business by "sitting next to Nellie". Modern transport professionals must be able to adapt to, and anticipate the implications of, changes in the industry. Perhaps one of the most important aspects of modern management is the ability to manage change and it is hoped that this book will give an insight as to how port management has coped with change over the last century. This book also endeavours to stress the importance of ports, a factor which is often overlooked. When Gary Crook of UNCTAD was asked for a suitable title, he suggested "Ports: The misunderstood key to prosperity".

Such an approach has become an integral part of most of the professional and academic courses that are concerned with Shipping, Ports and Transport. The structure and content of this book are based on the lectures given to, and the interaction I have had with, students in London and at the World Maritime University in Malmö over the last 25 years.

In this second edition I have taken the opportunity to update the material, include any new developments (such as the ISPS code), and respond to user comments and any criticisms arising from the first edition.

I have tried to avoid the unnecessary use of jargon in this book and hope that the text will be readily understandable to those with little knowledge of ports but yet have sufficient depth to be of interest and value to those professionally engaged in the industry.

Where possible I have quoted actual figures and statistics, as I have found it easier for students to grasp the relative merits of the size, importance and value of a thing or concept by giving actual data. However, students should be aware that even the highest authorities will not always agree on statistics as, in their collection and selection, different assumptions may be possible; the precise control of the laboratory is not usually available in the actual commercial situation.

It is not anticipated that this book will answer all the reader's questions on ports but it is hoped that it will stimulate their curiosity on the subject. I have also personally found that disagreement on a subject can provide as valuable an educational insight as agreement.

When discussing various aspects of those persons engaged in ports and shipping, I have tended to use the pronouns he and him, rather than she or her. This is not meant to be sexist but merely an attempt to save paper and to avoid being verbally tedious. Although the world of ports and shipping has tended to be a male dominated business, women do now occupy many of the highest positions in the industry and the terms he and she can in nearly all cases be considered interchangeable.

PATRICK M. ALDERTON
December 2004

ACKNOWLEDGEMENTS

I would like to thank my colleagues and friends at the World Maritime University in Malmö and those at what was the London Guildhall University and is now the London Metropolitan University. I would also like to thank those professionally working in the industry who have helped me, not only with data but who have exchanged views with me over coffee during the last 25 years or so. A special acknowledgement of gratitude is also due to those students who have been so helpful and usually so patient in developing and testing not only the material, but also the emphasis and structure.

It would of course be invidious to mention any particular names from the many experienced and talented persons I have been fortunate enough to be associated with during the period of compiling this book, but I must thank Professor Ted Samson for his section on the "Basic Argument" in the Chapter on Port Environmental Matters.

Finally, I must thank my wife, Mary, for the time she has spent correcting the manuscripts.

CONTENTS

Preface	v
Acknowledgements	vii
List of figures	xiii

CHAPTER ONE: PORTS ✓   1
Introduction—Definitions—the importance of ports—fundamental observations—the main functions and features of a port—the main facilities and services provided—different types of port—information about ports—conclusion.

CHAPTER TWO: PORT DEVELOPMENT   17
Introduction—Factors constraining port development—growth of world trade—growth of the world's leading ports—changes in growth—leading ports for specific cargoes—physical development of a major port—developments in port location—financing port development—developments in terminal design and operation from 1800 to present day.

CHAPTER THREE: IMPACT OF CHANGING
SHIP TECHNOLOGY ON PORTS   43
Ship Developments which influence Port Development—tonnage—growth of tonnage—development of propulsion—ship size—ship type and specialisation—increasing size of container ships—Hatchsize, perhaps the most significant technical development—effect of port time on ships' speed—changes in management attitudes.

CHAPTER FOUR: SEA APPROACHES
AND MARITIME SERVICES   61
Vessel traffic services—organisations concerned with the sea approaches of a port—agents—safety at the ship/port interface-port security—port security & the ISPS Code—port state control—dangerous cargoes—environmental protection provided by the port—Dock Regulations 1988

relating to Marine Department's operations—licensing of river works and dredging—hydrographic surveying—pilotage—tugs—bunker supply —customs, immigration and health officials.—changing water depth— tides—Inland Transport—as an alternative to sea transport—shoreside distribution and analysis of modal split—logistics and/or intermodal transport—comparison of transport modes, i.e. which is best suited for what—modal split.

CHAPTER FIVE: PORT ADMINISTRATION,
OWNERSHIP AND MANAGEMENT   91
Basic problems for port management—types of port ownership and administration—survey of ownership of port activities—why increased private sector participation—ways of increasing private sector participation—boards governing ports—port development from a transport centre to a logistic platform—the rise and fall of ports—a free port or zone— port management objectives—the port as an economic multiplier—competition between ports—information technology (it) in logistics—port efficiency—port safety and security.

CHAPTER SIX: PORT POLICY   117
General points on maritime policy-corruption—national port planning —EU port and transport policy—relationship between port and state— constraining influences on port management—port ownership—port and state financial assistance—port pricing.

CHAPTER SEVEN: BERTHS & TERMINALS   131
Number of berths required in a port—terminal productivity definitions— how to reduce waiting time—land productivity—berth size, type and layout—equipment and terminal layout—cruise ship terminals—dry bulk terminals—tanker terminals—berth maintenance—alternatives to formal port systems—port logistics and distriparks.

CHAPTER EIGHT: CARGO & CARGO HANDLING   149
Definitions—stowage factors—pre-shipment planning, stowage plan and on-board stowage—ship stresses and stability—developments in cargo-handling and terminal operation—benchmarking for quality standards —cargo positioning and stowage on the terminal—facts concerning the container—equipment development and definitions—purchase, maintenance and control of equipment—safety of labour and cargo— cargo security—warehouse technology.

CHAPTER NINE: PORT LABOUR   175
Labour development—how dockers were employed—how dockers were

paid—unions—numbers employed—labour split—gang size—labour versus technology—tonnage and labour—technological change and improved operation—how labour is managed—training.

CHAPTER TEN: TIME IN PORT & SPEED
OF CARGO HANDLING   189
Port time and cargo handling speeds for sailing vessels, general cargoes, containers, bulk cargoes, tankers—general operational delays—strikes —port time other than berth time—weather delays—congestion— compensation—port productivity -basic data a port should collect—safety of cargo.

CHAPTER ELEVEN: PORT COSTS, PRICES & REVENUE   209
How much does a port cost—development of port costs—shipowners' major costs—total port charges—average port disbursements—cargo- handling costs—stevedoring rates—typical port revenue and expendi- ture—port pricing—who sets the prices—costs and cost centres—port finance and profitability.

CHAPTER TWELVE: PORT ENVIRONMENTAL
MATTERS—SUSTAINABLE DEVELOPMENT   223
Port environmental matters—sustainable development—the organisa- tions concerned and their involvement—causes of port environmental pollution—port and harbour related pollution types, sources and environmental effects—policies for sustainable development in a port— emergency plans, personnel and training.

Index   241

LIST OF FIGURES

Figure 1:   The Port of Sines 11

Figure 2:   The Port of London 14

Figure 3:   Factors constraining port development 18

Figure 4:   Growth in world trade 19

Figure 5:   A "model" port 28

Figure 6:   Layout for a typical berth (1850–1900) 31

Figure 7:   Typical breakbulk general cargo terminals
             (1900, 1920, 1960) 34

Figure 8:   Growth in world container tonnage 35

Figure 9a: Container Terminal, 1970 38

Figure 9b: Container Terminal, 1980 39

Figure 9c: Container Terminal, 1990 40

Figure 10:   Ship and cargo tons 44

Figure 11:   Typical relationship between LOA and Dwt 46

Figure 12:   Growth of world GRT 47

Figure 13:   Growth of the average ship size (GT) showing the
             number of ships with a draft greater than 13 metres 52

Figure 14:   Increasing size of container ships 53

Figure 15:   Economies of scale expected for larger container ships .. 55

Figure 16:   Direct and better "spotting" with open hatches 56

Figure 17:   Sea approaches 62

Figure 18:   Vessel traffic services 65

Figure 19:   Modes of distribution 86

Figure 20:   Private Sector involvement in Ports 97

Figure 21:   Constraining influences on port management 124

Figure 22:   Optimum of berths required in a port 131

Figure 23:   Relationship between berth occupancy ratio and
             waiting ratio 133

Figure 24:   Conventional breakbulk general cargo berth 137

Figure 25:   General layout of a container terminal 137

Figure 26:   Traffic Paths 138

xiv List of Figures

Figure 27: Tanker berth 143
Figure 28: Distance from ship/shore interface to storage 144
Figure 29: Cross section of a ship inclined by external forces 155
Figure 30: London—cargo tons v dockers 165
Figure 31: Types of cranes 167
Figure 32: Some of the many varieties of cargo gear available
from a specialist stevedore supplier 168
Figure 33: Gross average speed of cargo-handling per hatch for
the entire stay in port 191
Figure 34: Relationship between ship size and cargo
handling speed 191
Figure 35: If using several cranes to load and discharge 193
Figure 36: Scale loading speed for Richard's Bay 195
Figure 37: Basic data a port should collect 205
Figure 38: Port productivity 206
Figure 39: Development of port costs 211
Figure 40: Shipowners' major costs expressed as a percentage 212
Figure 41: Comparison of oil consumption per person around
the world 224
Figure 42: Global population and oil consumption in 2025 225
Figure 43: Who arranges for reception facilities 234

CHAPTER ONE

PORTS

Introduction—some basic points—the importance of ports—fundamental observations concerning ports—main functions and features of a port—main facilities and services provided by a port—some definitions—different types of port—information about ports—conclusion.

INTRODUCTION

The purpose of this introductory chapter is to introduce and stress a few basic points which need to be made at the beginning. Many of these points will be repeated and amplified at later stages throughout the book where the analysis of the topic requires greater detail.

Throughout the book I have included some historical details going back to the beginning of the last century. This is included not just to entertain those with historical interests but to try to give an understanding to those wishing to grasp how and why a modern port operates and functions. Most of the world's major ports invested heavily in developing their infrastructure during the last century. Much of this is still visible and in many cases this heritage still forms part of the infrastructure that the modern port manager and port operator has to deal with. There can be very few, if any, large commercial undertakings which have to perform in the modern world encumbered with such a legacy from the past and until plastic disposable ports are developed, presumably this problem will continue. This is why port management needs to get its forecasting right. However, it is not just the geographical location and physical design that history can explain but also, and perhaps more importantly, the Zeitgeist and working culture of port labour can in most cases be really understood only when studied in its historical context. Further, as stressed in the introduction, modern transport professionals must be able to adapt to, and anticipate the implications of changes in the industry. Perhaps one of the most important aspects of modern management is the ability to manage change and it is hoped that this book will give an insight as to how port management has coped with change over the last century. The analysis of past performance is the basis of virtually all forecasting and our ability to anticipate the optimum solutions to the port decisions required in the next century can be focused by insights gained from the last.

SOME BASIC POINTS

Seaports are areas where there are facilities for berthing or anchoring ships and where there is the equipment for the transfer of goods from ship to shore or ship to ship. To use more modern jargon, it is a ship/shore interface or a maritime intermodal interface. From an historical point of view the customs facility is important because without it no international commercial intercourse was legally possible. In many older ports the most imposing piece of architecture on the waterfront is the Custom House.

The major reference books on ports list between 3,500 to 9,000 ports in the world. The reason why the figure varies is that the meaning and definition of a port can vary. At one end of the scale a large estuarial port may contain many terminals which may be listed as separate ports. At the other end of the scale not every place where a small vessel anchors to offload cargo may be listed as a port.

THE IMPORTANCE OF PORTS

Ports should be considered as one of the most vital aspects of a national transport infrastructure. For most trading nations they are:

— The main transport link with their trading partners and thus a focal point for motorways and railway systems.
— A major economic multiplier for the nation's prosperity. Not only is a port a gateway for trade but most ports attract commercial infrastructure in the form of banks, agencies, etc, as well as industrial activity.

Ports should also be considered as one of the most important aspects of maritime transport because they are the location:

— Where most maritime accidents happen. This is inevitable, as it is a focal point, usually in shallow water, where ships converge.

— Where cargo is damaged or stolen. Again this is inevitable as a port is a place where the cargo is handled and a place where valuables are concentrated. One of the initial reasons for building enclosed docks at the beginning of the last century was to reduce theft. However, with full container loads reducing handling in port and the increasing speed of throughput the significance of this element should be reducing.

— Where repairs are carried out. Although a port is obviously the only place where many repairs can be attempted the more modern practice of planned maintenance means that shipowners can plan at which port the repairs or maintenance will be done.

— Where most costs are incurred. Although some of these costs and delays form part of the essential and inevitable activities of a port, others, such as documentary costs and delays, are simply part of an historical tradition which could and should be changed.

— Where delays are most likely to occur.

— Where surveys take place.

— Where most shipping services are located, e.g. agents, brokers, etc. This still seems to be the case in spite of modern communication systems

— Where industries are situated. This has greatly accelerated since World War II.

— Where cargoes come from.

— Where customs and government policies are implemented.

Dr Ernst Frankel, in his book *Port Planning and Development* (1986), estimates that "... only 40–45% of all transport costs in international trade are payable for productive transportation. For general cargo the figure is probably only 33%". Much of the extra cost and delay occurs in ports (but is not necessarily caused by ports). As indicated, ports are places where numerous controls are imposed, such as documentary controls, finance controls, import controls, etc. For obvious reasons ports have developed as areas of storage while cargo waits for distribution, further processing or onward movement.

4   Ports

In Japan where there are officially classified 1,100 ports and harbours (21 of which are rated as major ports for international trading) the multiple role of a port is well recognised as a:

— Distribution centre
— Industrial zone and energy supply base.
— Mercantile trading centre – attracting banks, brokers and traders.
— Urbanisation and city redevelopment centre.
— Life activity base – this is particularly the case for the smaller rural ports.
— Maritime leisure base – yacht marinas, dockside recreation facilities, cruise ship terminal.

Note of the 21 ports rated as major ports in Japan, Yokohama, Tokyo, Kobe, Nagoya and Osaka handle the greater percentage of foreign containerised trade. Kobe had been number 6 in the world league of container ports before the great Hanshin earthquake in the early 1990s reduced its position seriously. However, by 1997 it had recovered 80% of its previous container throughput and by 2002 was rated number around 24 in the container traffic league. This is a good example of the effect of a natural catastrophe on a port and the ability of good management to overcome such disaster.

FUNDAMENTAL OBSERVATIONS CONCERNING PORTS

— Ports tend to be large civil engineering undertakings with huge sunk costs. They also tend to last much longer than the vehicles that use them. If a shipowner makes a mistake in the type or size of ship he buys he can usually recoup his losses by selling his mistake. A port manager will usually find it more difficult and costly to dispose of his mistakes.
— A ship is an entity, whereas a port is simply a collection of activities. This makes it more difficult to talk about ports in general. A small ship has many technical and operational features in common with a large ship but it is some times difficult to see what a small fishing port in a developing country has in common with, say, Rotterdam.
— Most ships and ship operators are international in their design and ways of working, whereas ports tend to be more parochial in that they reflect their local commercial attitudes, practices,

laws and working practices. The duties of, say, the ship's captain are similar regardless of flag, whereas the duties of the port harbour master can differ considerably between countries.

— Since the advent of intermodalism, ports now have to compete for cargo very much more than in the past – hence the great interest in increasing port efficiency and value-added activities over the last few years. (Value-added activities are described by UNCTAD as – "The term added value signifies value newly added or created in the productive process of an enterprise. Loading and discharging are certainly value-adding activities, so are the industrial services of a port noted earlier. In a distribution centre, added value can take different forms such as cargo-consolidation and deconsolidation – providing up-to-date information on the inventory and cargo movements, stuffing/unstuffing containers, crating; palletisation, shrink-wrapping, labelling, weighing, repackaging etc.")

— Ports provide an economic multiplier for a region and many ports now carry out Economic Impact Studies to determine which aspects of their work should be encouraged. It should also be remembered that ports are not only "gateways" for cargo but also obvious sites for industry, banks, agents, storage depots and distribution centres. They have in addition been large employers of labour.

— Ports are also an important part of a nation's transport infrastructure and must be part of national transport planning, which is why any national government or local government will wish to have some input into the general port strategic planning.

— Up to the mid-nineteenth century ships were small and could approach most creeks and estuaries. Since then they have grown steadily until the 1950s, after which ship size increased rapidly. This increase in size created problems for most ports, particularly as regards water depth, the width of dock entrances and berth length. Many terminals became obsolete.

— The increase in ship size caused changes in trading patterns in order to gain the advantages of economies of scale. Large ships must trade between large ports, with ample deep water, leaving smaller ships (feeder vessels) to distribute the cargo to smaller ports. Ships used to go to the cargo – now cargo goes to the ship. These large ports are now referred to as *centre* ports and the trading pattern as *hub and spoke*. It is also important to note that it is the large powerful liner shipowners who ultimately decide whether or not a port becomes a centre port, not the port management. The port management can, however, create a milieu that is attractive to the big multinational container carriers.

MAIN FUNCTIONS AND FEATURES OF A PORT

Civil engineering features

— Sea and land access.
— Infrastructures for ships berthing.
— Road and rail network.
— Industrial area management.

Administrative functions

— Control of vehicles, all modes, entering and leaving the port.
— Environmental control.
— Control of dangerous cargo.
— Safety and security within the port area.
— Immigration, health, customs and commercial documentary control.

Operational functions

— Pilotage, tugging and mooring activities.
— Use of berths, sheds, etc.
— Loading, discharging, storage and distribution of cargo.

MAIN FACILITIES AND SERVICES PROVIDED BY A PORT

Services and Facilities for Ships	Services and Facilities for Cargo
Arrival and departure	*Basic*
Navigation aids and VTS	Cargo handling on ship and on quay
Approach channel	Transport to/from storage
Pilotage, tugs and mooring gangs	Storage/warehousing
Locks (if tidal)	Tallying, marking, weighing, surveying
Berths	Surveillance, protection, sanitary measures
Administrative formalities	Dangerous cargo segregation
Police, immigration, customs, health	Customs and documentary control
Supplies, water, bunkers	Receiving and delivery
Telephone, repairs, medical, waste disposal	**Additional "added value" services**
Port state control	Repackaging, labelling, sorting, assembling
Cargo transfer	Cleaning and preparing cargo
Opening/closing of hatches	Setting up a logistic network
Breaking out/stowing	Setting up a marketing package

One of the important points to be underlined on reading through these lists of functions, features, facilities and services that exist within most ports, is the breadth and variety of skills and activities that are taking place, bearing in mind the preceding list only contains the more important and significant factors.

SOME DEFINITIONS

Operational definitions

Port. A town with a harbour and facilities for a ship/shore interface and customs facilities.

Harbour. A shelter, either natural or artificial, for ships.

Dock. An artificially constructed shelter for shipping.

Lock. In tidal waters the majority of docks have been maintained at a fixed depth of water by making the access to them through a lock, which allows the ship to be raised or lowered as it enters or leaves the dock.

The advantages are:
1. A constant depth of water can be maintained.
2. Cargo handling between ship and shore is easier.
3. The ship's mooring lines do not need constant attention.

The disadvantages are:
1. Increase in capital cost. It is also a constructional feature difficult to alter if changes in ship design make it too short or narrow. This has been a problem with many ageing ports in tidal waters.
2. Extra time and possible delays for the ship when arriving and leaving.

Breakwater or Mole. A long solid structure, built on the seaward side of the harbour, for protection against the weather, rough seas and swell.

Wharf. A structure built along the shore where vessels can berth alongside.

Pier or Jetty. A structure built out from the shore or river bank on masonry, steel or wooden piles for berthing ships. It is not a solid structure and should not greatly impede the flow of tide or current. However, both these terms are often used with considerable variations.

Dolphin. An isolated islet of piles or masonry to assist in the berthing or manoeuvring of ships.

Stevedore. A person employed in moving the cargo on or off the ship. This is again a term with many local variations. For instance, in London it was the term for one of the skilled team who stowed the cargo on board the ship but after Lord Devlin's report the many traditional functional terms used in this area were abandoned in favour of the all-embracing term "docker".

Tug. A small power-driven vessel used in ports and harbours to:

— Tow barges and other unpowered craft between required locations within the harbour. In the early days of sail they were among the first steam vessels to be developed as they were very useful in helping sailing craft in and out of port.

— Help large vessels to manoeuvre in and out of locks and on and off their berths.

— Help in salvage and rescue situations. Many will be equipped with fire fighting and pollution control equipment.

A modern harbour tug will probably have a bollard pull of somewhere between 20 to 70 tons.

Legal definitions

Port means an area within which ships are loaded with and/or discharged of cargo and includes the usual places where ships wait for their turn or are ordered or obliged to wait for their turn no matter the distance from that area.

If the word *port* is not used, but the port is (or is to be) identified by its name, this definition shall still apply.

Safe Port (see chapter four) means a port which, during the relevant period of time, the ship can reach, enter, remain at and depart from without, in the absence of some abnormal occurrence, being exposed to danger which cannot be avoided by good navigation and seamanship.

Berth means the specific place where the ship is to load and/or discharge. If the word *berth* is not used, but the specific place is (or is to be) identified by its name, this definition shall still apply.

Safe Berth means a berth which, during the relevant period of time, the ship can reach, remain at and depart from without, in the absence of some abnormal occurrence, being exposed to danger which cannot be avoided by good navigation and seamanship.

DIFFERENT TYPES OF PORT

Ports can be classified in two large groups – by Function and by Geographic Type:

By function

(A) A cargo interface

(1) *Hub or centre port,* also sometimes referred to as a mega port, direct-call port, hub and load centre port, megahub (greater than 4mn TEUs per annum where a TEU = Twenty-foot Equivalent Unit), superhub (greater than 1 million TEUs per annum), load centre port, pivot port, etc. The variations are almost endless but different authors can use them with subtle variations. (See comment at end of section.)

In the past ports tended to be either simply large major ports dealing with international trade or smaller local ports serving the needs of its own hinterland with mainly coastal or short sea shipping. As inland transport developed larger ports became larger and smaller ports smaller. The advent of intermodal transport and larger ships meant a change in the economics of international transport. Cargo began to move by feeder ships or inland transport modes to large hub or centre ports where large fast container ships moved the containers to other strategically located hub ports around the world.

The concept of hub ports has developed since it was first introduced a couple of decades ago. Originally the general consensus seemed to be that the hub port would naturally be formed by the largest container port in the region or the port for which ships had the most cargo. The idea of creating a major hub port which was neither the origin or destination of any cargo would have been firmly squashed, as it was in the case of Falmouth in the early 1980s.

However, ideas are changing, and we are now seeing hubs located at an intermediate point along a pendulum route with zero local cargo to offer, e.g. Malta (Marsaxlokk), Freeport (Bahamas) and Salalah (Oman). Such ports as these tend to be interchange ports for large vessels rather than hub and spoke ports for large vessels and feeders.

According to an H.P. Drewry Report in 1997, 78% of container throughput at the Port of Singapore in 1996 consisted of transshipment containers, while at Algeciras it was 90%. The same report estimated that two-thirds of the rise at the 20 major hub ports was not due to global traffic growth but caused by an increase in transhipment. It was also estimated that between 1980 and 1990 the number of transhipment containers had been growing at an average of 14% per annum. In 2003 it was estimated that 82% of all containers are trans-shipped

When considering the economics of hub and spoke feeder services one should remember that in the late 1990s the minimum terminal handling cost per trans-shipment container was probably be in the region of 500 USD.

As the large international liner companies are the major decision-makers when it comes to designating a hub port, they will not want one port to achieve monopoly status in a region. One would anticipate therefore that they will endeavour to ensure that at least two ports of hub port status are competing in a region to safeguard their bargaining position.

Relationship between total cost of direct-call and feeder alternatives

One of the major points of discussion concerning ports is whether this division of ports into centre ports and feeder ports will continue indefinitely. It may be that it is a passing phase of development in the early stages of the growth of containerisation, together with unbalanced global trade at the end of the 20th century. If the volume of trade is large enough, distribution via feeder vessels is obviously not the optimum solution. On the one hand, trading between centre ports enables the carrier to take advantage of the economies of scale offered by large container ships. On the other hand there are the extra costs and potential delays caused by having to re-ship the containers on to a smaller feeder ship for distribution. The volume of traffic therefore becomes the decisive factor. The volume in this context is, for a particular port, the number of obtainable TEUs per week by a shipping line in relation to a specified maritime route. Thus a shipping line should use feeder services as long as the traffic at its disposal on a maritime route is fewer than "x" TEUs per week (both import and export). Professor Shuo Ma suggested in the early 1990s that between an Asian and a European port x=580.

A case study of a possible new hub/centre port

The town of Sines, in the south of Portugal, is quite small but has a long history as a fishing port with a small general cargo terminal.

It was the birth place of Vasco de Gama. Over the last few years it has taken advantage of its deep water to develop as a tanker terminal but its small hinterland and relatively poor inland transport connections had made the port management of Sines before, around 1997, not sure whether the port could make any major development into containerisation. However, with the increasing success of the new generation of hub ports on pendulum routes, the port of Sines reassessed its potential. In June 1999, a concession was given to PSA to run a deep water container terminal which opened in 2003 with 320 metres of quay

The port of Sines has:

— An excellent geographical position. In fact it is virtually on
   the point where the main shipping routes to and from
   Asia, Africa and the Americas converge on north-western
   Europe.
— Deep water approaches and terminals.
— Room to expand – see sketch maps of Sines.
— An enthusiastic and competent management.

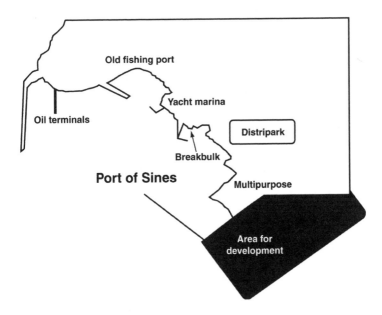

Figure 1: The Port of Sines

Another good example of a newly developed hub port is Gioia Tauro. It is situated in Southern Italy and handled its first container in August 1995. By 1997 the new port had a throughput of over a million TEUs. By the end of 1997 Gioia Tauro had a quay length of over three kilometres, a depth alongside ranging from 12.5 metres to 15 metres and 14 post-Panamax cranes. This is not a development in an old established port but a new purpose-built transport investment.

The port of Sepetiba, which is situated on the Brazilian coast between Rio de Janeiro and Santos, was reported in the maritime press in April 1998 to have plans to be a major hub for the east coast of South America.

In February 2003 *Lloyd's List* reported a possible new $390 mn project for a new deepwater Tangier-Med. port.

(2) *Feeder port* – to feed and distribute cargo from 1.
(3) *Entrepot or transit port.*
(4) *Domestic port*, i.e. a natural outlet for surrounding hinterland.

(B) A MIDAS (Maritime Industrial Development Area)

This was a term that became part of port jargon in the mid 1960s to cover the port development which had been taking place gradually since World War II. Industries such as petro-chemicals, oil refineries, steel works saw the advantages of locating themselves in port areas to take advantage of cheap transport of bulk raw materials. For this to occur there had to be deep water access, available land and demand for the product. A MIDAS can be one or more of the following:

(5) *Large industrial zone* with its own marine transport terminal.
(6) *Custom free port*
(7) *Oil port.*

(C) Specific Ship/Shore Interface

(8) *Naval port*
(9) *Fishing port*
(10) *Specific Commodity Export Port*, for example (quoting 2000 tonnages)
    Coal—Qinhuangdao (China) 83.8 million tonnes, Richards Bay (South Africa) 68.9 million tonnes, Hay Point

(Australia) 69.4 million tonnes, Port of Virginia (USA) 20.3 million tonnes.

Iron Ore—Tubarao Praia, Mole (Brazil) 68.3 million tonnes, Port Hedland (Australia) 68.5 million tonnes, Dampier (Australia) 65.9 million tonnes, Saldanha Bay (South Africa) 24 million tonnes, Narvik (Norway) 11.8 million tonnes.

A large port such as Rotterdam can be many of these.

By geographic type

This classification is almost endless, so only the more important types are considered here.

(1) Coastal submergence—New York and Southampton.
(2) Ryas (submerged estuaries)—Falmouth, Rio.
(3) Tidal estuaries—Bristol, London, Antwerp.
(4) Artificial harbours—Dover.
(5) Rivers (non-tidal)—Montreal.

The recognition of a geographic type may give one an insight into its operating advantages or disadvantages, e.g. a tidal estuarial port will probably require more expensive surveying and dredging, than a closed dock system.

The port of London is a good example of an estuarial port. Note that the ports on the Medway are under a different authority. The port of London also illustrates the process described in Chapter Two of how, as ports develop, their centres of operation tend to move towards the sea. It started in Roman times at London Bridge and would have moved to the Maplin Sands in the 1970s if the port management had had its way. Note also the sheer size of the port and the diversity of activities that take place within its boundaries.

INFORMATION ABOUT PORTS

Most large ports will of course have their own web page on the internet and there are several comprehensive reference books on world ports. However, over the last five years or so Fairplay has compiled this information on a computer disk and it is available both in the *Fairplay World Shipping Encyclopaedia* or on the disc called *World Ports*. By being available in disc form the information is not only easier and cheaper to send around the world and be kept

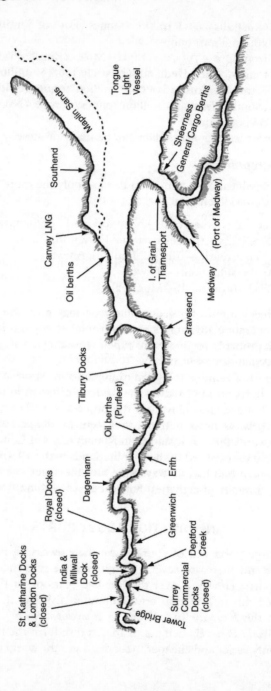

Figure 2: The Port of London

up to date, but the search facilities enable the user to easily find and select the data that is really needed. The information on each port includes a complete port description with charts and photographs (the latter only on the *World Ports* disc), pre-arrival information for ships, navigational considerations, information on berths , cargoes and port dues. It concludes with a comprehensive list of general information and addresses.

There is also a *Guide to Port Entry* which is available on disc.

CONCLUSION

One must also remember that ports have not developed simply as industrial and commercial trading centres. They have also been the points where foreign cultures and ideas have impacted on a nation. Shanghai, Bombay, Rio, Liverpool and a hundred other great port cities owe much of their flamboyant past to their maritime connections. Large modern ships with small crews, berthed well away from populated zones will no longer create the dynamic if racy waterfront areas so well described by maritime authors of yore. Such traces as are now left are being preserved as tourist areas, such as the Nyhaven in Copenhagen or the Reeperbahn in Hamburg.

The conclusion to this first introductory chapter is therefore that ports as such are a very loose and diverse concept. They are often more than a transport interface and a focal point of an areas inland transport infrastructure as they will invariably involve a large capital investment, be a regional economic multiplier and a large employer of labour. All of this will make them important pawns in the political arena of the area. I hope that this book will help to clarify the concept of a port and give a clearer understanding as to its function, purpose, operation and possible future development.

CHAPTER TWO

PORT DEVELOPMENT

Introduction—factors constraining port development—growth of world trade—growth of the world's leading ports—changes in growth—leading ports for specific cargoes—physical development of a major port—developments in port location—financing port development—developments in terminal design and operation from 1800 to the present day

INTRODUCTION

Ports, like most other commercial activities, are constantly changing. Their design and infrastructure change as the vehicles using them change and their functions develop and alter as the trade passing through them varies in type and quantity. Cargo-handling technology and changes in labour requirements and culture have also seen radical developments. In order to understand ports and to try to develop a general conceptual model for ports, it is important to grasp the general pattern and causes of these developments and the solutions, good or bad, attempted by various port managers. In London these developments have been evolving over 2,000 years but other ports in other parts of the world may have gone through the same process in just a few decades. As already stressed, if this process of evolution can be analysed, then it will be easier to forecast the future changes.

FACTORS CONSTRAINING PORT DEVELOPMENT

Many factors can cause ports to change, evolve or die:

— *Changes in the inland transport infrastructure.* For instance, the coming of the railways tended to make large ports like London and Liverpool larger and small ports smaller. Road

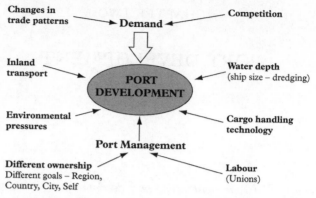

Figure 3: Factors constraining port development

- transport had the opposite effect in the UK where the post-World War II motorways saw a revival in many of the country's smaller ports. Many would argue however that it was not the motorway in itself that attracted the shipowner to the smaller ports, but that in the smaller ports the labour unions were less militant. However, the development of large container ships has again encouraged the growth of large regional ports.

— *Changes in trade patterns.* The UK joining the EU had a negative effect on Liverpool but a positive effect on Felixstowe as the UK traded more with its EU partners and less with the old members of the Commonwealth. Port analysts need to consider carefully the effect which the current trend of regional co-operation in trade and industry will have on port growth.

— *Changes in financial and logistic thinking.* London at its peak was an enormous warehouse for Europe. Since World War II the tendency is not to store "things" but to use ports as industrial areas, such as Rotterdam. More recently the trend has been to develop "value-added activities" and become a sophisticated marketing and distribution centre, such as for example Hamburg or Bremen. Students might like to discuss why London apparently failed in this development as compared with Rotterdam.

— *Length of life.* Unlike ships, ports often have to last a long time, sometimes for centuries. They therefore have to adapt and change over the course of time. Many of the traditional British ports were developed and built well over a century ago which means that many are now faced with a legacy of small antiquated docks.

GROWTH IN WORLD TRADE

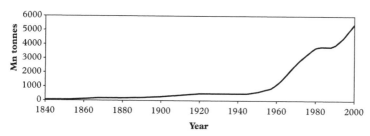

Figure 4: Growth in world trade

Figure 4 shows that growth has been continuous since reliable statistics began, and that there has been a tremendous upsurge since the 1950s, when a more efficient and productive system provided by containerisation and bulk carriage was evolved to meet the growing demand.

World Trade in million tonnes							
Year	Crude Oil	Oil Prods	Iron Ore	Coal	Grain	Other	Total
1975	1263	233	292	127	137	995	3047
1980	1170	262	314	188	198	1255	3387
1985	871	288	321	272	181	1360	3293
1990	1190	336	347	342	192	1570	3977
1995	1415	381	402	423	196	1870	4687
2000	1612	412	455	520	225	2150	5374
Av. Growth 1975–97	0.9%	2.6%	1.7%	6%	1.8%	3.4%	2.3%
Av. Growth 1975–97 tonne/miles	-0.7%	4.1%	2.3%	6.1%	2.1%	3.5%	1.5%
% of Total 1985–1999	37%	8.2%	9.6%	4.2%	41%	100	
World Trade in Billion tonne-miles							
2000	8,180	2,085	2,545	2,590	1,244	6,440	23,251

The table above, which tabulates the major individual products that go to make up world trade, indicates a fluctuating demand over the last quarter of a century for some commodities. As the price of crude oil increased in the early 1980s the demand for it reduced slightly. Grain will always fluctuate depending on the success or otherwise of local harvests. From the above table coal can be seen to have shown the most successful growth.

In 1980 the world trade in general cargo was 28% of total trade. In 2000 the world trade in general cargo was 981 million tonnes, of which 57.6% was containerised. In 2005 this is estimated to be 1,200 million tonnes of which 60% is expected to be containerised.

The phenomenal growth of the Chinese economy is affecting most of the world's trade routes. The port traffic through Chinese ports has been increasing at around 11% a year since 1998.

For the purpose of measuring world trade one can use the actual tonnes carried or the tonne/miles involved. For the purpose of gauging the impact of world trade on shipping activity tonne/miles is obviously more relevant, but for assessing the global impact on ports, actual tonnes carried would seem more useful.

The important question for port management is what of the future? Demand and personal consumption will almost certainly increase – for example if India and China increase their energy per capita to only half that of, say, Europe or Japan the demand in this sector will be tremendous. The table below is for 2000 but in 2004 China's demand for energy and raw materials was well in excess of previous optimistic forecasts and the demand for crude oil in India is growing fast.

Country	Energy (bbls per capita)	Oil consumption bbls per capita
India	2	0.8
China	4.4	1.3
Korea	28.5	17.2
Japan	29	16.4
UK	27.6	10.7
Germany	29.1	12.6
USA	58.6	24.6

Source: Poten & Partners.

LNG Trade in 2000 was 100 million tonnes. 15 LNG export terminals and 38 import terminals.

However, how will this demand be met? There are various scenarios:

— Will large bulk carriers continue to carry raw material long distances to be processed or will it be processed nearer its source? If so, will it affect the type of ship and terminal required?
— Will goods be moved, or will the factories and know-how be relocated, as the Japanese have done with their car factories?
— In 2001 it was estimated that there will be a 59% increase in energy requirements by 2020.

Structural changes in logistics

— Include greater flexibility rather than to achieve economies of scale by spreading the fixed costs.
— Larger product variety with a shorter life scale.
— Higher insecurity and risk.
— Outsourcing of the production of components, of transport and warehousing.

Political factors affecting world trade and port development

World trade may grow naturally as a consequence of growing industrial activity and of all the other factors which one can normally expect to form part of a nation's economic development. Such economic growth can be stimulated and controlled by national and international policy measures such as WTO (World Trade Organisation). Further, ports may be either the natural gateway through which this growth in trade is channelled or they may be developed, as Hong Kong and Shanghai largely were in the last century, to create access to a virtually new market. In other words, a port may be developed by trade or vice versa.

While political factors are causing trade to grow, the port has usually no serious problems except perhaps for congestion if the growth is too fast and unexpected. A more serious situation is when political factors cause a massive loss in trade passing through a port. For instance, Hong Kong's trade was severely hit in 1950 when the United Nations clamped its embargo upon trade with communist China. It is much to Hong Kong's credit that it switched from a port-based economy and turned itself into one of the world's great manufacturers.

Rostock on the German Baltic coast has suffered on more than one occasion from political changes. Before the Iron Curtain came down more than 50 years ago it was the premier German seaport in the Baltic. While in the GDR it built up a large international breakbulk trade of around 20 million tons. When the Iron Curtain was lifted in 1990 its cargo throughput dropped to 8 million tons per annum as the breakbulk cargo moved to better equipped and positioned Western ports. However, by 1996 its annual throughput was up to 18 million tons but this time by catering for the North South Ro/Ro trade across the Baltic. This latest development should continue, greatly helped by the parallel development of better road and rail connections.

There could be a possible development of regionalisation, as the EU produces more local trading in favour of international trading.

A paper produced in 2001 suggested that in a decade the number of hub ports could be reduced from 6000 to 100-200.

Swot analysis (strengths, weaknesses, opportunities and threats)

A swot analysis is a useful way of assessing the potential development concerning a port's competitive edge and threats from rival ports in the area. The elements to be considered in such an analysis will vary but such a list should include:

— Geographical position.
— Nautical access.
— Hinterland connections.
— Port facilities including information technology.
— Port costs.
— Output.
— Value added.
— Labour force and social climate.
— Institutional structure – its efficiency and its flexibility to change.

Some other "wildcards" that can affect growth

Labour—for instance, the port of Colombo having turned itself into a transit port in the early 1980s had moved up the container port league table from 75th position in 1983 to 26th position in 1988. However, labour unrest (which often follows success) in the late 1980s caused a major container line customer to pull out, and it was 1996 before the port was able to regain a similar rating in the world port container league.

Exceptional bad weather—has also damaged many ports, many of which have been under-insured and been unable to find the necessary capital to make good the damage.

Changes in cargo-moving technology—for instance in the 1970s some ports made large capital investments in terminals for the handling of LNG only to find a change of policy in some areas to move the commodity by pipeline.

Why some ports become major ports

In 1995 20 ports handled 52% of the world's terminal throughput. There are two main requirements for a port to achieve success:

1. A good natural harbour and deep water approaches, i.e. site considerations. For example, with Rotterdam, as with most large river deltas, silting was a major problem and the direction of the channels was constantly changing. To try to stabilise the situation a canal was cut in 1830. This attempt did not succeed but in 1870 the New Waterway was constructed to provided a direct outlet to the sea. This was successful and formed the basis of the modern port of Rotterdam. Amsterdam had an even greater problem when after World War II it lost the sea altogether when the Zuider Zee was reclaimed.
2. A strong traffic-generating location, i.e. the port must be central to an area and on the way to a meaningful destination.

The above two factors can be enhanced by human, corporate and government contrivance.

Growth of the world's leading ports

Many historians consider Bruges to have been the leading port in northern Europe in the thirteenth century. This title passed in the fifteenth century to Antwerp until the Spanish invasion and the closure of the Scheldt in 1585. After this the mantle was worn by Amsterdam for perhaps a century, before being claimed by London, when industrial capitalism assumed more significance than mercantile capitalism. The Table on page 24 shows how the port which could claim to be the world's largest port has altered. In 2001 the Port of Tanjung Pelepas in Malaysia was the fastest growing port.

There are many different ways port size can be compared, such as the physical area, the length of waterfront, the value of cargo passing through the port, number and or tonnage of vessels calling, etc.

Million metric ton (cargo) port comparison					
Year	London	New York	Hamburg	Rotterdam	Antwerp
1840	2	0.5			0.18
1850	3	1	0.8	0.68	0.24
1860	3.9	2.3	1.3	1	0.5
1870	5	4.5	1.8	1.7	1.3
1880	7	5.3	4.1	3	2
1890	10	7.6	7.5	4.5	4
1900	**16**	12.4	14.4	10	6.7
1910	25	24.5	22.1	15	16
1920	20	60.6	5.8	11.9	18.6
1930	36.4	**109.2**	25.8	35.1	21.3
1939`	41.6	**110.2**	18.7	42.4	23.6
1950	40.7	**131.4**	11.0	29.7	21.5
1960	57.1	**138.9**	30.7	83.4	37.5
1970	59.5	157.8	47.0	**225.8**	80.7
1980	48.1	125	63.1	**276.9**	81.9
1990	54.0	140	61.4	**287.8**	102.0
1997	55.7 (67% bulk)	52 (82% bulk	76.5 (bulk 50%)	**303.3** (bulk 76%)	111.8 (bulk 53%)
2000	47.9	64.8	85.9	**320**	130.5

However, as a crude indicator of size, the total cargo throughput of the port is the statistic preferred by most people working in the port industry. As can be seen from the figures in brackets in the table above, bulk cargoes do form a very large proportion of the total in all cases, particularly with the leading ports.

The Table above indicates how the size of the ports shown has altered. All have grown, but some have grown more and faster than others. In most cases the figures could be challenged as regards their precision and consistency of methodology, and what has been included and excluded. For instance, until recently London figures used to include several million tons of sludge which were shipped out to the North Sea for dumping. However, the trends should be sufficiently accurate to allow general conclusions to be made.

The Table also shows that over the last century the majority of the world's largest ports were in the Atlantic basin but in 1995 Singapore appeared in the Statistical Tables as the world's largest port and the latest world league tables shows that the Pacific basin can now claim this honour.

Singapore's growth in the last decade has been truly phenomenal. It has in fact trebled its tonnage throughput since 1985 and doubled it since 1990. In the October 1996 edition of the *ISL*

Shipping Statistics and Market Review, Singapore was listed first with an annual throughput of 305.5 million *freight* tons (the only port shown in the list to use freight tons). Rotterdam was number two but Antwerp, which was number three in our table above, lies in tenth place. There are some who would contest Singapore's claim to this leading place, because if the throughput were measured in metric rather than freight tons one would expect the figure to be smaller. For instance, in figures given in the *Baltic Magazine* for November 1997, the throughput weights in *metric* tonnes for 1995 are given as Rotterdam 293.4 and Singapore 235.2. There are also many who would not allow the extent of double counting which occurs in the Singapore methodology. Nevertheless, everyone must be truly impressed by Singapore's growth and success.

By 1997 Rotterdam had claimed back its lead position by achieving an annual throughput of 307.3 million metric tonnes. However, in 1999 Singapore annual throughput was claimed 326 mn freight tons of which 42% was bulk cargo.

CHANGES IN GROWTH

From the Table on page 24, comparing London and New York, it can be estimated that New York finally draws well clear of London in 1915, after the start of World War I. This same conclusion would seem to be arrived at no matter whether one uses values or tonnages. This was rather sad from the British point of view as London had long been proud of its claim to be the world's greatest port, so proud in fact that it continued to make this claim though the 1920s and 30s. London did, however, continue to grow, though considerably more slowly than its rivals, and reached its zenith with regard to tonnage in 1964 when it peaked at over 60 million tons. It must be underlined that these tables and graphs are considering only the size of ports. London can still lay claim to be the world's premier maritime commercial centre.

The same Table shows how, in the late 1960s, New York passed the largest-port baton onto Rotterdam which had continued to grow at a phenomenal speed following World War II. Like London before it, New York was proud of its leading position and in the 1997 *Guinness Book of Records* it was still listed as the world's greatest port.

Leading ports for specific cargoes

Ports can of course be classified by size with reference to specific activities or cargoes. Miami claims, for instance, to be the biggest when it comes to cruise shipping and in the various shipping trades claims are made that a port is the largest fishing port, coal export port, etc. However, within the containerised shipping trade, league tables are published annually by *Containerisation International* and these are copied into numerous publications .

See also the section on the "Rise and Fall of Ports" in Chapter 5.

The physical development of a major port

The table below is based on Professor Bird's summary given in his book *Major Seaports in the UK* and its purpose is to show the general physical stages through which most ports have passed.

	Era	Comments
1	Primitive	The ships approach chosen discharge point as closely as possible, lying aground if necessary. A port grows around this point. In London this point would have been just below Old London Bridge. Professor Bird says that this era comes to an end when demand causes this basic nucleus to expand or relocate itself. He suggests that in London this happened around AD 200.
2	Marginal Quay Extension	There is now a series of purpose-built quay walls for ships to berth at. In London this was the system until the end of the ninth century.
3	Marginal Quay Elaboration	Number of berths extended by artificial embayments. In London this appears to have happened at Queenhithe in 899.
4	Dock Elaboration	Artificial docks constructed with tidal basins and complicated quay patterns. In London this started in 1802 with the opening of the West India Dock. It is interesting that very many of the traditional ports arrived at this point about the same time. Liverpool was the first in the UK in 1712.
5	Simple Lineal Quayage	Long straight quays built in docks purpose-built for the large steel steamships. These docks may be located in places more suitable for the ships. In London this can be seen in the building of the Royal Docks and Tilbury Docks.
6	Specialised Quayage	Quays and jetties built in specific areas to accommodate large tankers such as VLCCs, and specific cargoes. Specialised Container and Ro/Ro berths could be considered in this category.

The dates given for London are mentioned only for interest. The important fact to recognise is the general evolutionary process. Los Angeles, for instance, went through the whole process in about a century and a half.

The reasons why London is chosen as an example frequently throughout this book are:

1. It is universally well known and has been reasonably well researched
2. There are many older ports, such as Alexandria, but probably few where the development can be traced on such a continuous and consistent basis.

Developments in port location

Figure 5 (overleaf) represents a simple "model" port which shows how many estuarial ports have developed. Originally the ships approached as far upriver as possible and were generally forced to stop where the first bridge had been built. This was usually no problem as the bridge marked a main thoroughfare and a large trading city had probably developed there.

In the case of London, the Romans built the bridge and developed the city of London. The ships would anchor or berth below the bridge and discharge. By the beginning of the nineteenth century the river had become congested by ships and much of the cargo was being stolen. (The London River Police were the city's first police force.) To ease congestion and increase security various docks were built along the river. As ships got bigger with deeper drafts, the new docks and terminals moved down-river to the sea. In London by the 1870s Tilbury docks were built, 35 miles down-river from the city. With the advent of containerisation and faster cargo-handling, more terminal space was needed as well as good access to inland transport systems so old terminals were closed and new ones constructed. In the 1970s the Port of London Authority had plans to develop a new port system right at the mouth of the Thames on Maplin Sands but this plan hit several problems, some of them environmental (it would have meant destroying an important bird sanctuary) so the plans were shelved.

Some elements of the process indicated by the model can in fact be observed in most ports that have not been lucky enough to be built on a virgin site within the last three decades. Dubai is an interesting variation, as there in a creek can be seen sailing vessels

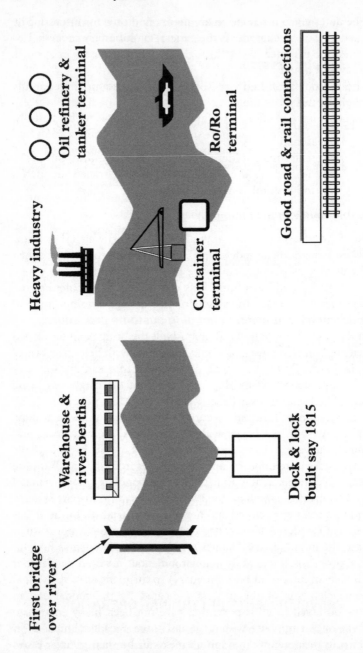

Figure 5: A "model" port (see Professor J. Bird's Major Seaports of the UK).

berthed and trading in a manner seemingly untouched by the passing of time, while almost alongside lies a new state-of-the-art container port.

Financing port development

Since an old established port often owned land in the old city centre, now very desirable for development as high rent offices, many ports have been able to fund their new projects by skilfully developing their redundant port sites. Good land management has therefore become an essential management function for many of the traditional port administrations. One can see good examples of this in London, New York, Copenhagen, Hamburg, Antwerp, etc., where old warehouses have been converted to trendy luxury hotels, office blocks, shopping malls or apartment areas.

A relatively new development in port financing and control is the growing practice of large powerful ports, such as the ports of Singapore and Hamburg, investing their profits and skills in new port development in other parts of the world. Large shipping groups have also been involved in port investment

Developments caused by changing customs procedures

In 1803 in London a law was passed allowing ships to discharge to customs warehouses. This is very significant date as it meant that until this time the ship was virtually the warehouse, and the consignee had to collect the cargo from the ship. So before this time merchant warehouses were often outside the docks. Communication was very limited so a ship's arrival could seldom be anticipated with any precision. Consignees had to wait until the Master notified them that the ship had arrived and where she was berthed. Even towards the end of the 1800s in the UK, sailing ships had to give shippers three days' notice before working cargo, to allow them time to make arrangements for collecting or delivering the cargo.

This very significant change in customs procedure affected the whole concept of port cargo-handling and terminal design. Even today in many developing countries the customs procedures can be the major cause of low productivity.

DEVELOPMENTS IN TERMINAL OPERATION

The dates and modes of operation given in the following section are only indications of the methods employed in many major ports about that time. The descriptions are largely based on London which until 1908 was really a collection of private unregulated terminals. Thus at any one time the practices adopted at one terminal or dock were often quite different to those practised at other terminals in the vicinity. However, the importance of locating precisely when things happened is not so important as identifying why the changes occurred.

The period before 1800

Prior to 1800 port operation had remained in general unchanged for centuries. The standard ship around 1800 was in the region of 300 tons and was of course sail-powered. Most ports would have quays or wharves. (By 1805 26 miles of vaults existed in London for wine storage.)

Cargoes were usually loaded and discharged on and off the ship by the crew, though the Master or agent could employ extra labour if they needed or wished to. The cargo would be handled manually, though tackle often seems to have been used to lift the cargo vertically out of the hold to the ship's deck. John Pudney in his book *London Docks* says that towards the end of the 1700s the London watermen opposed the use of cranes. These were of course hand-operated cranes as hydraulic and steam cranes were still in their theoretical or experimental stage.

However, although this had not been a dynamic period of changes for ports, efforts to improve port facilities were beginning. For instance in 1780 Hull Dock Company developed a 2-horse-power operated dredger capable of shifting 22 tons per hour.

1800–1850

During this period the tonnage entering the port of London more than doubled over the previous century . The industrial revolution was under way, and by 1840 the UK had a national railway system. In the UK the railways were one of the major forces in port development, making large ports larger and small ports smaller. For ports exporting coal during this century and the UK was one of the world's largest coal suppliers, their rise or fall was almost entirely in the hands of the private railway companies .

Unfortunately, the introduction of the steamship during this introductory period caused problems for the dock designer. Gordon Jackson in his book *History and Archaeology of Ports* makes the point that steamers could not be crowded into a dock. A dock for 140 sailing ships would take only 35 steamers. Jackson also notes that "The aversion to dockside warehouses that had been growing since the 1840s became, as far as is known, universal, with new docks favouring one and two-storey transit sheds, often with built-in gantry cranes, and with more emphasis than hitherto on open spaces for the handling of minerals and machinery. There was a growing tendency for goods to be stored outside the docks. Railways and docks were increasingly interdependent. However, in London and many other ports ships discharged directly into barges which lay alongside – some docks had a width problem." The dockside warehouse did remain at many terminals until the end of the century and the evolution of the transit shed was in many places slow.

During this period steamships appeared, though they could only be used for short distance and coastal traffic because the engines were inefficient and their coal consumption considerable. However, in 1818 the *Savannah* was the first auxiliary ship to cross the Atlantic and by 1837 the steamships *Great Western* and *Sirius* did establish a regular trans-Atlantic service. In 1850 steamers formed 41% of foreign-going ships arriving at Hull, but only 28% of those arriving at London. Therefore the sailing ships were still the predominant commercial long-distance carrier. Anticipating the approaching threat from the steamship, sailing ships were however improving their speed and efficiency.

By 1850 the average sailing ship size was 210 tons and the average size steamship was 250 tons.

1850–1900

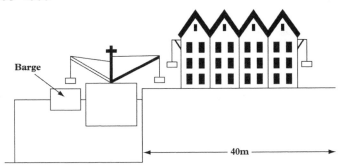

Figure 6: Layout for a typical berth (1850–1900)

Figure 6 illustrates a possible layout for a typical berth during this period. The ship discharged her cargo onto the wharf or into a barge. The warehouse probably had cranes fitted to her walls to lift the cargo to the required floor. Cargo movement on the wharf or in the warehouse would be by hand truck and distribution to and from warehouse would be by horse and cart or railway.

During the second half of the century the tonnage of ships arriving in London increased by over 12 times that of the first half. So this was obviously a period of rapid expansion for London. Not only was world trade growing fast, but the railways made London the transport focal point of Britain and also, to use modern jargon, it became the centre port for Europe. This was almost certainly helped by its political and financial stability compared to most of its European rivals, and its empire trade.

In 1888 the *Report from the Select Committee on Sweating* gives a complete insight into the operational working of the London Docks for that moment of time, with employers, union officials and dock workers being cross-examined about the working practices of the moment. Most seem to take mechanisation (cranes) for granted in the docks (though not on the smaller river wharves) and some made wistful comments about how good it was 15 or so years ago before the cranes brought unemployment and lower wages into the docks. When asked what had made the greatest changes in the docks, two of the senior employers said the Suez Canal, which they blamed for increasing the competition from the continent, and the telegraph which greatly facilitated communication over large areas within the port. It was also noted that the improvement in international communication had reduced the amount of speculative importing and storage in the London warehouses. (Is this the first indication of JIT?) Comments were also made concerning the growth in the number of steam tugs which had done much to even out the ship arrivals, hitherto so dependent on the wind to manoeuvre upriver. The growth in steamships was also noted as well as the fact that they were nearly all geared and needed little extra equipment to work cargo. Sailing vessels on the other hand were seldom at berths with cranes and would often need a barge with a portable steam winch and boiler.

1900–1960

By the early 1900s, the port had reached a stage of development that is easily recognisable even today. From then until the greater utilisation of dry bulk cargoes in the fifties and the onset of unitisation in the sixties, its development was one of gradual evolution as it adapted to increases in ship size and the steady improvement in cargo-handling technology. In 1913 a survey comparing major world ports rated Hamburg as the best equipped port in the world and New York one of the worst. In spite of this, New York was rated the best as regards ship turn-round times, because the labour force worked at high speed at all hours. This illustrates even at this point how labour-intensive ports were and how labour-dependent for their productivity. This probably remains true and will continue to be the most important factor in productivity as long as this "traditional" type of breakbulk general cargo terminal remains in existence.

In the UK, London and Liverpool were established as the major ports. In 1913 London handled 29.3% of the national trade and Liverpool 26%. By 1920 road haulage had arrived but it was not perhaps until after the Second World War and the building of the motorways that road transport started to reverse the effect the railways had had a century before, and in the UK made the small ports bigger and big ports smaller. The devastation of the Second World War gave many continental ports that rare opportunity offered to port management, that is "to start again". This new start combined with a new surge in growth in ship size, improved transport and commercial communications and a steep post-war rise in demand for raw materials, gave rise to a change in the basic port function. The storage and warehousing function decreased but the port as an area of industrial activity increased. In Rotterdam for instance the south bank of the waterway was covered in two swift stages to become 50 kilometres of heavy industry with access by large bulk carriers.

To illustrate the evolution in this period figures for a typical breakbulk general cargo terminal for 1900, 1920 and 1960 are shown for comparison in Figure 7 (on page 34).

In the 1960s dock transit sheds were about 500ft by 120ft. They originally had low roofs, but fork lift trucks could now stack high easily and cheaply, therefore sheds were now built with higher roofs.

A new era for dry cargo shipping and ports

From about the mid-sixties it could be argued that ports and shipping were entering a new phase of operation. The "traditional" cargo ships continued in operation but were in decline and would continue to be marginalised to the lesser ports of the world with

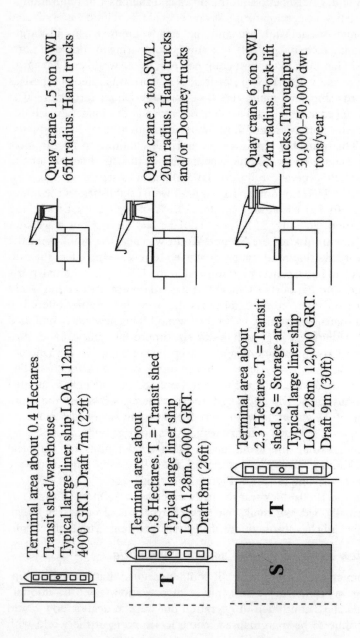

Figure 7: Typical breakbulk general cargo terminals (1900, 1920, 1960).

less lucrative cargoes, in the same way that sailing ships had been a century earlier.

General cargo moved to container ships, and bulk cargo to bulk carriers. Both ship types grew rapidly and considerably in size as ports found the water to match their draft and the cargo-handling technology to maintain a rapid turn-round in port. In addition to these major new ship types, many new specialist types emerged such as:

1965	PCCs (Pure Car Carriers) and PCTCs (Pure Car and Truck Carriers). These require the port to have large parking facilities and their large "windage" may cause berthing problems.
1970s	Introduction of barge-carrying ships such as Lash and Seabees. Originally it was thought that these ships could manage with little or no terminal facilities. In fact some special terminals were developed for them. Because of their very sophisticated barge-lifting gear there were also occasional labour problems in ports as to who had the "right" to operate them.
1976	First Semi-submersible.
1985	First Fruit Juice Carrier. These ships do of course require specialist terminal facilities.

The container age

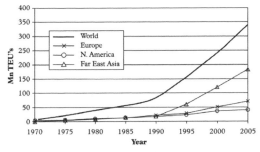

Figure 8: Growth in world container tonnage.

Figure 8, showing the growth in the world container traffic, illustrates that although the global growth has been consistently increasing the growth has varied in the three main trading regions.

In 2000 world container ports handling increased by 8.7% but in S.E. Asia and S. America the growth would be nearer 25%. Note that some 17% of container traffic is in empty containers.

Development of unitisation

This started between the developed countries in the late sixties (in Australia and USA perhaps a decade earlier) but very often with only makeshift ships and hurriedly converted terminals. The pioneering spirit behind this development was a truck operator, not a shipowner.

By the mid-seventies, containers were moving to developing countries in self-sustaining vessels and although cranes were not needed at the port, the lack of facilities for the final inland transport leg led to many problems. By 1980 the second generation of container vessels was now well-established and the concept of a well-developed container terminal became better defined. However, ships continued to grow and by the late 80s there were the fourth generation ships which required larger gantry cranes to reach across them. New container sizes were also introduced and all these changes required large capital investment which for developing countries meant further difficulties.

Containers brought with them other problems for port operators:

— The large investment necessary to containerise a route meant that liner shipowners had to form themselves into larger financial units and hence were more powerful customers from the point of view of the port.
— The increase in size and complexity of ships meant an increase in the cost of the ship's time. Also the cargo was now intermodal so the cargo started to move to the ship rather than the ship to the cargo.
— Because the cargo was now intermodal, adjacent ports on the same land mass could now compete with each other and the choice of port was, and often still is, in the hands of the large multinational liner-operator.
— There was a need for a comprehensive information system and greater efficiency.
— A significantly smaller but better trained work force was needed.
— Faster customs clearance, better documentation procedure, and a review of much of the country's transportation law was required.

The table on page 37 shows that the above ports, though all relatively close to each other, have all developed their container traffic at different rates.

North European Container Port Traffic 1971–2002 by TEU (mns)					
Year	Hamburg	Rotterdam	Antwerp	Felixstowe	Le Havre
1971	0.1	0.4	0.2	0.1	
1975	0.3	1.1	0.3	0.2	
1980	0.8	1.9	0.7	0.6	0.5
1985	1.2	2.7	1.2	0.5	0.6
1990	1.9	3.7	1.5	1.0	0.9
1992	2.3	4.1	1.8	1.4	0.8
1997	3.3	5.3	3.0	1.6	1.2
2000	4.3	6.3	4.1	1.8	1.4
2002	5.4	6.5	4.8	1.8	1.7

Leading 10 Euro Container Ports 1970–2002 (% of Europe Container Traffic)						
Port	1970	1975	1980	1985	1990	2002
Rotterdam	19.8	21.7	18.6	18.6	17.6	13.2
Hamburg	2.9	6.7	7.7	8.1	9.5	10.8
Antwerp	9	6	7.1	8.7	7.5	9.6
Felixstowe	6.7	4.6	3.9	5.1	6.9	3.4
Bremen	9.3	8.3	6.9	6.8	5.8	6
Le Havre	4.1	4.8	5.0	4.0	4.1	3.4
Algeciras	0.5	1.0	2.4	2.5	2.7	4.4
Marseilles-Fos	0.4	1.9	2.9	3.4	2.3	1.6
Barcelona	0.5	1.6	1.8	2.5	2.2	3
Leghorn	1	1.3	3.0	3.3	2.0	GioiaTauro 5.8
Total	54.2	57.9	59.3	63	60.6	61.2

Development of container terminals

Omitting ferry terminals which have developed specialisms of their own, many of the earlier container terminals contained some facilities for Ro/Ro loading and discharging and many of the packaged lumber berths were of this nature. This type of cargo-handling was often referred to as STO/RO procedure. However, to give themselves world-wide flexibility, most of the ships that now offer this type of facility have their own very expensive and sophisticated ramps.

By 2000 the outreach of the new cranes at the larger terminals, as Yokohama, reached 63 metres to reach across 22 boxes, which is a possible athwartship stow in the current larger generation of container ships.

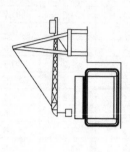

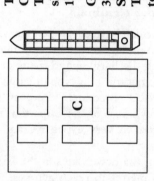

1970

Terminal area about 5.7 hectares
C = Container Stacks
Typical first generation container
ship LOA 128m, 1000 TEU,
19000 GRT, Draft 10.5m (34ft).

Gantry crane 30 tons SWL.
35m outreach.
Straddle carriers, sideloaders.
Throughput 500000–1000000 dwt
tons/year.

Figure 9a: Container Terminal, 1970.

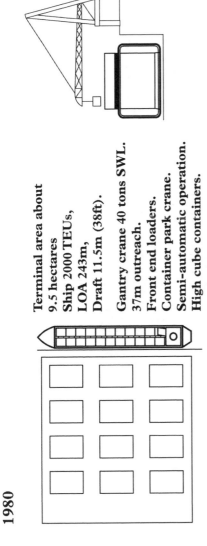

1980

Terminal area about
9.5 hectares
Ship 2000 TEUs,
LOA 243m,
Draft 11.5m (38ft).

Gantry crane 40 tons SWL.
37m outreach.
Front end loaders.
Container park crane.
Semi-automatic operation.
High cube containers.

Figure 9b: Container Terminal, 1980.

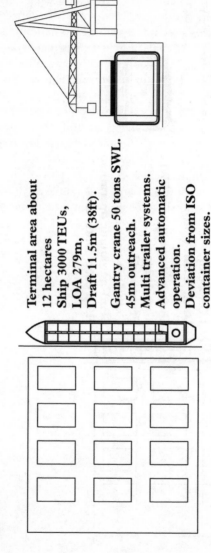

Terminal area about
12 hectares
Ship 3000 TEUs,
LOA 279m,
Draft 11.5m (38ft).

Gantry crane 50 tons SWL.
45m outreach.
Multi trailer systems.
Advanced automatic
operation.
Deviation from ISO
container sizes.

1990

Figure 9b: Container Terminal, 1990.

Bulk cargo terminals

The development in size of these terminals is very similar to that of container vessel terminals, with the Panamax (65,000 dwt) size being popular in both groups. However, at the higher end of the scale the bulk carriers are larger, with some ore-carriers in the VLCC size. (See Analysis section re bulk cargo-handling speed.)

Bulk cargo-loading terminals are usually situated as near as possible to the source or with good rail connection to the source, and loading will be some variation of controlled gravity fall into the hold.

This will be fast and often very dusty which may now bring environmental claims from people living nearby. Cement dust for instance can be troublesome to people living many miles away downwind.

The discharging terminals will now often be part of an industrial complex situated in the port area and the complex will often have its own dedicated terminal, discharge equipment and conveyor belts.

CHAPTER THREE

IMPACT OF CHANGING SHIP TECHNOLOGY ON PORTS

Introduction–tonnage—growth of tonnage–relationship between LOA & GT–relationship between tonnage and draft–ship type and specialisation—growth in ship size—increasing size of container ships—hatch size, perhaps the most significant technical development—effect of port time on ships' speed—changes in management attitude—safety—changes in port requirements caused by changes in ships' requirements

INTRODUCTION

Although this is a book about ports there are certain facts about ships which anyone interested in ports must be aware of, such as tonnage which usually forms a vital part of a ports pricing system and terminal berth organisation. The driving force for changes in port infrastructure, superstructure and operations have been the changes in certain aspects of ship technology and changes in ship management's attitude and expectations.

SHIP KNOWLEDGE

Tonnage (ship size is usually expressed in NT, GT, DWT or LOA)

In shipping the term tonnage can indicate many different measures and anyone working in ports should be familiar with most of them. The following gives a brief summary of the basic terms.

A tun was a barrel holding 252 gallons of wine. Remember that for hundreds of years the tun was a much valued container for the transport of many cargoes. A 100-tun vessel was one that could carry a hundred tuns. Hence the word ton in shipping can denote both weight and capacity.

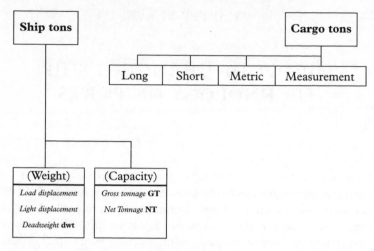

Figure 10: Ship and cargo tons.

Before 1982 GT was known as GRT and NT as NRT. The R
meant Registered, as up to 1982 these tonnages were given when
the ship was registered.

Brief history

In 1849 a Royal Commission originated the concept that assessment of dues should be based on the vessel's potential earning
capacity. It was known as the Moorsom system after the secretary
of the Commission, George Moorsom, and came into force in
1854. The idea was that gross tonnage would be a measure of the
vessel's volume and that net tonnage would be a measure of the
ship's earning capacity. Port dues and taxes were paid on these
tonnages so shipowners looked for ways of reducing them. Governments, to encourage safety, would also offer various exempted
spaces as an inducement to good building practices. For instance,
the double bottom was exempted from gross tonnage if it was used
only for water ballast. The precise definitions of measurement
tonnage had therefore become long, detailed and complex and varied from country to country.

In 1873 an International Tonnage Commission met in Con-
stantinople. Its findings were not followed, except by the authorities of the newly opened Suez Canal.

In 1930 the League of Nations tried to obtain universal agreement but it was not followed by either the British or Americans, though adopted by most other countries.

In 1967 the Merchant Shipping (Tonnage) Regulations were passed.

In 1969 the UN Agency, IMO (The International Maritime Organisation) held an International Convention on Tonnage Measurement of Ships. This convention at long last brought in a universally accepted system of gross and net tonnage on 18 July 1982.

Note: as these tonnages are independent of the nationality of the ship they no longer need to be linked to the registration of the ship, so their official title is Gross Tonnage (GT) instead of Gross Registered Tonnage (GRT). Likewise the post 1982 NET tonnage is abbreviated to NT instead of NRT.

Ship tonnage

Loaded displacement tonnage is the actual weight of the ship and cargo. Light displacement tonnage is the actual weight of the ship. The difference between the loaded displacement and the light displacement is the *weight* that the ship can actually carry and is known as the deadweight tonnage. Gross tonnage is, very simply, a measure of the total enclosed *volume* of the ship in cubic metres multiplied by a constant. The net tonnage is the total enclosed *volume* available for cargo in cubic metres multiplied by a constant.

Displacement tonnage has little or no commercial use. The size of tankers is usually expressed in deadweight tonnage, i.e. a 250,000 ton dwt tanker means it can carry 250,000 tons of oil, bunkers and stores at its summer draft. It is more convenient when transporting liquids to charge for the ton weight carried, not only because it is a relatively heavy cargo but the volume of 250,000 tons of oil can appreciably change with a ten-degree variation in temperature.

On the other hand most general cargo ships are usually full before they are down to their marks, so a shipowner is usually concerned with selling space and he is more interested in the volume of his ship rather than the weight it can carry. Hence one usually talks of a cargo ship of, for example, 9,000 gross tonnage.

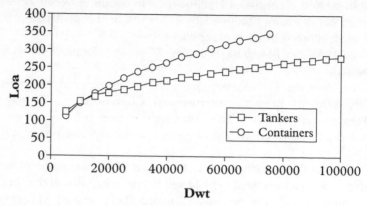

Figure 11: Typical relationship between LOA and Dwt.

LOA = Length of ship overall in metres
An approximate deadweight of a container ship could be estimated from the following empirical equation: Dwt = 8 x teu capacity + 6000

When considering berth allocation and assessing various dues, a vessel's length over all is obviously an important factor. The above graph shows the typical relationship that can be expected between a ship's length and her dwt tonnage. Note that the length does not increase at the same rate as the tonnage. In fact P&O's *Grand Princess*, which entered service in mid 1998 and was hailed by the press as the world's largest passenger liner, had a GT of 109,000 and a length of almost 950 feet.

Relationship between tonnage, grt and draft

Draft for sailing ships

Due to its deeper keel the sailing vessel had a deeper draft than the steamship, so water depth was not the problem when steam took over from sail, but it became a major headache for port administrations with the new ship types that were introduced in the 1960s and 1970s.

The table on page 47 shows that ports' problems with water depth came when ships started to exceed 20,000 dwt and had drafts in excess of 10 metres, as few ports in the 1950s could offer entrance channels of that depth.

Naturally enough there are designs for special "reduced draft" large vessels. For instance the majority of cruise liners, regardless of their tonnage, are designed with a maximum draft of less than 9 metres, as many of the best terminals nearest historical sites have only limited depths of water. Gas carriers are also often designed so that their loaded draft is less than 13 metres, while naval architects designing container ships are conscious of the limited outreach of many gantry cranes, so may reduce the breadth for larger ships.

The approximate correlation between ship draft and tonnage					
Older smaller ships			Larger more modern ships		
GRT	Draft in feet	Draft in decimetres	Dead-weight	Draft in feet	Draft in decimetres
1,000	17.9	54.56	10,000	26	79
2,000	20	60.96	20,000	30	91
3,000	21.8	66.45	50,000	38	116
4,000	23.6	71.93	100,000	48	146
5,000	25.4	77.42	200,000	60	183
6,000	26.6	81.08	300,000	72	219
7,000	27.4	83.52	500,000	90	274

SHIP DEVELOPMENTS WHICH INFLUENCE PORT DEVELOPMENT

Three major factors which have influenced port development are:

(1) increase in the supply of ship tonnage;
(2) specialisation in ship types. Cargo-handling features;
(3) increasing ship size.

1. Increase in the supply of ship tonnage

As already stated, the GRT gives an indication of the carrying capacity of the world's merchant fleet.

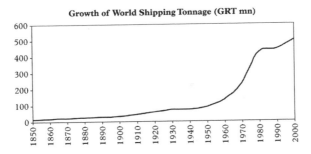

Figure 12: Growth of world GRT.

As one would expect, the graph on page 47, showing the development of the supply of ship tonnage, reflects very closely the graph in Chapter Two showing the increase in world maritime trade. What the graph does not indicate is that this increase in supply of tonnage is made up of a slow increase in the size of ships until the 1960s, when ship size increased rapidly.

2. Development in ship type specialisation and equipment

The development in power-driven vessels

Year	Sail	Power	GRT (mn.)
1850	7.88	0.7	8.58
1870	14.8	2.8	17.6
1890	13.7	11.6	25.3
1900	6.5	22.4	28.9
1920	3.3	53.9	57.3
1940	0.9	66.9	67.8
1960			129.8
1980			419.9
2000			497.0

1878 was the year when the number of steamships equalled the number of sailing ships but the table above shows that it was in the last decade of the century that steam tonnage exceeded sail tonnage. This tells us that it was therefore the latter part of the century before the large steamship became the long distance trading vessel. It was, of course, the large steamships that forced ports to develop and change, as almost a century later it would be the large bulkers and large container ships which had a similar effect. It can also be noted that steamships required a different dock infrastructure to that of sailing ships, just as container ships require an even more radical change to terminal design.

Development in type specialisation

The term specialised ship is not a precise technical expression but rather a term used to cover ship types built and designed to fit a specific or dedicated purpose. They may be built for a variety of reasons, such as allowing cargo, like heavy lifts, to move that which would not be able to move otherwise. Alternatively, they may be introduced, like wine tankers in 1946, as a way of moving that specific cargo more productively. In most cases a specialised ship type will require specialised terminal facilities to handle and store the cargo. It may require special additions to the dock architecture. In Rotterdam the large PCTC (pure car and truck carriers) with their high superstructure became very difficult to manoeuvre in certain areas of the port in cross-winds. To overcome this problem the Port of Rotterdam had to design and build elaborate windbreaks along the side of a dock entrance.

Date	Details
1800	Around this time, when enclosed docks first developed, the standard vessel was a 300-ton sailing ship.
1812	First steamship on Clyde. In 1820 Glasgow directory listed 28 steamers out of Glasgow with passengers and stores to islands and highlands. **Steamships required new designs in dock and terminal construction.**
1818	*Savannah*, an auxiliary steamer, crosses the Atlantic.
1858	*Great Eastern* launched, 692ft long, 18,914 GRT.
1860	Steam with sail, 4 hatches, booms for sails as derricks.
1871	**Telegraph communication to Far East** (Shanghai) 1888 Hong Kong has local telephone system. The importance of world-wide communication in international maritime trade is often not appreciated.
1882	Dunedin, one of the first **refrigerated** vessels for frozen meat.
1884	Some liners equipped with 1.5 ton cranes at hatch corners, 20ft radius.
1885	**First purpose built tanker, the** *Glückauf.*
1890	**Union purchase** introduced on the W. Coast of America. (Note mast-table and cross-tree required).
1892	Gt. Lakes have specialised **self-unloader** *Samuel Mitchell*. 1916 converted to self-unloading cement carrier. Still in service in 1981.
1910	**Steel hatch** covers fitted in large colliers and ore-carriers.
1920	First **Heavy Lift Vessel** *Belfri* (3,400 dwt).
1920	Early 1920s last sailing ship discharges in PLA.
1924	Harwich to Zeebrugge Ro/Ro Train ferry.
1949	First ship with bulk sugar, the *Bara Haig*, arrives in London with 5,073 tons.
1952	**Flush weathertight tweendeck covers – steel weatherdeck hatches commonplace.**
1954	Lloyd's Register assign a class for ore-carriers.
1955	**Introduction of car carriers.**
1969	**First purpose built international trading container ship. Sulphur tankers, phosphoric acid tankers.**
1976	**First Semi-submersible.**
1985	**First Fruit Juice Carrier.**
1986	**Hatchless design** in Australia. First Bell Pioneer in service Oct. 1990

The table on page 49 claims many firsts and I suspect that there will be readers who will disagree over some of them. However, although I am naturally concerned with accuracy, the real points I want to show with the table are:

— The date when a development was known to be in existence and could be expected to impinge on port operation.
— That technical developments were not just the steel steamship and container ship but were many, and almost continuous.

It should also be observed that some technical developments became universal almost immediately, some progressed very slowly while others, after a fanfare of publicity, disappeared without trace. For instance, in the 1970s many argued that integrated tug barges would revolutionise maritime transport and ports but little is heard of them now.

					Summary of the world's cargo-carrying ships by type					
	1965		1980		2000				2003	
Ship Type	No.	GT mn	No.	GT mn	No.	GT mn	Age	dwt mn	No.	GT mn
liquefied gas	5	0.059	631	7.4	1126	19.7	14	18.5	1,180	22.8
chemical			649	2.2	2,534	17.5	14	28.7	2,828	22.5
oil	5,307	55	7,112	175	7,009	155.5	16	283.7	6.946	159.3
other liquids			120	0.2	345	0.5	23	0.7	371	0.7
bulk dry	1,316	17.6	4,282	83.4	4,886	142.7	14	255	5,046	156.0
0/0 & OBOs	87	3.4	424	26.2	205	8.6	17	15	174	7.0
self dis. Bulk dry					165	3.2	26	5.4	168	3.3
other bulk dry					1,086	6.7	17	8.9	1,112	6.9
general cargo	22,000	50	22,676	81.3	16,755	54.9	22	78	16,253	51.2
container			662	11.3	2,590	60.2	10	69.1	3,055	78.4
refrigerated					1,414	7	18	7.4	1,272	6.4
Ro/Ro cargo					1,882	27.1	17	13.7	1,921	29.1
pass./ Ro/Ro cars					2,574	13.1	21	3.8	2,737	15.1
passenger					3,366	10	22	2.1	3,586	12.6
Other	500	2			268	2.1	24	2.2	268	1.9
Totals	29,215	128	36,556	387	46,205	528.8	19	792.2	46,917	573.2

The 2000 columns in the above table give a complete list of cargo-carrying ships as regards their number and their GT. The blanks in the 1965 and 1980 columns merely indicate that Lloyd's Register Annual Statistical Tables did not give so much detail in these years. These years are I think worth including as they do show, for the main types, where the increases and decreases are. General cargo ships for instance remained fairly constant in the seventies. Container ships have grown consistently throughout the period. O/Os and OBOs peaked around 1980 but as a type seem to be lacking popularity at the moment.

The average age figure is interesting. For all the cargo-carrying fleet it was around 19 years in 2000, while for both 1965 and 1980 the average age was less than 10 years. The world supply of ships would seem to be getting older – probably due to the relatively low freight rates since 1973, leaving insufficient margins for reinvestment. It should also indicate that during the next decade there must be either a reduction in supply or a boom in shipbuilding. However, the considerable rise in freight rates in most of the shipping markets during 2004 would suggest that the latter is very probable.

3. Development in ship size

See Chapter 4 on water depth.

	Home Trade Av. net tonnage		Foreign Going Av. net tonnage	
Year	Sail	Steam	Sail	Steam
1870	66.1	159.4	513.3	813.3
1900	61.1	143.4	1395.3	1837.9
1913	62.1	127.1	1567.7	2500

The above table shows that for Home Trade vessels (a term that was used to designate ships that could trade around UK and with Ireland and the near continent) average size decreased slightly – probably influenced by the growing competition from the railways. Foreign-going ships in both sail and steam steadily increased in size. Sailing ships are a good example of Professor Parkinson's Law which states that *things only achieve their optimum state just before they become obsolete.*

The table on page 52 shows that depth of water was not a major issue until the 1960s. Even in 1950 Rotterdam still had only 10 metres. In 1970 there were only eight ports in Europe which could accept the new class of VLCC tankers and there were no ports with sufficient depth of water on the east coast of North America. By 1975, following a period of energetic dredging, there were 22 ports in north-west Europe which could accept such ships. Dredging is a very expensive activity and the question facing port managers is:

Year	Average size of ship built and registered in UK				Largest ships in world
	Steam	Draft (m)	Depth Rotterdam	Sail	Power
1850	250	4.3		210	2,900 GT (6.5m draft) 1858 *The Great Eastern* 18,914 GT
1870	580	5.5		775	4,000 GT (7.2m draft)
1890	1,580	5.8	7.6	1,570	7,000 GT (8.3m draft)
1900	1,640	5.9		912	11,000 GT (10.2m draft)
1910	1,981	6.1	9.4	782	30,000 GT (12.3m draft) 1911 *The Olympic* 46,000 GT 1914 *Vaterland* 54,000 GT
1930	2,586	6.4			1936 *Queen Mary* 81,237 GT
1950	3,006	6.6	10		
1960	4,027	7.2	12.8		100,000 dwt (14.6m draft)
1970	6,757	8.2	18.9		1967 200,000 dwt (19m draft) 1969 350,000 dwt (23m draft) 1972 500,000 dwt (27m draft)
1997	Suez Canal 16.2 m but starting to dredge to 20.4m (*Mashour* world's largest cutter dredger)				
2000	11,400		24.8		

— Will ships continue to get bigger? The graph showing average ship size since 1850 does indicate a levelling off in average ship size after 1980. If the average of the five largest tankers are considered for each year it can be seen tanker size peaked around 1975. If the same exercise is considered for dry bulk carriers their size seems to have peaked around 1985–89.

— If so, should one dredge the old channel or develop a new terminal in an area which enjoys deeper water?

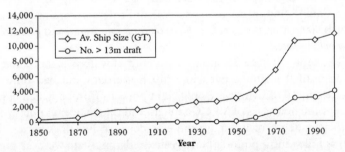

Figure 13: Growth of the average ship size (GT) showing the number of ships with a draft greater than 13 metres.

Ship size and container terminal

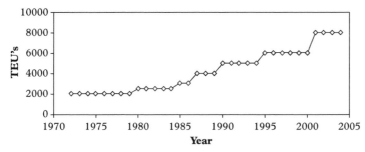

Figure 14: Increasing size of container ships.

The graph above, showing the increasing size of container ships, does not indicate steady continuous growth but sudden rises followed by long plateaux. If container ship size continues to rise then radical changes will be required for terminals needed to service such ships.

The increasing size of the container ship						
Date	*Generation*	*No. of TEUs*	*Speed*	*Length (m)*	*Draft(m)*	*No – 1999*
1960–1970	1st Generation	<1,000	16	200	9	831
1970–1980	2nd Generation	1,000–2,999	23	275	10	1,136
1987	3rd Generation	3,000–4,000	23	290	11.5	222
Start of Post Pamamax v/ls – Max. size for the Panama Canal = 289.5m loa, 32.3m beam 12.04 m.						
1988	4th Generation	4,000–6,000	23	320	14.3	172
1996	5th Generation*	6,000–8,000	23	310 -42.8b	14.5	22
2001	6th Generation	8,000 +	23	338 46b	13.0	P&O, Maersk

* Ships with a capacity greater than 6,000 TEUs are sometimes referred to as Super Post Panamax.
Lloyd's List Jan 2001 uses the term ULCS (Ultra Large Container Ships) of ships of 9000–10,000 TEU capacity. Also proposed terms: Suezmax container ship 12,000 TEU, Malaccamax 18,000 TEU.

The table at the top of page 54 shows the numbers of vessels in the accepted commercial sector classification. As can be seen the number of feeder vessels and their TEU capacity is quite small but so is the average length of their round voyage compared with the Post Panamax vessels which will be used on the longer routes.

From the 3,000-box ship of 1972, container ship size did not increase any further until 1982 when the 4000-box ship was introduced. From there another size plateau was sustained until the

World container fleet in operational categories at 1/2/2004					
Sector	TEU Range	No of Vessels	% of Vessels	No. of TEUs	% of TEU capacity
Feeder	000–499	416	13	131,374	2
Feedermax	500–999	575	18	408,827	6
Handy	1000–1999	915	29	1,289,675	20
Sub-Panamax	2000–2999	508	16	1,261,917	19
Panamax	3000–3999	273	9	944,055	14
Post Panamax	4000–4999	228	7	1,000,577	15
Post Panamax	5000–5999	142	4	783,995	12
Post Panamax	6000+	110	3	723,726	11
Total		3167		6,544,146	

early 1990s when the 6,500-box ship appeared. R.G. McLellan analyses this growth in container ship size in a paper in the *Maritime Policy and Management Journal,* Volume 2, of 1997. In this paper he concludes that:

— One serious constraint on building a 6000+ box vessel was the lack of an engine that could generate the necessary 90,000 bhp capable of driving such a vessel at 24.5 knots on a single screw. However, the development of the Sulzer 12RTA96C and the MAN B & W 12K98MC-C reduced this problem.

— As ship beam increases, cranes must increase in size. This involves increase in weight and there comes a point when the terminal cannot take the extra load without considerable civil engineering expense.

— As ship draft increases, depth of water in ports becomes a problem. Virtually all major ports have 10 metres, but few can offer over 15 metres. At present only two ports in the UK can take the largest container ships.

— For large ships to maintain the same schedules as their smaller brethren cargo-handling speeds will have to be increased. From this it follows that the terminal area will need to be increased and the inland distribution facilities improved.

— Increasing the size of ships may well also increase the peaking factor which can be a serious cost problem for a centre hub port.

— Large ships + expensive port facilities means more claims from pilot impact problems.

In 1999 a survey amongst container shipowners indicated that a major constraint to increasing ship size was terminal productivity. Large container ship operators are looking for 660 container moves per hour. Other factors include berth and channel draft, crane lift height-outreach and quay strength, peaking problems and turning circle availability.

The construction in 2003 of the Ceres terminal in Amsterdam, which can load/discharge containers from both sides and therefore improve port turnround time, was completed. However, although this was a bold management decision by the Port Authorities, the mega container shipowners have shown little interest.

One of the interesting questions therefore at the moment is whether container ships will continue to grow, or remain at around 8,000 TEU? Press reports have indicated that P&O NedLloyd have designs for 10,000 TEU ships. Dutch designers have plans for Malaccamax 18,000 TEU vessels with a 18m draft. Ports with 18 metres draft are Rotterdam, Marsaxlokk, Gioia Tauro, Salalah/Port Raysut, Singapore, HK. All ports would need improved facilities.

Larger container ships—lower unit costs
One of the effects of the increasing size of container ships is the reduction in unit costs. This reduction in unit costs for container carriage added to overcapacity on some routes and the efforts made to reduce the carriage of empty containers means more and more bulk cargoes are being moved in containers. It is estimated that

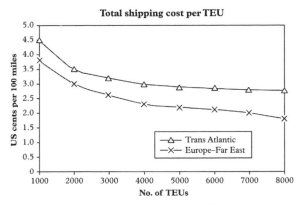

Figure 15: Economies of scale expected for larger container ships.

between 1980 and 2000 container carriers have trebled their market share of what previously would have been considered bulk cargo. In the minor bulk trades the percentage now moving in containers is even greater. Containerisation has made significant inroads into the grain, sugar, fertiliser, scrap, steel and forest products trades over the last two decades and this gain looks like increasing.

Hatch size—perhaps the most significant technical development affecting cargo handling

As can be seen in the diagram, ship A has a small hatch opening and therefore all cargo has to be dragged into the wings to be stowed and back into the hatch square for discharge. With ship B, however, the cargo can be dropped more or less into its required place. This fact is of course quite obvious but it was not possible to build ships with large openings until notch-toughened steel was developed during World War II. Such increases in cargo-handling productivity as seen in bulk carriers and container ships would not have been possible without the "open hatch" ship concept.

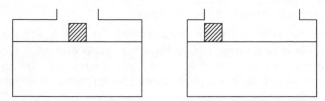

Figure 16: Direct and better "spotting" with open hatches.

H.A.C. = Hatch Area Coefficient See *HJW and Eben on Cargo-handling S.N.A.M.E.*, 16 July 16 1953. In this case HAC = Hatch Area/Hold Area expressed as a percentage.

Year	Sail		Power Driven Vessel
459	Roman trading vessel	9%	
1850	*Cutty Sark*	10%	
1930			17%
1940			20%
1960			28% to 30%
1970			open hatch 80%
1975			container 90%

Hatchless vessels

The advantages for a container vessel are obvious, as there is no time lost in either opening the hatches or in having to secure any containers stowed on top of the hatches.

FastShips

There has been an idea to start a FastShip service on the Transatlantic route between Cherbourg and Philadelphia. The ships would be capable of 38 knots but expensive at around $200 mn each. Annual container liftings on this route are around 24 million tons of which 3.4 million tons are high value or time sensitive. However, 1.8 million tonnes move by air.

Consideration is also being given to FastShip services between USA and Asia, and Europe to Asia.

Note that in 1989 the Japanese developed the design of a super liner carrying 1000 containers at 50 knots but considered the operation would not be economically viable.

The BIMCO Annual report 2000 gave the following possible door to door times for the different container services on the Europe Atlantic Trade:

Conventional Container ship	17–28 days.
FastShip	7 days.
Air Freight	4–6 days.
Express Air Freight	2–3 days.

EFFECT OF PORT TIME ON SHIP SPEED

Ship speed	Port Time	Voyage Time	Total Time	% Change by incr. Speed
10 knots	30 days	10 days	40 days	
20 knots	30 days	5 days	35 days	12.5
10 knots	1 day	10 days	11 days	
20 knots	1 day	5 days	6 days	45.5

As the figures in the above table simply illustrate, the shorter the port time the greater impact ship speed has on the total voyage time and ship productivity is increased. Therefore, as port time decreases, ship's speed should, in theory, increase. This is what happened when containerisation dramatically reduced port time.

This does lead to the rather curious conclusion that the longer the time spent in port the slower the ship's speed should be. To a great extent this is borne out by the facts, in that coastal ships which spend much of their time in port have always had relatively slow operating speeds, whereas ships designed for greater distances with smaller port time/sea time ratios are faster.

The same principle is of course true for any form of transport. In fact, shipping is the mode where one must be cautious in interpreting this principle because of the very high cost of speed for surface vessels – where the cost of increasing speed is higher than in any other mode. The trade-off between the increasing cost of speed against the increased revenue earned has to be considered and the revenue can usually be equated to the value of the cargo carried. This probably explains why container ships go faster than tankers.

Effect of port speed on ship size and hence port location

Faster cargo-handling has caused ship size to increase. Arising from this, shipowners wish to reduce pilotage time and hence look for port locations with these benefits. The same pressures cause shipowners to look for well-placed "centre ports".

OTHER TECHNICAL DEVELOPMENTS AFFECTING PORTS

Effects of the computer on communications

- Container control – there are often discussions as to how many containers can reasonably be handled by a manual system and many have argued that the figure lies between 50,000 to 100,000 per annum. Some would also argue that containerisation as we know it today could not have happened before computerisation.
- Co-ordination of the activities of all the stakeholders involved in port activity.
- Security, safety and environmental protection.

Changes in ship management attitudes and goals

In the days of sail an efficient ship manager liked to have his ship leaving port full and port time was a very secondary consideration. When loadlines were introduced his goal was refined to his ships leaving port "full and down". That is full up and loaded down to her load line marks. This created some intellectual confusion when unit loads were introduced, in particular with regard to Ro/Ro ships. In loading Ro/Ro ships considerable broken stowage (wasted space) is inevitable which was anathema to the manager with the goal of "full and down". With such ships the manager had to measure his efficiency in terms of cargo moved in units of time rather than per voyage.

With modern ships becoming such a major capital investment and yet becoming just one part of the total transport system, there is a growing tendency for ports and shipping to develop together as part of a combined transport strategy.

With the introduction of ISO Code 9000 (Quality Assurance) and the growth of management liability for poor operating practices, general operating culture, which in many ports often had a colourful individual air about it, will tend to become a standard universal material-handling procedure.

JIT (Just in Time) requirements in modern logistics put a greater onus on ports in regard to their reliability and cargo throughput procedures and should reduce the cargo-storage requirements.

Shift of certain cargo-loading aspects from ship to shore

In the last century during the era of the sailing ship, the crew loaded and discharged the cargo.

With the advent of steamships, the development of a workforce of professional dockers and their unions, the port labour took over full responsibility for the cargo transfer, but under the close supervision of the ship's officers.

One of the effects of containerisation has been to reduce port time. This reduction, combined with smaller ships' crews who are changed frequently, has meant that terminal staff take over many of the supervisory tasks of the ships' officers.

Safety

Ship safety is inevitably related to ports, as statistics show that only about 19% of ship unsafety occurs in open water. Most safety problems occur in the port environment or in the port approaches.

Changes in port requirements caused by changes in ships' requirements

Changes in bunkers and ballast are examples of this development. When ships still required coal bunkers large stocks were required and usually special berths provided. Although coal as cargo could be loaded quickly and easily, loading coal bunkers was usually slower as the opening to the ships coal bunker space was often small. Even after World War II there were still ports in the world where coal bunkering was performed by a human chain carrying baskets of coal. With oil bunkers there are few of these problems. These can now be supplied either from a barge or a flexible pipe can be passed aboard at the normal cargo handling berths.

Before ships used seawater as ballast or extra weight to give the vessel her seaworthy trim and stability, ships required solid ballast. For this solid ballast most ports had special ballast quays where the ballast could be loaded and discharged as required. These quays were supervised by the ballast master who was an important part of the ports' management hierarchy and usually one of the first to be appointed when a new port was being developed. However, over the last century ships have been built with double bottoms and special ballast tanks to enable them to ballast with sea water. Ballasting with sea water has obvious cost and time advantages. Less obvious perhaps is the increased safety factor provided by the double bottom skin. There are, however, disadvantages such as dirty and polluted ballast water being discharged. Also ballast water that has been pumped aboard the ship on the far side of the earth may contain micro organisms that cause problems when discharged into a new environment.

CHAPTER FOUR

PORT APPROACHES

Sea approaches and maritime services—vessel traffic services—organi-sations concerned with the sea approaches of a port—agents—safety at the ship/port interface-port security—port security & the ISPS Code—port state control—dangerous cargoes—environmental protection provid-ed by the port—Dock Regulations 1988 relating to Marine Department's operations—licensing of river works and dredging—hydrographic sur-veying—pilotage—tugs—bunker supply—customs, immigration and health officials—changing water depth—tides

Inland Transport—as an alternative to sea transport—shoreside distri-bution and analysis of modal split—logistics and/or intermodal trans-port—comparison of transport modes, i.e. which is best suited for what—modal split.

SEA APPROACHES

Activities, responsibilities and persons involved in the sea approaches and ship arrival

Harbour master/port captain

The International Harbour Masters' Association (IHMA) con-ducted a world-wide survey to identify the duties and functions of a harbour master. Forty functions were listed and every function was performed by at least one of those harbour masters consulted. However, there were only five functions listed that everyone who responded to the questionnaire carried out. This exercise revealed the range and diversity of the responsibilities that are imposed on those who perform the harbour-mastering role. These variations in

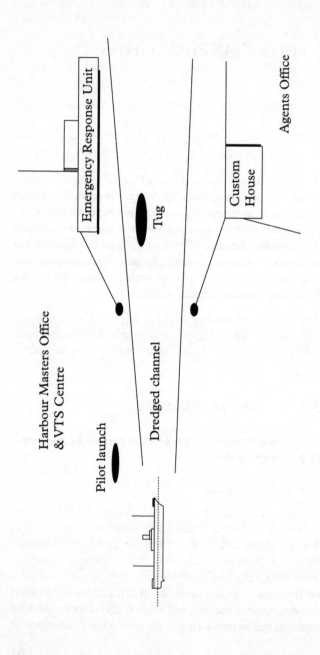

Figure 17: Sea approaches.

the job description are not only explained by differing national traditions and structures as large variations can exist within one country. Factors such as the port's size, its specific function and how it is owned and administered will also make a difference.

There are, however, two basic ways in which harbour masters may be appointed:

— As an employee of the port and hopefully a member of the Board.
— As an external appointment, as in the USA, where the harbour master's (or ports captain's) role is discharged by an officer of the US Coast Guard.

Both systems have their merits. Some argue that in his safety regulatory role the harbour master can function better if free from commercial pressures. Others argue that for the port to optimise its performance the harbour master must be part of the operational team. In practice the choice is seldom so stark, as each system has developed over the years to cope with the situation it finds itself in and hence provides a further reason for the variations in the functions of harbour masters.

On the basis of the questionnaire response the IHMA definition of a harbour master is:

"a harbour master is that person who, whatever may be his local title of office, is the principal person who normally exercises jurisdiction at a place and in ways that meet the following criteria:
— That the jurisdiction is exercised over the water area of a port or port approach;
— That in the exercise of this jurisdiction he should possess an authority conferred on him by national law, regulation or rules;
— That the duties should encompass a legal and/or operational responsibility for the movement of shipping; and
— That the duties should involve him significantly in ensuring that shipping moveme\nts within the area of jurisdiction are carried out safely."

The harbour master's wider role will also usually include:

— The safety of the port and the ships within the port.
— The sustainability of the environment encompassed by the port.
— Emergency planning and training.

The efficient operation of the sea access to the port. Controlling and co-ordinating the arrival and departure of ships from the port will also usually be the responsibility of the harbour master's office. The actual physical location of the harbour master's office will usually have a commanding view of the port entrance and the traffic control centre will often be located in the same building.

Vessel Traffic Services (VTS)

In November 1997 the IMO adopted Resolution A 857 (20) – *Guidelines for Vessel Traffic Service*. In this Resolution the IMO defines a VTS as a traffic monitoring service "Being implemented by a competent authority, designed to improve safety and efficiency of vessel traffic and to protect the environment". The resolution goes on to say that "such an authority may be a governmental maritime organisation, a single port authority, a pilotage organisation or any combination of these".

Most ports of a reasonable size will have a traffic control centre operated by experienced and qualified mariners who will be able to observe the movement of all vessels within the port by enhanced radar and video presentations. They will have continual access to updated weather, tidal and water depth information. The centre will also be in direct contact with all vessels within the port by VHF radio and with the rescue services and relevant commercial bodies, such as ship's agents, by direct-line telephones, etc. As indicated in the next section the actual degree of control exercised by such a centre will vary from country to country.

The World Vessel Traffic Services Guide (published jointly by IALA, IAPH and IMPA) is now available on its own Internet web site: *www.worldVTSguide.org* There are some 200 VTS operators in the UK.

Active VTS or passive VTS

Active VTS: Within a defined area the VTS traffic controller will regulate the conduct of vessels in accordance with port or regional legislation. Vessels are required to conform to a predetermined movement programme, based on such factors as size and type of vessel, cargo carried, berth availability, pilotage requirements and other vessel movements.

Passive VTS: Here the person in charge has only the role of traffic advisor and informing vessels in the area of current traffic movements and of any unusual circumstances.

However, in either case where movements of ships with dangerous cargoes are concerned its advice may become mandatory by virtue of local port by-laws. Most experts seemed to be agreed, that like air traffic controllers, VTS systems will in time extend the extent and degree of their control.

Many ports are now developing what is referred to as "silent VTS". In this system the pilot takes a laptop computer on board with him and all information required by him is relayed directly to his computer via satellite. This avoids relaying information via the VHF telephone.

The centre is also usually the control and co-ordinating centre in the event of any accident or catastrophe occurring within or near the port. As it will record all the visual and other technical data and communications that occur within its area of operation, it will obviously be the major source of information and evidence in any subsequent inquiry.

The port will also probably have regulations which will require the ship's master to give his ETA so many hours or days before arrival.

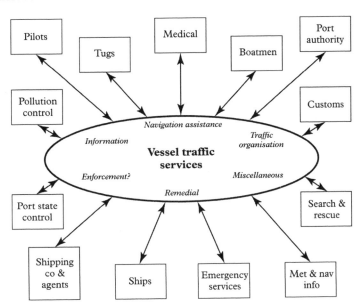

Figure 18: Vessel traffic services.

The VTS will in fact co-ordinate most of the safety and important commercial activities that take place in a port, i.e. those shown outside the ellipse in the diagram on page 65. The functions within the ellipse indicate those functions traditionally associated with the Port Authority.

The BIMCO Bulletin in Volume 93 No.1 98 identified three basic types of VTS:

(1) Coastal VTS – which is mainly for surveillance purposes carried out in sensitive areas such as the Dover Straits. Many will have ship-reporting schemes.

(2) Estuarial VTS, which is provided to ensure the safe transit of vessels in rivers and estuaries on their way to the port or a terminal situated in that estuary.

(3) Harbour VTS to monitor ships entering or leaving a port with little or no pilotage run-in.

Organisations concerned with the sea approaches of a port

IAPH – International Association of Ports and Harbours.

IHMA – International Harbour Masters' Association.

EHMA – European Harbour Masters' Association.

IMPA – International Marine Pilots' Association

The ship's agent

The shipowner cannot always have an office in the port to which his ship trades but the owner will usually want a person on the spot to look after his interests. These interests will fall into two distinct categories.

Firstly the owner will need a "mister fix it" or ship's husband. Such a person will need to know every aspect of the port, such as a good dentist for a crew member with toothache or where and how to get some vital repair effected. In other words the agent has to be able to find an answer to all problems concerning the welfare and smooth running of the ship and crew during its stay in port. In addition, before the vessel arrives the agent will need to notify the port authorities, order a berth, pilot and boatmen. The stevedoring company will also need to be supplied with the vessel's stowage plan and any necessary documents prepared for the many interested authorities such as Customs, Immigration, Health, etc. This service is usually paid for by a fee assessed in most countries by a nationally agreed formula.

Secondly, liner owners in particular will need an agent and loading brokers to market their services in that geographical area and to deal with the huge amounts of cargo documentation that liner shipments generate. Even in this modern computerised era I suspect that there are more people involved in moving the documents around the world than in moving the actual cargo. Further documentary delays and costs may well seriously impede a port's productivity and competitive position. This service is usually paid for on a commission basis.

In many ports the port itself will offer a ship's agency service, though hopefully there will be more than once agency in the port as owners prefer a choice. For ships on charter it may make good commercial sense for the ship to employ two separate agents. One to look after the owner's interests and the other to take care of the charterer's interests, as this avoids any problems that might arise out of any "conflicts of interest".

Development

At the beginning of the last century before the telegraph was developed worldwide the agents in the port virtually controlled the trade out of that particular geographical area. Once quick and reliable communications developed they became less involved with decisions made with the ship's master and more service and information providers to the ship's owners. During the early part of this century they developed slowly but for the most part profitably. The 1970s however produced several problems for agencies. This was a bad period for shipping in general following the oil price rise in 1973 and most aspects of the industry were involved in cost cutting. Further it was a period of major change in the liner industry. Containerisation enabled shipping lines to streamline their operation. Up to the 1960s and early 1970s, lines generally operated a large number of liner services. But by the end of the decade the lines were increasingly merging their operations and reducing the number of agents that they employed around the world. Many lines also set up dedicated offices in all the major ports that they served, eliminating the need for ship agents in all but the smallest feeder ports. To counter this problem many agencies agreed to join forces and set up large international networks of agents. The largest of these was Multiport which held its first meeting in Athens in 1978 with agencies from Australia, Lebanon, Jordan, the UK, France,

Greece, Singapore, Egypt, Germany and Holland. In 1998 Multiport represents more than 3,000 different principals in some 98 countries and territories. The advantage of joining forces in this manner is that it can offer a single marketing strategy for its members and by applying an overall quality control it can offer a quality and reliable service. The Multiport association gained ISO 9002 certification in March 1993. However, Multiport is an affiliation of agencies but in 2004 many long-standing agencies have considered merging into a single entity to be known as S5. It seems that the five Ss indicate shipping, service, systems, solutions and security.

The forwarding agent

The forwarding agent is a logistic expert who traditionally advises the cargo owner on the best way to move the cargo from A to B and to assist in the preparation of the necessary documentation. Like the ship's agent, their development over recent years has been greatly affected by the container but many have met the challenge by setting up as NVOCC (Non Vessel Owning Common Carriers) in their own right. From a ports point of view they are in important as:

— They may be the basic decision maker as regards whether the cargo is routed through your port or not.
— If your port has or is considering "adding value" to the services you offer through a distribution centre, then you will almost certainly be taking on many of the activities associated with the forwarding agent.

Safety at the ship/port interface

On 23 November 1995 at the nineteenth Assembly of the IMO, Resolution A.786 was adopted which brings all matters concerning the ship/shore interface under the wing of the IMO. There were, however, a number of countries which did not believe that the IMO should be dealing with ports. But there is a certain logic to IMO's involvement as IMO is concerned with safer ships and cleaner oceans, and ports are areas where ships need most regulation and can do the greatest amount of damage. However, since the implementation of the ISPS Code on 1 July 2004 the role of the IMO to standardise and enforce international security in ports can no longer be questioned.

Port security and the ISPS Code

In order to mitigate terrorist attack to maritime industry, The International Ship and Port Facility Security Code (ISPS Code) was adopted by a Conference of Contracting Governments to the International Convention for the Safety of Life at Sea (SOLAS), 1974, convened in London from 9 to 13 December 2002. The ISPS Code came into force on 1/7/04. The speed of implementation of the Code was without precedent and many thought it was verging on the impossible, however July the 1st came and went without too much confusion but only after a great deal of hard work and expense. The final bottom line concerning the increased cost to maritime transport has yet to be determined though it will certainly be significant. See *www.bimco.dk* concerning the responsibility and cost issues arising out of the implementation of the ISPS Code in the charterparty context. However, not all the aspects of the ISPS Code are new, and in fact it has enabled the IMO to put all the security issues under one set of standard rules and procedures.

In theory the purpose of the Code is to provide a standardised, consistent framework for evaluating risk, enabling governments to offset changes in threat with changes in vulnerability for ships and port facilities. To quote from the IMO website: "To begin the process, each contracting Government will conduct port facility security assessments. Security assessments will have three essential components. First, they must identify and evaluate important assets and infrastructures that are critical to the port facility as well as those areas or structures that, if damaged, could cause significant loss of life or damage to the port facility's economy or environment. Then, the assessment must identify the actual threats to those critical assets and infrastructure in order to prioritise security measures. Finally, the assessment must address vulnerability of the port facility by identifying its weaknesses in physical security, structural integrity, protection systems, procedural policies, communications systems, transportation infrastructure, utilities, and other areas within a port facility that may be a likely target. Once this assessment has been completed the contracting Government can accurately evaluate any possible risk."

This risk management concept will be embodied in the Code through a number of minimum functional security requirements for ships and port facilities. For ships, these requirements will include:

— ship security plans;
— ship security officers;
— company security officers;
— certain onboard equipment such as Ship Security Alert System (SSAS).

For port facilities, the requirements will include:

— port facility security plans
— port facility security officers
— certain security equipment

(The IMO Global Integrated Shipping Information System (GISIS) contains a country by country search tool which lists each port by an ID number and a UN Locator Code also gives a note on compliance status. *http://www2.imo.org/ISPSCode/ISPSInformation.aspx*)

In addition the requirements for ships and for port facilities include:

— monitoring and controlling access
— monitoring the activities of people and cargo
— ensuring security communications are readily available

Because each ship (or class of ship) and each port facility present different risks, the method in which they will meet the specific requirements of this Code will be determined and eventually be approved by the Administration or Contracting Government, as the case may be.

In order to communicate the threat at a port facility or for a ship, the Contracting Government will set the appropriate security level. Security levels 1, 2, and 3 correspond to normal, medium, and high threat situations, respectively. The security level creates a link between the ship and the port facility, since it triggers the implementation of appropriate security measures for the ship and for the port facility. The implications and liabilities that will be involved when a port announces a security level of 2 or 3 at their port will only be determined over time as precedents are established. Will a port in a period of high risk be a "safe port"?

Ships will have to carry an International Ship Security Certificate indicating that they comply with the requirements of SOLAS chapter XI-2 and part A of the ISPS Code. When a ship is at a port or is proceeding to a port of a Contracting Government, the contracting Government has the right, under the provisions of regulation XI-2/9, to exercise various control and compliance measures with respect to that ship. The ship is subject to Port State control inspections but such inspections will not normally extend to examination of the Ship Security Plan itself except in "specific circumstances".

Facilities for crew to enjoy much needed shore leave in certain ports, particularly in the USA, has been a difficulty facing those responsible for ensuring that possible terrorists can not enter their country. Hopefully a way round this problem can be achieved.

At the same time, the USA implemented a number of new maritime security initiatives after September 11, 2001 attacks on the World Trade Centre and the Pentagon. These new security initiatives form part of the Maritime Transportation Security Act 2002, which was designed to protect United States ports and the public from acts of terrorism as well as prevent the use of maritime trade as a way to transport weapons of mass destruction to the United States. United States Customs and Border Protection (CBP) are responsible for three new initiatives: the Container Security Initiative (CSI), Customs-Trade Partnership Against Terrorism (C-TPAT), and the 24-Hour Rule.

Container Security Initiative (CSI)

Under this program inspectors are placed at foreign ports enrolled in CSI to pre-screen cargo containers being shipped to the United States. CSI has four core elements: Using automated information to identify and target high-risk containers, pre-screening containers identified as high-risk before they arrive at US ports, using detection technology to quickly pre-screen high-risk containers and using smart, tamper-proof containers.

24-Hour Rule

The US Customs instituted the 24-Hour Rule requiring information on cargo destined for the United States to be submitted through the Automated Manifest System (AMS) by the carrier. This rule requires detailed descriptive information for all cargo; so vague cargo descriptions as commonly used in the past, such as "Freight of All Kinds" (FAK), are no longer acceptable. "Do not load" orders are issued to the carriers at the foreign port for cargo that does not meet the 24-Hour Rule.

In order to ensure that the carriers can meet the new 24-Hour Rule requirements for filing detailed manifests at least 24 hours before loading at a foreign port, carriers are requiring shippers to deliver containers to the port several days before loading. Four days is typical, although the required advance delivery time varies among shippers.

Problems and help for developing countries. A report by an American consultant in September 2004 indicated that the ports in developing countries have difficulties with the ISPS code due to its cost and corruption. However, in June 2003 the IMO established an International Maritime Security Trust Fund (IMST Fund) to give related assistance to developing countries. Further, by October 2004, the IMO had set up 74 National Training courses on security issues.

Port State control

The major practical problem of safety re ships is not the lack of adequate legislation but the enforcement of existing legislation. Traditionally this has been done by the Flag State – but not all States have the will or the trained staff to enforce the legal safety requirements. To overcome this problem the 1978 SOLAS Protocol extends this enforcement to Port states. In 1982 14 West European nations signed the Paris Memorandum as a bid to operate Port State enforcement in a uniform manner on foreign ships. Details of Port State inspections are kept on the Computer Centre which is located at Saint-Malo, France.

In the 1994 BIMCO Review, Mr W. O'Neil, the then Secretary General of the IMO, writing on the implementation of safety said "There is a two pronged approach to ensuring this is done – by flag state control and port state control.... *Port state* control is designed as a secondary line of defence. Whenever a ship goes to a port in a foreign country it can be inspected to check that it complies with IMO requirements. In extreme cases the inspectors can order repairs to be carried out before the ship is permitted to sail." In 2002 the average detention rate varied between 2.7% to just over 9% giving an average detention rate of around 6%.

Although regional PSC authorities have set targets for inspecting between 15 and 50% of the ships trading in their waters, a report by the UK P&I Club in 1998 shows that the actual inspection rates vary between less than 0.05% and 37%. Such a variation in standards could allow critics to apply the term "Ports of Convenience" to those ports where sub-standard ships run a reduced risk of detection, e.g. countries with inspection rates below 5% include Hong Kong, Singapore, Malaysia, Papua New Guinea, and Thailand.

Ports which appear to be over-zealous in inspecting ships run the risk of becoming unpopular, not only to sub-standard shipowners but also those with ships of the highest standards. Inspections take time and increase pressure on hard worked senior ship staff.

Dangerous cargoes

The legislation concerning dangerous cargoes is fortunately mostly international in character and substance, as most countries have based their legislation on the IMO Dangerous Goods Code – the IMDG code. In addition there are other international codes which amplify and extend the IMDG Code. To avoid complications which have arisen in the past, correct technical names should be used to describe cargo rather than trade names, and to reduce the risk of confusion all dangerous cargoes are given a UN number. The relevant international codes and regulations are:

— International Bulk Chemical Code.
— Bulk Chemical Handling Code.
— Gas-carrier Code.
— SOLAS/MARPOL Regulations.

Most maritime countries will have in addition their own national legislation which may well be more stringent than the internationally agreed codes. There may also be local by-laws.

The British law based on the IMDG Code appeared in 1965, and is now updated by the Merchant Shipping (Dangerous Goods) Rules 1982, but the practical detailed advice on the Carriage of Dangerous Goods by Sea is given by the *Blue Book*. This is an official publication which gives the relevant characteristics and properties of the goods, details of packaging, advice on stowage and how such problems as the prevention and fighting of fires should be tackled.

As crude oil and most other petroleum products are dangerous cargoes it is not surprising that a substantial percentage of the cargo entering a large modern port is dangerous cargo. For instance, at Rotterdam around 45% of the total cargo handled comes under the heading of dangerous cargo.

Most ports require at least 24 hours' notice for a ship planning to enter with dangerous cargo and will require precise details concerning such cargo. The port may well put restrictions on when and how a vessel with dangerous cargo on board may enter and leave the port and will also have allocated certain areas of the port for the storage and handling of certain goods. Certain toxic cargoes may require specialised handling equipment and carefully trained labour.

Containers loaded with dangerous cargoes are allocated a specific area on the terminal and ship's officers may wish to ensure that the containers have been safely packed and they will give strict instructions as regards their stowage. Containers carrying dangerous cargoes are usually carried on deck on the top layer at the side where they can be jettisoned if necessary. The Code does, however, contain details as regards constraints as to where dangerous cargoes can be stowed.

Goods classified as dangerous are not allowed on passenger ships and they must always be declared by the shipper and the packages clearly marked with the agreed international symbols. They must be accompanied with a Dangerous Goods Note (DGN).

The Times Law Report of 9 January 1998 does indicate that the term dangerous can in certain circumstances take on an additional significance. This report concerns a parcel of infested ground nuts which eventually had to be dumped along with an adjacent parcel of wheat. The ground nuts were held to be dangerous because it was liable to give rise to the loss of other cargoes loaded on the same vessel. Infestation can be a big problem in ports where large quantities of food stuffs are stored for long periods.

Safe ports/safe berths

The legal opinion

Charterparty disputes between shipowners and charterers regarding safe ports/berths are very common. The vast majority of these disputes concern physical damage to vessels which in turn incurs delays and extra costs. The classic definition of a "safe port" given by Sellers LJ in the case of *The Eastern City* (1958): "... a port will not be safe unless, in the relevant period of time, the particular ship can reach it and return from it without, in the absence of some abnormal occurrence, being exposed to danger which cannot be avoided by good navigation and seamanship...".

A good example of a safe port dispute is where a vessel runs aground in the Mississippi River (as many do) in circumstances where the shoaling of the river gives rise to a potential unsafe port claim by shipowners where their vessel has been ordered to, say, New Orleans. Under a time charterparty and the charterers warrant in the charterparty, it is required that any port to which the vessel is ordered should be safe. When a vessel goes aground in such circumstances the shipowner may claim against the charterer for damage to the vessel by grounding and also for any general average expenses and delay. Providing of course that the charterer cannot prove negligence on the part of the master or pilot. Further, a good many safe port/berth claims take place concerning damage to a vessel alongside a berth. Winds blow up rapidly and before a vessel can get out of the berth/port she suffers damage while ranging alongside the berth.

While port managers and authorities are not involved directly in safe port/berth charterparty claims, they do become involved behind the scenes in many of the disputes between owners and charterers for the obvious reason that the charterers of the vessel may have a claim against a port authority/ berth owner on the basis that they may be entitled to an indemnity from the port authority/ berth owner.

Elements of safety

The elements of safety that make a safe port are:

— It is safe during the time the particular ship will be using it.
— It must be safe for that particular ship. It does not matter if it is unsafe for other ship types and ships of other sizes.
— The ship must be able to approach safely.
— The ship must be able to enjoy safety during its stay or at least be able to leave in safety should the port be liable to become dangerous.
— The ship must also be able to make a safe departure.
— Abnormal occurrences will not make a charterer liable for damage to the ship in port if they are unrelated to the prevailing characteristics of the particular port.
— A port may also be unsafe because of danger created by a political situation or an existing state of war.

Port safety following the *Sea Empress*

The Marine Accident Investigation Report on the *Sea Empress* caused many to ponder anew on the whole aspect of port safety and stirred the UK government to launch in 1997 a review of the arrangements for harbour pilotage under the Pilotage Act 1987.

The main conclusions of this review were:

— A Marine Operations Code for Ports should be developed, covering all port safety functions and not just pilotage.
— Pilotage should become fully integrated with other port safety services under harbour authority control.
— Harbour authorities should use their powers to ensure that there is a clear practical assignment of responsibility for the safety of piloted vessels.
— Harbour authorities should be made more accountable for all their port safety functions.
— The IMO recommendations on pilot training and examination should be supported.
— Performance measures should be developed to monitor port safety improvements.

In January 1999 the Port Authorities of Milford Haven were fined £4 million following a judgment on the *Sea Empress* affair.

Environmental protection provided by the port

This may include some or all of the following:

— Setting maximum speeds for surface effect vessels in close proximity to land. Waves from high speed ferries have presented an increased risk of damage to small vessels in the vicinity and can affect the balance between the movement of the sediment in both directions along the coast. In shallow water the waves produced by high-speed ferries distinguish themselves from waves generated by conventional vessels and ferries. Conventional ferries generate short periodic waves with a period of 4–5 seconds. High speed ferries typically generate a wave pattern comprising groups of short and long periodic waves. The long periodic waves cannot normally be observed near the route of the vessel due to the flatness of the wave profile, but the waves cause problems in shallow water and along the shore. See

"The Impact of High Speed Ferries On the External Environment" by the Nautical Division of the Danish Maritime Authority 1996.

— Provision of a range of practical services such as diving, salvage, driftwood and rubbish collection.

— Encouragement of self-help by groups interested in maintaining the water frontage and foreshore.

— Enforcement of international, national and local regulations in regard to Environmental Protection.

— Assessment of the long term impact of all new developments, since the port is the Licensing Authority for all works undertaken in the "water" area under the port's jurisdiction.

Note that APELL (Awareness and Preparedness for Emergencies at Local Level) has been revised to include ports—also *Guiding Principles for Emergency Preparedness and Response* by IMO, OECD and UNEP has been revised and contains an amendment which covers ports.

Dock Regulations 1988, Relating to Marine Department's operations

— Ensure that all areas are adequately lit.

— Provide a safe means of access to/from all vessels and berths.

— Provide safe access by water where necessary.

— Ensure that all vehicles are safe and suitable, and provided with competent and well-trained personnel.

— Ensure that all lifting plant is safe, properly maintained and properly used. Note: all lifting-plant should be tested before being used for the first time and after repair or modification and have a thorough examination by a competent person at least every 12 months. Lifting-plant should be marked with its SWL (Safe Working Load) and a means of identity. Records of tests and thorough examinations of lifting-plant should be obtained and kept for at least two years.

— Ensure that precautions are observed concerning the entering of confined spaces.

— Provide and maintain suitable and adequate welfare amenities.

— Ensure that the correct protective clothing is issued and worn.

Harbour patrol service

This service may be operated by the Port Authority, Police or Customs. Its main function will be to enforce security and the various laws and regulations that govern all activities within the port.

Turning basins

At strategic locations throughout the port system there will need to be turning basins. As a rough guide the diameter of such a basin should be twice the length of the largest vessel anticipated to use that area of the port.

Licensing of river works and dredging

In many ports, dredging can be one of the major costs and in estuarial ports in particular any new structure on the river banks or within the water may cause serious siltation problems. Nowadays it would be usual to do a comprehensive hydraulic simulation study to assess the impact of any changes.

In ports such as Rotterdam situated on waterways which discharge from highly industrialised hinterlands, the dredged silt may contain toxic material which must be disposed of with caution and in a manner that incurs even further expense.

The port will also probably be responsible for enforcing all the environmental regulations throughout the area over which it has responsibility.

Dredgers

Present-day dredging equipment can be divided into two categories. The first embraces vessels, which literally scoop up the soil (mechanical dredgers), while the second type is equipped to dredge by suction (hydraulic dredgers).

The bucket dredger is one of the most common forms of mechanical dredger. Its basic design has remained much the same for many years. Some 13% of all dredgers are of the bucket type, with a heavy concentration in Europe.

About 50% of bucket dredgers have a bucket capacity of 200 to 400 litres and some 20% of the fleet can be called large-sized, with bucket capacities of 800 litres or more. The advantages of this type of dredger are that it can cope with a variety of soils ranging from mud to soft rock. It can also be used for the removal of rock pieces after blasting. It is noisy, however, and tends to block the channel, and it is unsuitable in swell conditions.

The trailing suction hopper dredger was used for the first time during the construction of the New Waterway, the new entrance to the Port of Rotterdam, around 1878. This type is ideal for working on busy shipping channels. It does not dredge in a fixed position but sails slowly under its own power up and down the channel.

In August 1996 *Dredging and Port Construction* gave the following data on dredger types and the approximate numbers in service around the world:

1. 236 Cutter Section and Bucket Wheel Dredgers with dredging depth potential ranging from 3 to 35 metres.
2. 213 Trailing Suction Dredgers with capacities between 23,425 and 45 m^3, some with depths to over 100 metres.
3. 168 Grab and Clamshell Dredgers.
4. 80 Bucket and Ladder Dredgers where the largest can dredge to a depth of 40 metres but where the average for this type would be half that.
5. 77 Dipper and Backhoe Dredgers where the largest can dredge to a depth of 30.5 metres but where the average for this type would be half that.
6. 30 Suction Dredgers.

Hydrographic surveying

Many ports will also need to be able to undertake hydrographic surveys to ensure that their navigation channels are as depicted on the charts. Grounded vessels can not only greatly impede the commercial operation of a port but may also be a cause of environmental danger and a source of expensive legal actions. For instance, it is worth remembering that in the judgment of the *Hermes* case, the port authorities were held solely responsible for the collision, in that the navigational leading lights had been displaced.

Training and licensing of those working on the water

Pilotage

Most ports require ships over a certain size to employ an official pilot when entering, leaving or moving within the port, though certain classes of vessels, such as naval vessels, are exempt. In the past many pilots, as in many UK ports, were self-employed but licensed by some external authority such as Trinity House. However, over the last few years the trend has been for the pilots to be licensed, trained and employed directly by the port. Ports in the UK have only been responsible for pilots since 1988. (The port of Rotterdam has around 300 pilots with a similar number of back up staff. The port is also considering a shore-based pilotage for vessels meeting set quality criteria.)

In the majority of ports the legal position of the pilot is that he is there to give advice to the Master of the ship concerning the navigation of the ship within the port—in other words, in the event of any accident the responsibility is the Master's. However, the outcome of some recent court actions that have involved pilots would seem to indicate that pilots (and their port employers) are finding it less easy simply to walk away from their mistakes. R. P. A. Douglas and G. K. Geen, in their book *The Law of Harbours and Pilotage*, say that the obligation of harbour authorities is no longer to merely supply qualified pilots but to undertake with due care and skill the pilotage of the vessel. These authors also suggest that the harbour authorities may be vicariously liable for negligent navigation by pilots. Further, the UK Pilotage Act 1987 shifted the responsibility of licensing pilots from the General Lighthouse Authority to the Competent Harbour Authority.

The number of pilots in the UK in 1954 was 1,800, while in 2000 the numbers had reduced to 800. Of all the vessels using UK ports some 2/3rds of the vessels were exempted.

In 2002 IMO recommended that ships with drafts greater than 13 metres should use a pilot in the Great Belt between Denmark and Sweden but pilots are expected to report if vessels are unsafe.

Tugs

A modern harbour tug will have a steady bollard pull (SBP) of around 45 tons, whereas 25 years ago a typical harbour tug would have had a steady bollard pull of about 15 tons.

Boatmen/watermen/linesmen

As a large incoming vessel is approaching her berth there are usually boatmen in attendance, in small boats fore and aft, who will assist in passing the vessel's first mooring lines ashore. The vessel can then gentle warp herself into position. It is worth remembering that a large modern tanker may have a mass in excess of 300,000 tons, and 300,000 tons, even when moving slowly, can cause a significant impact. It is not surprising, therefore, that harbour masters will spend time shopping around for the best quality fenders or apparatus that will reduce the impacts of vessels arriving and control and reduce the speed of approach to the berth.

Barge/lighter

This is a flat-bottomed vessel with a large hatch used for lightening a vessel at anchor and/or distributing the cargo around the port or through rivers and canals to inland destinations. Some people use the terms as interchangeable, while for others a barge has some form of propulsion and crew, and a dumb barge or lighter is just a large floating container.

One of the great advantages of Rotterdam is that not only has it excellent road and rail connections but that it also has very good barge access to a huge inland waterway system.

Before containerisation London was very much a lighterage port where a large proportion of cargo was discharged into lighters, even from vessels alongside the berth. In Hong Kong, due to a shortage of container berths, containers are loaded and discharged by specially designed barges which are fitted with large cranes capable of handling loaded containers.

Customs, Immigration and Health Officials

All ports dealing with international trade will have a number of government agencies, usually in residence, which although not actually part of the port may exert a significant influence on aspects of its operation—particularly as regards the arrival and departure of ships.

Customs and Excise departments of governments have for centuries had the authority to say where internationally traded cargoes could be loaded and discharged, i.e. customs-approved wharves, and when and how it was allowed. Until recently the customs authorities were often the only body producing port trade statistics and the large imposing customs buildings which graced the ports waterfront were often the most dominant piece of architecture. In these buildings, which contained the "long room", the Masters of inbound ships "entered" their vessels by presenting the ship's cargo manifest and other official documents. In some ports these time-honoured procedures are still followed but many countries have now adopted more streamlined measures.

Immigration departments of government will often, for a variety of reasons, have a vested interest in preventing its own citizens from leaving or foreigners from entering. In the majority of ports, however, this problem can usually be handled by port security.

Port health and the fluttering yellow flag, whereby an arriving ship indicated its claim to be a healthy ship and made its request for "free pratique", has long been part of maritime tradition. However, now that jumbo jets transfer thousands of people an hour from one country to the next with all the attendant health risks involved, many maritime authorities consider that in comparison ships offer relatively little risk and have reduced the degree and level of inspection.

An "arrived" ship

A merchant vessel will not be able to commence trading until it has satisfied the procedures required by the Customs, Health and Immigration Authorities. Further, during the course of a vessel's stay in port, the Port State Control Authorities may need to check the ship's safety documents.

International bodies such as IMO, BIMCO and the International Chamber of Shipping have worked hard over the last few years through their facilitation committees to try to standardise and streamline these port entry procedures. However, it is one of the jobs of the local agent to ensure that all the necessary documents are prepared and ready for the ship's arrival.

Bunker supply

For a number of ports around the world, the bunker supply business is big business, employing thousands of people and generating many millions of dollars of revenue, both directly and indirectly, each year. Moreover, bunker supply facilities are part of the total package delivered by a port and can thus have an influence on its overall competitive position. Two of the biggest bunker supply centres are Singapore and Rotterdam. Ports that have a substantial bunker supply operation within their jurisdiction will inevitably become involved in the question of bunker quality in the event of any customer complaints as regards this issue. The port authorities in both

Singapore and Rotterdam have given the task of enhancing the quality of bunkers a high priority over the last few years. Singapore is pursuing a direct form of interventionist regulation, while Rotterdam is trying to encourage the industry to regulate itself.

Water depth (see also Chapter Three)

The changing depth of water at Rotterdam

Date	Water depth at port of Rotterdam in feet and metres	
1891	25 feet	7.6 metres
1911	31 feet	9.4 metres
1950	33 feet	10.0 metres
1960	42 feet	12.8 metres
1970	62 feet	18.9 metres
2000	81 feet	24.8 metres

The above table shows that water depth is not a constant factor and that with money, determination and technology it can be increased. However, increased water depth at a port may not necessarily be due to dredging. In many cases the port will move to deeper water or rather develop deep water terminals for its large ship customers.

Limiting water depth in entrance channel 1995 (in metres)						
Colombo	*London*	*Singapore*	*New York*	*Kharg I*	*Rotterdam*	*Antwerp*
13	11.4	22	14.6	32.3	22.5	14.9
Hamburg	*Le Havre*	*Sines*	*Lisbon*	*Setubal*	*Liverpool*	*Sligo*
13.4	28.8	22.5	13.7	11.9	12.8	6.4

In 1939 the majority of ports had no more than 9 metres of water. Only 23 major ports had depths greater than 40ft (12m) alongside the berth at all states of the tide. Even by 1970 finding ports with sufficient depth of water to be able to accept loaded 200,000 ton deadweight tankers was difficult. In 1970 (the early days of VLCCs) there were only eight ports in Europe which could accept such ships and none on the east coast of North America. Energetic dredging operations have improved on this, so by 1975 there were 22 such ports in north-western Europe (of which nine are in the UK), 15 in the Mediterranean, four in North America, 16 in Japan, four in South America, one in South and East Africa and one in south-east Asia. Since this initial surge of improvement the number of ports with sufficient depth of water has increased only gradually. In fact in 1995 only about 10% of major ports have channel depths at MLWS in excess of 15 metres.

It is not only a question of finding sufficient depth of water at the port and in the port, but also in getting to the port, and many of the continental shelf areas of the world present real problems for the larger ship. This problem is aggravated at the moment by the fact that when much of the world was surveyed during the end of the nineteenth century, the maximum draft that the surveyor conceived possible was 6 fathoms or 11 metres. Depths greater than this did not always get the attention many modern mariners would have wished.

Ports in Asia which have container berth with a water depth of 15 metres			
Country	*Port*	*1998*	*2000*
Japan	Kobe	2	5
	Osaka		3
	Yokohama		3
	Tokyo		3
Korea	Busen	4	4
	Kwangyang	4	4
China	Hong Kong	4	4
Malaysia	Port Klang	2	2
	Tanjung Pelepas (PTP)		2
Singapore		6	16

Source: *Lloyd's List.*

The previous table indicates the perceived need of leading container ports to be able to offer water depths of 15 metres at their terminals, to cater for the new generation of container vessels.

Nor is it enough simply to have sufficient water to float the ship. In 1961 the Permanent International Association of Navigation Congresses recommended that the depth of water in port approaches be at least the ship's draft plus 1.5–2.5 metres (sometimes referred to as UKC – Under Keel Clearance). In 1977 IMO recommended that all vessels should have 3.5 metres UKC. One of the reasons why IMO recommends a reasonable UKC is because of "squat". Squat is an effect in shallow water whereby the ship's draft can be increased. For a typical 15,000 dwt general cargo ship this could be up to 1.5 metres, and for a large tanker it could be more. Further, in shallow water the ship's speed will be reduced and if the shallow water is on one side of the vessel the steering may become erratic—a problem that can occur when a ship moves out of the centre of a narrow channel.

Tides

The moon is the major tide-raising force and because of this the Spring tides (the tide with the maximum range) occurs approximately at new and full moon, and Neap tides (the tide with the minimum range) about seven days later when the moon is in quadrature. Also because of the moon, the time from high water to high water is in theory about 12 hours 25 minutes. However, although the moon is the major tide-producing force, its effect will vary considerably from place to place depending on the size of the basin, the depth of water, the latitude and numerous other factors. The greatest tidal range in the world is at the Bay of Fundy, Newfoundland, where it exceeds 15 metres. In the Mediterranean it seldom exceeds half a metre. Just to emphasise how it does vary from place to place compare the following European ports.

	Spring Range	Neap Range
Avonmouth	12.2 m	6.4 m
London Bridge	6.7 m	4.6 m
Southampton	4.0 m	1.8 m
Le Havre	6.7 m	3.7 m
Antwerp	5.2 m	4.0 m
Hook of Holland	1.8 m	1.2 m

Note that at Southampton and Le Havre there is a prolonged stand of tide at high water.

Where there are significant tides it may be considered necessary to build enclosed docks, approached only through *locks*, because apart from the undesirability of the vessel going aground at low water there are problems of cargo-handling when the vessel is rising and falling 6 to 12 metres twice a day. Although these docks do have some advantages in that security is easier and that the depth can be increased by pumping in more water, they do have many disadvantages:

   (a) they are expensive to construct, maintain and modernise.
   (b) there are delays in moving through the locks and possibly in waiting for the necessary tidal conditions.
   (c) there is the possibility of catastrophic delay and expense if the lock gate is damaged.

The size of the lock is often the factor that limits the size of ships which can enter many of the older docks, though modern ports looking ahead have built enormous ones. The largest lock in the world at the moment is at Le Havre, where it was completed in December 1971 at a total cost of about £20 million. It takes on average about 45 minutes for a large vessel to pass through.

INLAND TRANSPORT

As alternative to sea transport

Good examples of this are the trans-continental land bridges such as the Trans Siberian Railway (TSR) or the equally long 7,000 mile Eurasian Continental Bridge which has linked Lianyungang with Rotterdam since 1992. At the moment neither of these routes offer great advantages over the sea passage but their scope for improvement is tremendous. There are also numerous other land bridges in operation across Europe from north to south and across North America and a land bridge is also proposed linking the Red Sea to the Gulf by a fast rail link between Jeddah to Dammam. Pipelines for oil and gas have also been built and their potential for future development should also be carefully considered by those trying to forecast future trade flows. In 1997 there were over 30,000 kilometres of long distance transport pipelines world-wide increasing at around 6-8% a year.

Shoreside distribution

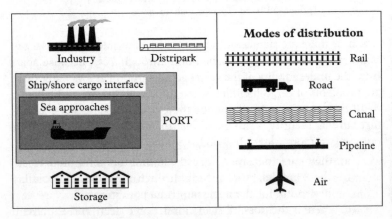

Figure 19: Modes of distribution.

Logistics and/or intermodal transport

Logistics is an even more refined transport concept and can be defined as "an optimisation process of the *location, movement* and *storage of resources* from the point of origin, through various economic activities, to the final consumer". Not all processes are sufficiently integrated to be optimised over the total process from start to finish, though the transport of the banana would seem to be a good example of one that is.

With the advent of containers and other intermodal devices, liner shipping should no longer be considered simply as part of sea transport but as an integral part of a logistics or systems approach to transport. The introduction of intermodal devices, such as the container, not only involves new technology but also the need for new legislation, new documents, new information systems, and perhaps above all , a new way of looking at the transport problem. The liner ship now becomes just one of the modal carriers as the container moves between modes on its hopefully uninterrupted journey from source to destination

Once the cargo arrives at a port it will be moved on by other modes.

An important jargon expression that occurs frequently in port and logistic discussions is JIT (Just in Time) or an alternative expression is MRP (Manufacturing Resource Planning) and the Japanese refer to it as *Kanban*. In short, the idea is the suppliers deliver the needed items to an assembly line or manufacturing process "Just in Time". The purpose of such an approach is that it saves capital in storing expensive items and in the construction of expensive storage facilities. An economist would also point out that it is a demand-led process, as in theory the items need only be produced to order and not on a speculative basis.

Comparison of transport modes, i.e. which is best suited for what

The figures shown in the table at the top of page 88 are not only very approximate but could vary depending on a number of circumstances. They do, however, enable one to make rough comparisons and draw general conclusions, such as that ships are very energy-efficient and safe. (I have found, however, that few students are prepared to accept that aircraft are 20 times safer than buses!)

Mode	Energy efficiency index	Speed	Average haul (USA)	Deaths per billion passenger kms	Date introduced	Vehicle life (years)
Air	1	400 *	1,000	0.02	1958 (Jet)	22
Truck	15	55 *	265	2.4	1920	10
Rail	50	20 (200)	500	0.55	1830 (1970)	20
Barge	64	5.5	330	very small	17thC	50
Pipeline	75	4.5	300	negligible	1856 (1970)	?
Ship (Liner)	100	16.5	1500	1.0	1870 (1970)	15

* In the speed column the figures are specific to the USA.

Other comparative modal safety measures:

Bus	Car	Bicycle	Pedestrian
0.4	3.3	44	62

Where I have put two dates, as with rail, I am trying to indicate that a transport *mutation* took place about that time and that modern high-speed block trains present different transport opportunities to the previous systems. The speed column can also be misleading; for instance, a barge is relatively slow but it can move slowly for 24 hours a day whereas a truck is usually limited in the number of hours a day it can move. From Duisburg to Mannheim is around 300 km and is a stretch of the Rhine where road and rail follow the Rhine. Along this route road haulage averages 43 kph, block trains 38 kph, freight trains 20 kph while barges average 8 kph upstream and 13 kph downstream.

However, research shows what has been a demonstrable fact for decades, that decision makers in favour of road transport are highly influenced by non-price variables such as the control/flexibility factor.

Some comparisons of modal costs

Mode	Commodity and route	US cents per tonne/mile
Sea	Capesize with iron ore from Australia to Rotterdam	0.067
Air	Australia to Europe	12.0
Rail	Coal by rail in the USA	2.17

Source: *Intercargo Annual Review 1996/97.*

The modal cost table on page 88 illustrates how cheap sea transport can be compared with other modes.

Modal split

Year	Port	Road %	Rail %	Barge %	Coaster/ lighter %	Pipeline %	Air %
1913	Hamburg	20	18	17	45		
1958	USA	12.5	39.3	31.7	31.7	16.5	
1970	USA	15.9	35.9	28.4	28.4	19.6	0.2
1984	Rotterdam	70	15	15			
1990	USA	19.4	31.3	26.7	26.7	21.8	0.8
1992	Hamburg	48	37	15			
1995	Rotterdam	60	11	29			
2010	Rotterdam	33	33	33			

— In 1913 road refers to transport by dray, and the lighter served much the same purpose in delivering cargo from ship to warehouse.

— Liverpool in 1922: half horse-drawn, half motor vehicles.

— Competition from railways forced coastal services to improve port turnaround, and also the greater capital of the larger coastal steamships needed higher productivity.

— Rotterdam has good rail connections. First railway from Rotterdam to The Hague and Amsterdam built 1847. New York has poor rail connections but is considering improving. Most US ports have good rail connections.

— In 1991 Hamburg moved only 43% of its cargo by road, whereas the average for France was 58% and Italy 63%.

— In Hamburg in 1997 three out of four containers going distances greater than 150 km travelled by train.

— Modal split Thamesport 1999: Rail 20%, Road 74%, Ship 6%.

— In UK (and much of Europe) there is a policy to shift cargo from road to water, e.g. to carry containers to nearest port and to situate freight stations at canals, rivers, etc.

— In UK 34% of energy consumed by transport.

Modal Shares in EU 15 (tkm in %) projected to 2020			
Year	Road	Rail	Inland waters	Total in billion tkm
1952	35	42	23	
1970	56.0	32.3	11.7	872
1980	64.5	26.0	9.5	1,116
1990	72.9	19.1	8.0	1,338
2000	78.6	14.3	7.1	1,754
2020	45	20	30	

Source: European Commission, ERF.

The preceding tables on modal split show, as one would expect, a growth in the road mode (the percentage road mode for the UK was 88.9% in 2001). The projections for the future, also as one would expect, show a decrease in road transport and an increase in rail and water transport.

Comparative European inland waterway traffics 1975–95 (billion tonne-kilometres)			
Nation	1975	1985	1995
Belgium	5.1	5.1	5.6
Germany	50.0	50.6	64
Finland	4.4	4.2	3.3
France	11.9	8.4	5.9
Netherlands	29.5	32.8	34.5
UK	0.4	0.4	0.2

Source ECMT (1997).

Air transport—a few interesting facts and features

— 1998: the 560 major airports around the world handled 58.2 million tons of cargo and it is anticipated by the industry that this sector will over the next 20 years grow 2% faster than the passenger sector.

— BA invested £250 million in the construction and fitting out of its new World Cargo Centre on the south side of Heathrow (300 metres long, 95 metres wide). It can handle up to a millions tons of cargo a year.

— The carriage of fresh produce has grown at 15% a year over the past 3 years and is worth £45 million annually to BA.

— 1997: 20 airlines and 17 freight forwarders banded together to create CARGO 2000. This has replaced air waybills with electronic messages. Forwarders label all cargo with bar codes before it enters an airline network. This allows cargo to be traced immediately to its status in the system. Since 1996 BA has offered a track and trace service over its world wide website.

— Much of the documentation can be completed and bar codes obtained via the internet.

— Airlines also own, operate and co-ordinate trucking operations. BA spends £19 million annually in extending its flights along the motorways.

— Boeing World Air Cargo Forecast expects cargo traffic to increase at an annual average annual rate of 6.2% for the next two decades.

CHAPTER FIVE

PORT ADMINISTRATION, OWNERSHIP AND MANAGEMENT

Basic problems for port management—types of port ownership and administration—survey of ownership of port activities—why increased private sector participation—ways of increasing private sector participation—boards governing ports—port development from a transport centre to a logistic platform—the rise and fall of ports—a free port or zone—port management objectives—the port as an economic multiplier—competition between ports—information technology (IT) in logistics—port efficiency—port safety and security.

Many would argue that administration and management functions should be considered separately, and that port administration should be responsible for the regulatory functions of the port while the management is responsible for the commercial operations. However, this simple dichotomy may be simplistic and much will depend on the type of ownership adopted and the interpretation given to the term administration which does seem to vary throughout the world.

PORT MANAGEMENT BASIC PROBLEMS

Ports last longer than ships. This is an obvious fact but a very significant one. Most of the UK ports and docks, for instance, were designed and developed between one and two centuries ago when ships were small and much dockside distribution was done by horse and cart.

It is difficult to escape from bad decisions. In other businesses one can often escape from the worst effects of erroneous decisions. For instance in shipping, if one were to buy the wrong size or type of ship, one can with any luck find a buyer for your mistake and start again. It is obviously very much more difficult, if not impossible, to sell a terminal or dock that is in the wrong place or the wrong size or of unsatisfactory design.

A port is not a coherent entity like a ship, but a loose collection of trading activities within a fairly arbitrary boundary. This makes it more difficult to theorise about it and develop universal concepts concerning ports.

TYPES OF PORT OWNERSHIP AND ADMINISTRATION

Ports can be classified as to their type of ownership or administration—in fact, over the last decade this has been one of the most debated topics concerning port efficiency. Before considering port ownership in any detail there are one or two points that should be made:

Traditionally, British textbooks classified port ownership under the following headings:

(1) *State ownership.* However, this heading can cover everything from absolute political supervision to State ownership of majority shares.

(2) *Autonomous.* Public Trusts such as London and Liverpool were before privatisation. Many UK port used to have this type of administration before they were privatised in the late eighties. Such a Trust is a quasi-governmental organisation set up by Act of Parliament. It is non-profit-making and offers a unified functional administration over a functionally defined area. It may suffer from insufficiency of funds and may be burdened with unnecessary restrictions.

(3) *Municipal ownership* such as Rotterdam, Hamburg, Kobe and Yokohama. It has as one of its major advantages, complete co-operation on all the local needs of the port. The municipality may also agree to subsidise the port, because by offering competitive port charges and encouraging trade, the overall prosperity of the region can be greatly increased. One of its major disadvantages is a natural unwillingness to co-operate in any national plan. The term can be confusing because the expression "municipal" can alter its significance in different countries.

(4) *Private ownership ports.* In 1947 about 30% of UK ports were brought into public ownership. During the 1980s various UK ports followed Felixstowe's example and were privatised. Under the 1991 Ports Act, the then Conservative government outlined its intention to privatise several trust ports with an annual turnover in excess of £5m. The UK is one of the few countries to have adopted this approach in its extreme. In 1983 ABP (Associated British Ports), consisting of 19 UK ports, was privatised with most employees owning at least 1000 shares. Since then labour productivity has increased by 40%. Privatisation also caused re-allocation of port property which was put to new use—doubling its capital value and stimulating local economies. However, a paper published in *Maritime Policy and Management* by Saundry and Turnbull in 1997, indicated that the promises of greater competition, greater capital investment and general improved commercial efficiency had not occurred in UK ports—at least not as a result of privatisation.

It is worth remembering that "port privatisation" is not a new concept. In the last century the Port of London was a chaotic jumble of private creeks, terminals and docks and the Port of London Authority was established, largely by popular demand, in order to bring some form of order to the free-wheeling entrepreneurial jungle.

In many modern ports such a classification as outlined above might be considered simplistic, as the ownership might in fact consist of a combination of two or three of the above. One of the most common growing forms of port ownership/operation is the *Landlord* port. In this type the State or the City own the land and the port's sea approaches, and lease out the terminals to private stevedoring firms to operate. There are several variations to this approach. In the Landlord port the landlord provides the infrastructure (i.e. a paved terminal with deep water access) and the tenant provides his own superstructure (i.e. cranes and cargo handling equipment).

In what is often referred to as a *Tool* port the landlord provides both the infrastructure and the superstructure. Where the Port Authority wishes to provides all the services and facilities for ships and cargo within the port it is known as a *Service* port and although many State-owned ports are considering moving away from this type of operation they should consider that this was the type of operation used at Singapore, until it transformed itself into a private company in 1997. However, as a state-owned port Singapore was considered by many to be one of the most efficient ports in the world.

Nowadays most ports will be governed or controlled by a *Port Authority* which in the case of the Landlord port will be the landlord. The Port Authority therefore is a body with juridical status in charge of the management of the port according to the rules defined in its constitution.

Port Authority Responsibilities			
Port Type	Infrastructure	Superstructure	Stevedoring
Landlord	Yes	No	No
Tool	Yes	Yes	No
Service	Yes	Yes	Yes

Another variation might be Build, Operate and Transfer (BOT)

With BOT, the private sector is involved in building, financing and operating a port facility for a certain period of time. The ownership is transferred to the public sector at the end of the agreement. The build-operate-transfer method gives the private sector a large role in developing and operating new port capacity. This method was used by 19% of the ports privatised. As an instance, in India, the Jawaharlal Nehru Port Trust (JNPT) made a BOT contract for construction of a 600 metre container-handling quay over a 30-year period.

A few developing countries have also favoured the method of Corporation (13%) or Management contracts (2%).

The preferred UK solution has been to sell the land and all the infrastructure and superstructure but has few imitators elsewhere. It is difficult to see what advantage is gained by this option, from a policy point of view, compared with the landlord options, particularly as in most cases where this has happened the ports have been sold off at "bargain" prices.

Another variation might be Sullom Voe Harbour, owned by Shetland Islands Council, which is the harbour authority, while the SV Terminal is owned by the oil industry partnership of more than

30 participating oil companies and operated on their behalf by BP under an evergreen contract

Who might own what within a port

In 1992 the Editor of the *Port Development International* seems to have summed up a general world-wide attitude when he wrote "for too long the inefficiencies and excesses of the dockers have been mirrored by top-heavy administrations—over-manned, under-talented and equally obdurate to change". In general the trend world-wide—in Europe, China, Africa, Asia, etc., is to decentralise direct government control and to place the port on a more commercial footing. In the Harris Survey of the late 80s around 80% of ports indicated that private sector participation was increasing in their country's port sector.

A survey conducted by F.R. Harris and summarised in *Fairplay* 21/28 December 1988 looked at over 60 ports in 20 countries. Four out five of the ports surveyed replied that private involvement was increasing or being promoted, although the forms this participation took varied considerably from country to country. The port of Antwerp when replying to the survey made the following very pertinent observation: "you will no doubt agree that it is very difficult to answer your questionnaire as privatisation means so many different things to so many different ports."

The reasons behind this universal urge to privatise the ports is the anticipation that putting the port on a commercial footing will improve the productivity and reduce the size of public sector financial commitments, though, as indicated below, considerable state involvement in the port in one form or another is inevitable.

Survey of some 30 ports world-wide comparing the ownership of the activities involved

The data for the table on page 96 was taken from ports selected from Europe, Asia, Africa and North and South America. As the sample was small and those filling out the questionnaire may not always have been certain which category best fitted the different activities for their particular port, the results should be treated as a general indication rather than a definitive picture. However, the table does illustrate the complex network of activities that goes to make up a port and also shows:

Activity	Type of Ownership %			
	Private	Independent Body	Local Port Authority	Ministry-Govt. Navy
The ship				
Channels, breakwaters, docks etc.	4	4	72	20
Aids to navigation—VTS	0	16	72	12
Pilotage	12	28	52	8
Tugs and boatmen	32	0	52	16
Stores and bunkering	84	0	8	8
Repairs	40	12	28	20
Cargo and passengers				
Terminals	16	12	68	4
Tank farms	44	16	28	12
Cranes etc.	28	0	64	8
Cargo-handling	44	0	48	8
Lighterage	32	8	44	16
Land carriers				
Roads	8	8	64	20
Lorry and car-parks	36	8	40	16
Railway tracks and depots	0	40	36	24
Inland waterways (within port)	0	8	66	26
Pipelines	44	16	24	16
General services				
Conservancy	0	8	52	40
Lighting	0	16	74	10
Firefighting	0	24	60	16
Police force	0	28	48	24
Labour amenities	0	40	48	12
Sanitation	4	24	60	12

(a) That virtually every conceivable type of "ownership" can co-exist within a port, e.g. private, state, municipal, etc.

(b) That who pays for the costs will vary considerably from port to port and state to state. This is the reason for the accusations of unfair competition which are so frequently made and the cause of the problems that exist for, say, the EU authorities when trying to ensure a "level playing field" for all ports within the community. A 1997 report commissioned for the ILO "indicated that in most ports, wet areas (63%) and quays (76%) are in public ownership without competition, while the operation of quays is fairly evenly distributed between the public and private sector".

Arguments for increased private sector participation in the port industry

These are, in descending order of perceived importance, according to a survey:

(1) Reduce size of public sector financial commitments. See the following example of Keelung.
(2) Improve productivity through competition.
(3) Raise funds for other public activities.
(3) Escape the problems of bureaucracy.
(4) Reduce the size of the port labour force—hence the general lack of enthusiasm of unions to privatisation.

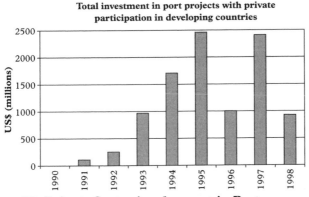

Total investment in port projects with private participation in developing countries

Figure 20: Private Sector involvement in Ports

Of this investment in 1998, 58% was in East Asia and the Pacific, 27% in Latin America and the Caribbean, 4% in the Middle East and North America, but only 0.3% in Sub-Saharan Africa.

A few examples of privatisation

Port Klang (known as Port Swettenham until 1972) started privatisation in 1986 when the government gave a 21-year contract to Port Klang's container terminal as a private consortium. In December 1992 the remaining North & South Ports terminals were privatised under the Landlord system. Since then, repair, maintenance and administration costs have been halved—container tonnage increased 75% and wages increased 85 %.

A report by the American Association of Port Authorities shows that 30% of the 66 US public port authorities operate at a loss!

The report says "weak incentives to operate efficiently and exposure to political interference are the main problems facing US ports".

In 1986 the port of Shanghai was decentralised and operated as a municipal type port. Since 1994 Shanghai Container Terminal has been operated as a joint venture between HIT Hong Kong and the Port of Shanghai. Between 1994 and 1997 the terminals throughput doubled as did the dockers' wages, the costs were reduced by around 10%, the productivity increased around 30% and the average ships time in port was in 1997 around 30% of the average for 1994.

Operation performance—before and after privatisation in Colombian ports

Indicator	Before 93	1996
Average vessel waiting time (days)	10	Virtually no waiting
Working days per year	280	365
Working hours per day	16	24
Bulk cargo (tons per vessel per day)	500	2,500 (minimum)
General cargo (tons per vessel per day)	750	1,700
Containers per vessel per hour (gross)	16	25

Source: Colombia General Port Superintendent, July 1997.

ORGANISATIONS CONCERNING PORTS

IAPH (International Association of Ports & Harbours)

Founded on 7 November 1955 in Los Angeles where 126 delegates from 38 ports and 15 countries had gathered. It is a non-profit making and non-governmental organisation with its headquarters in Tokyo, Japan. In 2000 IAPH had some 230 members. The members include leading ports in 89 countries, which accounts for almost 60% of the world's seaborne trade. This includes 90% of the world's container traffic. In addition, over 100 ancillary maritime businesses are represented as associate members.

BOARDS GOVERNING A PORT

In 1979 Dr Richard Goss published *A Comparative Study of Seaport Management and Administration*. In this study he observes that most ports were under the immediate control of Boards whose members were appointed or elected.

The composition of the Board governing a Port Authority will vary considerably from country to country and on how the port is owned. Because of the wide range of interests and activities that make up a large and modern port there has been a tendency, at least in the past in the UK, for the Board to be too large and unwieldy. Fortunately, the trend since the Harbours Act 1964 has been to reorganise ports on principal estuaries into larger units and reduce the size of the management boards.

Possible constitution of a board for a harbour authority might be:

- *Representative Board.* A Board consisting of persons representing interests concerned with the operation of the port. Their appointment will probably be for a fixed term. The problem may be that such members have little knowledge of port operations and that their primary loyalty may well remain with the interest that appointed them.
- *Board of Experts.* Here the members of the Board may be appointed for their proven expertise in some aspect of port operations. If the appointee is the Government the appointments may be made on political grounds.
- *Two-tier Boards.* Where there is a large Board it could appoint a small executive Board of five or six persons to run the port on a day-to-day basis . The top tier Board would only be concerned with major matters of policy.
- Where the port is a private company its Board will be that of a private company but there are very few of these outside the UK.

Dr Goss in his Study also makes the point that some Board meetings were public. "At some of these, notably in the USA, it is illegal for three or more Board members to meet to discuss port matters without the public having an opportunity to attend..."

PORT MANAGEMENT DEVELOPMENT—FROM A TRANSPORT CENTRE TO A LOGISTIC PLATFORM *

First generation port

Up to 1960 a port is merely the cargo interface location between land and sea transport and can usually be recognised by the following features:

*See UNCTAD Report 1990.

— It is usually isolated from the transport and trade activities, and sees its function in terms of cargo transfer from ship to shore. It may have an EDI system but this may well be incompatible with port users' systems.
— It considers itself an "independent kingdom" with little or no co-operation with local authorities.
— The different port activities are isolated from each other.
— It is usually either a breakbulk or bulk port.

Second generation port

This port has developed as a transport, industrial and commercial service centre. It can be recognised by the following features:

— It undertakes and offers industrial and commercial services to its users which are not directly connected with their loading/discharging activity.
— Port policies and development strategies are based on broader concepts and more sophisticated management attitudes.
— Industrial facilities are set up within the port area.
— It enjoys a closer relationship with transport and trade partners who have built their cargo transformation facilities in the port area. However, only big shippers benefit.
— It develops a closer relationship with the locality.
— Different activities become more integrated within the port organisation.

Third generation port

This emerged in the 1980s principally due to world-wide containerisation and intermodalism combined with the growing requirements of international trade. This port type can be recognised by the following features:

— The port is seen as the hub of the international production and distribution network. Management is proactive rather than reactive.
— As well as traditional activities, activities are specialised, variable and integrated.
— Port infrastructure is planned with equal consideration to structure and information processing facilities.
— The port adds value to the primary product. As mentioned before, the term added value signifies value newly added or created in the productive process of an enterprise. Loading

and discharging are certainly value-adding activities, so are the industrial services of a port noted earlier. In a distribution centre, added value can take different forms such as cargo consolidation and deconsolidation—providing up-to-date information on the inventory and cargo movements, stuffing/unstuffing containers, crating, palletisation, shrink-wrapping, labelling, weighing, repackaging, etc.

— The port works towards environmental protection.
— It works to users' convenience rather than its own.
— It tries to simplify customs' procedures.
— Organisational structures are integrated.

Fourth generation port

A development that appeared in the 1990s and as shown in the summary is the focus on globalisation, especially among the large international operating companies. This same globalisation has seen a standardisation of information and procedures and a greater and more sophisticated use of automation.

Summary of differences

	First Generation	Second Generation	Third Generation	Fourth Generation
Period of development	Before 1960	After 1960s	After 1980s	After 1990s
Main Cargo	Break bulk (bb)	bb and Bulk	Bulk and unitised. Larger ships hence more space for cargo.	Unitisation of a large % of the cargo.
Attitude and strategy re port development	Conservative. Changing point of transport mode.	Expansionist transport, industrial and commercial centre.	Commercially orientated. Integrated transport node & logistic centre.	More sophisticated use of automation.
Scope of activities	1) ship/shore cargo interface	1+ 2) Cargo transformation. Industrial activities.	1+2 + cargo & info distribution. Full logistic potential.	Standardisation of information
Organisation characteristics	Independent activities. Informal relationships.	Closer relationship to port and user. Loose relationship in port activities. Casual relationship with port and municipality.	United and integrated relationships. Move to privatise.	Globalisation of port communities. Greater environmental environmental control.
Production characteristics	Cargo flow. Low value added.	Cargo flow and transformation. Combined services. Improved value added.	Cargo/info flow and distribution. Multiple service package. High value added.	Emphasis on quality of service and trained work force.
Decisive factors	Labour/capital.	Capital.	Technology/ know-how.	Info technology.

Source: Based on *Port Marketing & the Challenge of the 3rd Generation Port*, UNCTAD Report 1990. See also *Maritime Policy & Management*, Volume 31, No. 2, on the Workport Model.

Trend for ports to assume more risks and liabilities

Demand for liability insurance and effective risk management is set to grow as port authorities and terminal operators are increasingly held liable for loss or damage on their premises. For the past 100 years, shippers have taken the attitude that they ought to insure their own product. The attitude is now changing and they do not think they should insure a product entrusted to the care of someone else.

This trend is partly a sign of the times, where the growth in liability can be seen in virtually all areas of commerce. In ports the trend becomes more noticeable as ports "privatise" (government organisations are always difficult to sue) and commercialise, as ports may be forced to accept liability rather than lose trade to the competition ports.

THE RISE AND FALL OF PORTS

Throughout most of the last century (the 20th) the number of UK shipping companies decreased in number and tended to centralise, moving their head offices to London. However, in the last few years we have seen some companies move out of the high rent "City" offices to locations nearer London Airport.

The success and failure of ports is indicated by some of the following league tables:

World leaders in 1937			
Rank	**Port (1937)**	**No. of vessels**	**Million NRT**
1	New York	92,032	68.6
2	London	59,000	61.5
3	Kobe	26,776	28.3
4	Yokohama	5,757	26.8
5	Rotterdam	110,406	22.4
6	Baltimore	56,067	21.0
7	Colombo	2,708	20.4
8	Osaka	18,999	19.6
9	Antwerp	11,125	18.7
10	Hamburg	16,141	18.4

This table shows the dominance of the Atlantic basin in 1937.

Port Size League 1995					
Rank	*Port*	*mn tons*		*Port*	*mn tonnes*
1	Singapore	305.5 FT		Rotterdam	293.4
2	Rotterdam	291.2 MT		Singapore	235.2
3	Chiba	176.2 MT		Shanghai	165.0
4	Shanghai	166 MT		Hong Kong	127.8
5	Nagoya	142.6 MT		Nagoya	124.5
6	Yokohama	131.5 MT		Antwerp	108.1
7	Ulsan	127.3 MT		Yokohama	106.5
8	Hong Kong	127.3 MT		Pusan	93.4
9	Kwangyang	108.4 MT		Long Beach	89.8
10	Antwerp	108.1 MT		Marseilles	86.6

Source: *Shipping Stats and Market Review*, Oct. 1996   Source: *Baltic Magazine*, November 1997.

The above tables give the 1995 figures showing the total through-put figures for the worlds 10 largest ports. It also shows differences between different sources. However, disregarding the differences, what both tables show is the complete dominance of the Far East and the Pacific.

Growth of ports world wide between 1970 and 2002 (million TEUs) (R= rank)					
Port	*2002*	*2000 (R)*	*1990 (R)*	*1981 (R)*	*1970 (R)*
Hong Kong	18.6	18.1 (1)	5.1 (2)	1.6 (4)	0.036
Singapore	16.9	17.1 (2)	5.2 (1)	1.0 (6)	0.006
Busan	9.3	7.5 (3)	2.4 (6)		
Shanghai	8.6	5.6 (6)			
Kaohsiung	8.5	7.4 (4)	3.4 (4)	1.1 (5)	
Shenzhen	7.6	3.9 (11)			
Rotterdam	6.5	6.3 (5)	3.6 (3)	2.6 (1)	0.24 (4)
Los Angeles	6.1	5.0(7)	2.1 (7)		0.17 (6)
Hamburg	5.3	4.3 (9)	2.0 (8)	0.9 (7)	0.07
Antwerp	4.8	4.1 (10)	1.5 (14)	0.8 (12)	0.2 (5)
Long Beach	4.52	4.6 (8)	1.6 (12)		0.048
Port Klang	4.5	3.2 (12)			
Dubai	4.2	3.1 (13)			
New York	3.7	3.05 (14)	1.9 (9)	1.9 (2)	0.93 (1)
Qingdao	3.4				
Bremen	3.0	2.7 (16)	1.2 (18)	0.8 (10)	0.2 (5)
Gioia Tauro	2.97	2.65 (17)			
Manila	2.95	2.29 (19)			
Tokyo		2.9	2.9 (15)	1.6 (13)	0.054
Felixstowe	2.8	1.8 (28)	1.4 (15)	0.5 (22)	0.09
PTP	2.6	Tanjung			
Yokohama	2.3	2.3 (18)	1.6 (11)	0.8 (9)	0.148
Kobe	2.0	2.26 (20)	2.6 (5)	1.6 (3)	0.09

Sources various, and not always in agreement.

In 2002 London was in position 37, handling 1.6 million TEUs.

The table at the bottom of page 103 looks at the container TEU movements between 1970 and 2002. The figures may not be precise but radical changes can be seen to have taken place in the late 1970s and early 1980s with port leadership and trade moving away from Europe, USA and the Atlantic to the Far East and the Pacific Rim. It also shows the phenomenal growth of ports such as Gioia Tauro, which only handled its first container in 1995.

Growth of container traffic in the Hamburg–Le Havre range 1990–2002 (in TEUs)				
Port	1990	1997	% growth 1990-97	2002 in mn teu
Antwerp	1,549,113	2,950,000	90.4	4.8
Zeebrugge	342,440	640,000	86.9	1.0
Hamburg	1,968,986	3,300,000	67.6	5.4
Rotterdam	3,666,666	5,340,000	45.6	6.5
Bremen	1,197,775	1,700,000	41.9	3.0
Le Havre	857,765	1,100,000	28.2	1.7

Source: Antwerp Port Authority.

The table above shows that competing ports in the same economic region have grown at different rates

Major World Ports—Cargo Traffic in Million tonnes and Number of Ships in 2002						
Port	Bulk	Container	Other Gen.	Total	Rank (tons)	Ships(no.)
Rotterdam	233.4	51.8	33	321	2	29,092
Singapore	137(FT)	184	14(FT)	326(FT)	1	142,745
Hong Kong	39.2	133	20	193	5	218,490
Houston	84	–	74	159	3rd USA	6,414
Port Hedland	82	.002	.5	82	3rd Aus.	693

Source: ISL Bremen.

This table again stresses that large ports can be large for different reasons.

A free port or zone

Dr Ernst Frankel distinguishes between several types of industrial free ports or zones but basically they are a small part of the national territory remaining under full sovereignty of the State but placed outside customs limits. Goods are still subject to other laws, for example, those involving the safety and sanitary aspects of the goods.

The advantages of a free port is that it reduces the time and effort required in customs formalities and avoids having large amounts of money deposited with the customs for duty on goods that are only in transit or being assembled in the area before being exported as part of a larger product. In 1986 T. F. B. Helm estimated that 20% of the world's trade was handled in the 478 free zones situated in more than 80 countries—compared with only 10% in 1981. Hamburg is perhaps the most famous, being established as such in 1888. In 1984 six areas in the UK were designated as free ports.

Port management objectives

In the past, few ports seem to have had clear and explicit management objectives. However, the adoption of the ISO Code 9000 and the development of Quality Management by ports in the early 1990s will have caused the minds of port Boards to focus on this problem and come up with a variation of the following:

1. Ways of minimising costs.
    (a) Minimise payments by users in the port—including ships' time at a port.
    (b) Minimise users' total through transport costs.
    (c) Minimise port costs.
2. Maximisation of benefits
    (a) They maximise benefits to the owners of the port.
    (b) They maximise benefits to the town, region or country.

The port as an economic multiplier

Employment as economic impact

The fact that ports have an economic impact on a region is obvious, but the difficult question is the scale of the impact. To do a full EIS (Economic Impact Study) is time-consuming, expensive, intricate and seldom precise, so why bother to try? The main reasons seem to be:

1. To persuade authorities to support their ports with money and favourable policies. One can note that ports as Antwerp, Amsterdam and New York have been the pioneers of such techniques, possibly because they have been ports that needed such assistance.
2. To convince the moneylenders, such as the World Bank, that the investment is worthwhile.

3. To assist port managers to understand which of their activities contributes most to wealth-generation and maximum employment.

The techniques for doing an EIS seem to have been developed just after the Second World War. This was a period of reconstruction and rapid trade growth, a time when ports worldwide had to make massive capital investments. However, possibly few developing countries could attempt such a complete analysis at the moment. It requires a very comprehensive amount of statistical data from many sectors of the economy.

Mr R. L. M. Vleugels in one of the earliest papers on the subject *The Economic Impact of Ports on the Regions they serve and the Role of Industrial Development*, given in 1969 identifies three approaches to calculating the impact:

1. *The added value.* A rough estimate of the impact of a port can be obtained by calculating the added value of all the industries, which can be listed under the term "port-related". For this purpose the net added value could be considered to be basically the gross profits of the enterprise and of the wages of the employees.
2. *Input-output analysis.* This is labour intensive and requires a considerable amount of statistical data, which may not be available in many countries.
3. The collation of the statistical data which show or suggest the relation between port activities and the socio-economic prosperity of the region

Examples

Le Havre

In the early 1990s the port of Le Havre estimated that it created:

— 7.2 billion francs value added in regional industries;
— 3.8 billion francs value added in regional transport;
— 2.3 billion francs value added in regional commercial services.

Hong Kong

The port of Hong Kong generates 20% of Hong Kong's GDP and supports 20% of all business establishments in the locality. In 1994 it provided employment for 350,000 people or 20% of its work force.

Callao (Peru)

The port and its hinterland generates 54% of the country's GDP.

Hamburg

Port dependent jobs made by Hamburg 1992			
Sector		*No. of Persons*	*Percentage*
Port based	Cargo-handling	5,637	4.0
Port based	Other	40,710	28.5
Trade, banking, insurance	22,290	15.6	
Miscellaneous	Customs, rail etc.	6,592	4.6
Port-based industries		19,774	13.9
Jobs indirectly dependent on port		47,545	33.3

15% of all jobs in Hamburg were dependent on the port.

In millions BEF 1992	Rotterdam	Antwerp
Direct value added	272	192
Total value added	404	293
Millions of tonnes handled	304	104
Direct value added per tonne	0.90	1.85
Total value added per tonne	1.33	2.82

Source: Port of Antwerp Policy Research 1995.

The value added per tonne shown in the table above is an interesting statistic. A study comparing the results for leading world ports would make a useful analysis.

COMPETITION BETWEEN PORTS

A recent survey of the Atlantic market indicates that the traditional approaches to explain inter-port competition, including the hinterland concept, are not particularly helpful. The competing ports must be viewed from the exporters' and importers' perspectives as seen in the table at the top of page 108.

Although the customers form the major decision makers as regards to which port to use, their decision will depend not only on the ability and willingness of the suppliers (as shown in the table), but also on the possibilities of new potential entrants into the game and the ability to find substitutes in economic alternatives formed by other transport modes.

Port selection criteria	Rank
Number of sailings	1
Inland freight rates	2
Proximity of port	3
Congestion	4
Intermodal links	5
Port equipment	6
Port charges	7
Customs handling	8
Port security	9
Port size	10

Port services criteria	Rank
Road and rail services	1
Container facilities	2
Tracking systems	3
Warehousing	4
Consolidation services	5
Heavy lift services	6
Marshalling yards	7
Bulk facilities	8
Cold storage facilities	9

Source: Strategic Planning Research done for the City of Rotterdam in 1989.

Strategic Planning Research done for the City of Rotterdam in 1989 concerning the criteria for selecting a port came to the conclusion that the most important factors in the decision to select a port revolve round the various aspects of *cost*, *service* and the *movement* of goods.

— *Cost*. Competitive costs and low freight rates
— *Service*. Reliable, fast, good communications, high number of sailings and low congestion.
— *Movement*. Road and rail access with good intermodal links.

Transhipment share in the Hamburg–Le Havre range of ports	
Year/Port	1990
Hamburg	9.3%
Bremen	4.6%
Amsterdam	4.8%
Rotterdam	43.7%
Antwerp	15.5%
Ghent	3.7%
Zeebrugge	4.6%
Dunkirk	5.6%
Le Havre	8.2%
Total	**100.0%**

The transhipment cargo does represent a segment of traffic that is most vulnerable to competition.

A report in *Lloyd's List* in November 1998 indicated that there was a possibility that a private company could end up as the major shareholder controlling a number of privatised terminals which handled over 25% of the deep sea container throughput in NW Europe. Regardless of such deals, it is certainly a possibility that the majority of terminals could in effect come under the control of one multinational organisation. Such a monopoly situation would not improve competition.

Co-operation between ports

In October 1998 the ports of London and Hamburg reported to the press that they had reached a joint working agreement, particularly in their marketing fields, to form a "trade bridge". This is just one example of many, where ports have decided to work together in various areas for their mutual advantage. So competition between ports is certainly growing but so is co-operation.

Hamburg and Bremerhaven Container Terminals combined in 1999 to fund the Eurogate venture. Also included in their influence are Gioia Tauro and La Spezia where they have controlling shares and 16% in Liscont at Lisbon.

Global marine container terminal operating companies

Twenty such major companies exist, five of which are global companies (as at April 1999):

1. PSA Corporation operates terminal facilities in Singapore, Dalian, Nantong, Fuzhou, Taicang, Cigadin, Aden, Genoa, Venice, Tuticorin.
2. Hutchison Port Holdings (HPH) (A.P. Moller owns 10% of shares) operates terminal facilities in Hong Kong, Shanghai, Yantian, Gaolan, Jiuzhou, Nanhai, Jiangmen, Shantou, Xiamen, Felixstowe, Thamesport, Harwich, Rotterdam, Freeport (Bahamas), Cristobal, Balboa, Yangon, Koja, Port Klang (Westport). HPH handles over 10% of world container liftings (18mn teus 1999) and owns 14% of the world's container terminals.
3. P&O Ports operates terminal facilities in Sydney, Melbourne, Fremantle, Southampton, Tilbury, Lame, Genoa, Naples, Cagliari, Manila, Shekou, Bangkok, Laem, Chabang, Vostochny, Port Qasim, Colombo, Nhava Sheva, Buenos Aires, Maputo.

4. Stevedoring Services of America (SSA) operates terminal facilities in Seattle, Portland, Tacoma, Oakland, San Francisco, Long Beach, Los Angeles, Mobile, Charleston, Savannah, Jacksonville, Manzanillo.
5. ICTSI operates terminal facilities in Manila, Buenos Aires, Rosario, Veracruz, Karachi, Dammam, Ensenada, Rosario.
6. "Vertically Operated" logistic operators as Maersk and Evergreen operate many terminals.

In 2003 Drewry Shipping Consultants of the UK published a multi-faceted analysis of global container terminal operators. Their Annual Review of Global Container Terminal Operators benchmarks the operators' performance and sets out current and future "league tables".

Analysis of confirmed expansion plans reveals that P&O Ports is set to join Hutchison, PSA and APM Terminals at the head of the global port operators' league table. Over the course of the next five years the gap between these four companies and the remaining global operators is set to widen further—by 2008, the top four operators will control over one-third of total world container port capacity.

The report adds that: "These companies have established a truly global presence—collectively operating in over 90 ports throughout 37 different countries. Consequently, the coming five years will see these leading operators not just continue to dominate the market, but also to increase the gap between them and the rest of the global operators."

INFORMATION TECHNOLOGY (IT) IN LOGISTICS

Reduced costs of IT hardware and increased capability have stimulated growth. For example in 1983 computer memory cost $300 per megabyte but by 1996 memory only cost $0.21 per megabyte. Also telecommunications costs overall have been reduced by a variety of new developments.

IT within the shipping industry between 1970–80 was mainly by mainframes but there were few on ships. Between 1980–90 the industry developed mini-computers and dedicated computers such as loadmasters and it was not until the 1990s that PCs were found on ships.

Management information systems

As in any commercial enterprise, the purpose of information technology is to optimise the use of resources, thus reducing costs. Such a system will usually monitor the overall performance of the enterprise, thus giving the management a total picture of what is happening as it happens, which previously could not be properly completed in a vast complex organisation such as a port.

Systems often found in ports

(1) Management of vessel operation facilitates management control over vessel arrival/departure and attendant facilities such as tugs, berths, pilots, etc.

(2) Management of cargo and terminals:

— centralise the management of cargo information and data;

— optimise the flow and control of cargo on the terminal;

— provide data and statistics;

— produce necessary documents;

— simplify reporting procedures to various agencies;

— calculate charges and issue invoices;

— help organise labour;

— assist management in quality and environmental control.

Electronic Data Interchange

— Predates the Internet but is more expensive than the Internet to use.

— Structured data can be transferred between organisations.

— Data transmission can be made secure.

— Audit trail can keep track of transactions.

— Banks can be connected into the system with automatic bill paying.

— UK companies use EDI—57% of users see this as a key way of improving productivity.

Definition of EDI

The computerised electronic exchange of information of structured data between computers in various organisations in the form of standard messages.

Development of EDI	
Date	*Development*
1968	L.A. and San Francisco clearing houses-Special Committee On Paperless Entries. SCOPE
1975	Development of EDIFACT Electronic Data Interchange for Transport and Commerce by UN/ECE
1982	Hamburg – DAKOSY
1983	Le Havre – Automated Customs Clearance of Goods ADEMAR
1984	Felixstowe – FCP80
1984	Singapore – PORTNET – early1990s TRADENET
1985	Rotterdam – INTIS – International Transport Information Systems
1985	P & O – DISH – Data Interchange for Shipping – INTIS Rotterdam
1986	Japan – SHIPNET – SEAGHA Antwerp
1987	ISO accepted UN/EDIFACT syntax
1988	Hong Kong – TRADELINK
1989	Australia – TRADEGATE
1993	Bremen BHT
1994	Gothenburg – EDIFACT – Korea KL-NET
1995	MARTRANS – an EU project to interconnect existing EDI Port Community Systems and implementing new EDI systems in non-automated ports. However since its inception the emphasis has shifted from maritime competitiveness to intermodal effectiveness, from European to International partnership and from EDI to the Information Highway
1997	MOSES – Modular and Scalable EDI System to provide an easy and cost effective system for small and medium size ports
1998	OOCL launch their Internet B/L service

See MPM, vol. 27, No. 2.

The table above gives a sample of international EDI development. It also shows that EDI started in the mid-sixties for banks and finance houses, but it was perhaps another decade before shipping and ports became involved. By the mid-eighties most major ports and shipping companies had systems up and running and by 1995 many of the local and regional systems had become global as information was exchanged around the world.

The Internet

Most ports in the world now have their own websites, which vary considerably in their use and effectiveness. Many of these provide email addresses so those specific customer queries can be satisfied. The number of logistic databases that can be found through the many search engines available is growing by the minute. The development of an intermodal information system based on the Internet is part of the MARTRANS project.

Maritime e-Commerce Association:

www.meca.org.uk
info@meca.org.uk
E-services by satellite from 2003.

The use of the internet. At the end of 2001 it was estimated that in a typical liner transaction the cost to the liner company for entering a new customer into the system was estimated to be $295 by phone, $83 by email, $ 11 via web self service

Conclusion

The impact of the computer on ports, as in most areas of activity, is still in its infancy and as in the development of most new technologies there is considerable variety in the software and hardware available. Because of this there is no standard model as regards its port application. Assuming technological development follows its normal course, one or two systems will probably eventually emerge dominant.

One of the few problems caused by not having a standardised system is that port statistics, which for most ports are now generated by their software systems, often contain subtle but significant differences in the precise details of their calculation.

PORT EFFICIENCY

As the main motive behind management and administration changes is the quest for greater efficiency, perhaps it is worth considering what this entails. If Efficiency is defined as the optimum use of resources within an acceptable context of safety, one has a reasonable starting point.

To optimise one has to be able to quantify, so the first step should be to define what can be quantified on a comparable basis. The comparable basis is necessary as there is no absolute measure of commercial efficiency, only that A is better than B or that A is better this year than last year.

At the moment most forms of financial comparability are not possible. Different ways of calculating the depreciation of port assets, different methods of allocating capital costs, different taxation systems, different forms of "financial assistance", etc., make comparing profitability a waste of time. Similar difficulties apply to cargo-handling costs, with the extra difficulty that actual costs are a matter of confidential negotiation with each client. However, one can try to produce an aggregated benchmark norm.

A starting-point would therefore seem to be to identify what can be precisely measured with the minimum of confusion. Apart from perhaps Port Dues there is little that can be measured on a whole-port basis. Most comparable data must concentrate on a terminal basis. See Chapter 10.

In November 2004 the Port of Rotterdam announced it is going paperless. Will this increase efficiency?

SAFETY
IMO and port safety

— 1964 Code of Safe Practice of Solid Bulk Cargoes.
— Adoption of the International Maritime Dangerous Goods (IMDG) Code in 1965.
— 1972 CSC (Container Safety Code) Convention.
— 1978 SOLAS Protocol extended safety enforcement by flag state to include the port states. This enforcement was made more uniform in 1982 when 14 European states signed the Paris Memorandum.
— 1978–1984 International Safety Guide for Oil Tankers and Terminals. Produced by ICS, OCIMF and IAPH.
— 1980 The Recommendations on the Safe Transport, Handling and Storage of Dangerous Substances in Port Areas.
— 1985 IMO/ILO Guidelines for Packing Cargo in Freight Containers or vehicles.
— 1995 Assembly resolution A.786(19) on Strategy for ship/port interface (SPI). The working group on SPI started work in 1992.
— 1996 The Sub-Committee on the Carriage of Dangerous Goods (CDG) was merged with the Sub-Committee on Containers and Cargo to form the new Sub-Committee on Dangerous Goods, Solid Cargoes and Containers (DSC).

Ports Marine Safety UK—Port Marine Safety Code

(1) Requires the publication of plans, accounts and performance reports.

(2) Allows minister to remove powers from Harbour Authority.

(3) Allows Harbour Authorities to regulate navigation within the port

(4) Amends restrictions from pilots exemption.

(5) Gives the Secretary of State powers to direct harbour authorities if they are failing in aspects of safety.

The Port Marine Safety Code represents an agreed national standard against which the policies, procedures and performance of harbour authorities may be measured. The harbour authorities, commissioners or trustees will in most cases be considered the corporate "duty holder" and as such must have a plan and policies encompassing the details of the safety code. They must ensure adequate resources exist to allow such a plan to function.

Note: In 1999 8 deaths and 695 injuries were reported in UK ports, which was four times higher than the average for all UK industries.

Port security

What precautions has the port implemented against unlawful acts as terrorism, theft, sabotage, stowaways and illegal immigrants, smuggling, etc.? Is security a port management problem or a matter for the local or state police force?

Has the port made a Port Vulnerability Assessment? This should include examination of the following:

— Type of security force.
— Physical security measures. types of fencing, barriers, lighting, IDS (Intrusion Detection Systems), etc.
— Routes of access/egress.
— Communications.
— Availability of additional port security resources.
— Response time/distance for security personnel.
— Proximity to urban areas.
— Geographic location.
— Proximity to international borders.
— Specific local problem—What are the port security problems?

See Chapter Four concerning the International Ship and Port Facility Security Code (ISPS Code).

Environmental safety

See Chapter Twelve on Port Environmental Matters.

The main problems are:

— Water quality—is the quality improving or getting worse?
— It has been estimated that some 10 billion tonnes of ballast water are carried between distant and dissimilar ports and may contain organisms that could cause problems at the discharge ports. The *Management of Water Ballast* was adopted in a New Annex VII to MARPOL 73/78 in the year 2000. This will make the mid-ocean ballast exchange mandatory unless the destination port gives exemption or the master reasonably determines that such an undertaking would jeopardise the safety of the ship. At the moment many ports and countries have their own restrictive water ballast change regulations. BIMCO has a database of the regulations for more than 100 countries which can be found on the Internet. The USA and Australia are among the foremost of nations which have developed comprehensive regulations covering this problem.
— Waste reception facilities—to charge or not to charge?
— Dry bulk handling facilities to reduce dust.
— Tankers—spill response unit.

After discussions with environmental experts, I am of the opinion that environmental safety, like profit, can only be self compared, e.g. is water quality improving or worsening each year?

There are, however, certain aspects, such as the percentage losses of environmentally dangerous commodities like bulk fertiliser at a terminal, which could be measured and compared.

CHAPTER SIX

PORT POLICY

*General points on maritime policy—corruption—national port plan-
ning—EU port and transport policy—relationship between port and
state—constraining influences on port management—port ownership—
port and state financial assistance—port pricing.*

GENERAL POINTS ON MARITIME POLICY

What is it?

"National shipping policy, an element of overall economic policy, expresses
the attitude of the State to Shipping. Shipping policy can be understood as
the totality of economic, legal and administrative measures by means of
which the State influences the position of its national fleet, that is, its place
and role in the national economy and in international freight markets....
The attitude of the State to its own merchant marine as a rule reflects indirectly its attitude to the fleets of other countries...

Shipping policy has then two aspects: foreign, expressing the attitude to
other fleets, and domestic, to own merchant marine."

Chrzanowski gives the above definition in his book on maritime
economics. It is very comprehensive but its meaning can take a
wider compass. It does concern Governments—but a government
has many departments. For example, the USA has the FMC,
Maritime Administration, US Department of Justice, Coast Guard,
Customs, etc. Each bureaucrat or official may also have his own
interpretation of a national policy.

Further it is not only governments that can have policies; organisations such as IMO and UNCTAD have policies, so one could
say: "Policy is a course of action adopted for the sake of expediency
to achieve a certain goal or offset a danger."

A policy maker is therefore an administrator trying to solve a
problem. There will nearly always be a problem but ports will only

117

turn to their national government when they have a problem, usually a financial problem. When all is going well with a port and it is making a reasonable amount of profit, the last thing it wants is interference from national or international bureaucrats.

Policies can usually be separated into two main groups:

1. Those concerned with safety, security and the environment. These are areas best suited to international agreement and are relatively simple in that some sort of agreement is usually possible. It would not be politically correct for a politician to be seen to be taking a stand against these issues.

2. Those concerned with commercial issues. These may place the politician in a dilemma. On the one hand there are often issues concerning justice and fair play between ports in a country or region; on the other hand the politician is concerned with his or her popularity amongst a specific group of voters. Policies in such areas usually end up with compromise solutions or working parties are set up to delay a decision.

However, once the policy maker has identified the problem the solution lies in a variety of options—all with good and bad effects.

See E. Frankel, "Hierarchical logic in shipping policy & decision-making", *Maritime Policy & Management*, 1992, Vol. 19, No. 3, pp. 211-221.

Policy makers must

— know what is happening and why;
— collect all available data;
— pursue the right goals;
— consider all the implications of the policy;
— ensure the policy is enforceable.

How can it achieve this policy ? Basically a government has one of two options: it can either help its own national industry or make things difficult for its foreign competitors.

Helping own nationals by subsidies or some form of financial assistance

Summary table of maritime subsidy measures (US Maritime Administration 1993)						
Type	USA	UK	Japan	Greece	Nigeria	Sweden
Operating Sub.	x					x
Construction Sub.		x	x			
Restructuring aid		x	x	x		
Financing aid	x		x	x		x
Cargo preference	x					
Bilateral agreements	x	x	x		x	x
Scrap & Build aid			x	x		
Export Aids			x	x		
Tax benefits	x	x	x	x		x
Customs preferences	x		x	x	x	x
Government Ownership		x	x			
Cabotage	x	x	x	x	x	x
R & D aids			x			
Insurance aids					x	
Other aids	x	x	x	x	x	

One of the major problems as regards subsidies or financial aid is that everyone has a different perception of what it entails and such help can take many forms. In the preceding table the US Administration attributes many types of financial aid that it sees offered by the UK Administration but the UK Administration would stoutly deny most of them, particularly the accusation that it practices cabotage.

CORRUPTION AND HIDDEN AGENDAS

The existence or not of corruption and hidden agendas does affect the attitude and approach of all those dealing with authority. Even in the "cleanest countries" there are often hidden agendas when it comes to a national plan for ports and other maritime issues. For instance on 12 January 1998 there appeared an article in *The Times* which suggested that the flurry of interest shown in mining the seabed for manganese nodules back in the 1970s was really just a cover for the US Intelligence services trying to raise a sunken Soviet submarine. Whether this is true or not, it does illustrate how a bureaucracy may have and use hidden agendas for what it would consider perfectly valid reasons.

The table below is not a serious analysis of corruption but it does reflect the perception of corruption by international journalists. There are many different ways of defining corruption and many different cultural perceptions of it. Such a table can, however, provide a good basis for discussion on corruption and hidden agendas. It is a good example of an attempt to measure the unmeasurable and to quantify a problem which many commentators prefer to ignore. Policy issues have many areas such as this and this does give an example of a simple methodology that might be tried.

Corruption Index (marked out of 10 for "cleanest countries")					
Cleanest Countries			Most Corrupt Countries		
Index	Country	Mark	Index	Country	Mark
1	Denmark	9.94	1	Nigeria	1.76
2	Finland	9.48	2	Bolivia	2.05
3	Sweden	9.35	3	Colombia	2.23
4	New Zealand	9.23	4	Russia	2.27
5	Canada	9.10	5	Pakistan	2.53
6	Netherlands	9.03	6	Mexico	2.66
7	Norway	8.92	7	Indonesia	2.72
8	Australia	8.86	8	India	2.75
9	Singapore	8.66	9	Venezuela	2.77
10	Luxembourg	8.61	10	Vietnam	2.79
11	Switzerland	8.61	11	Argentina	2.81
12	Ireland	8.28	12	China	2.88
13	Germany	8.23	13	Philippines	3.05
14	UK	8.22	14	Thailand	3.06

Source: Berlin based Transparency International Group survey, July 1997.

PORT POLICY

Port policy in this context considers those aspects of a port which, regardless of ownership, may be considered the concern of the central or federal government. The international agreements made by the WTO (World Trade Organisation) and their impact on trade and regional agreements, such as those of the EU, can also be considered under the general heading of Port Policy.

Although the EU is by far the most notable of the world's regional trading groups, it must not be forgotten that there are many others. The North American Free Trade Agreement is also very important and there are some 14 other Free Trade Areas and Customs Unions or Common Markets making a significant impact on world trade. It is also worth remembering that each of these bureaucracies will develop their own port policies, if they have not done so already.

The following points should be borne in mind:

— A port is a major national interface between a country and the outside world and as such it is a vital element in the national economy. (About 11% of GDP of the Netherlands is generated by the activities of the Port of Rotterdam alone.) It is an expensive capital investment with a large proportion of *sunk* costs—that is, once the investment is made, it involves a long term commitment.

— A port cannot exist in a vacuum. It should be the focal point of a national transport system of roads and rail—with access to an airport. It will attract industries and become an area of commercial and administrative activity. It will also attract tourists and undesirable elements such as terrorists and drug smugglers and be a constant source of anxiety to environmentalists.

— As ports evolve they will tend to retreat from their old city centre sites to new "out of town" locations. This means that for older ports real estate development in high-cost city centre sites becomes an important and often lucrative ancillary activity.

National port planning

From an academic point of view the most complete and coherent national transport plans were those produced by the centrally planned economies, such as those of the USSR and eastern Europe in the 1970s. In a modern liberal democracy it is possible to have plans but much more difficult to impose them. Private enterprise can be steered by national planners by prodding with taxes or coaxing with financial incentives but the results are to a large extent uncertain. So far, most attempts by most governments to reduce the use and growth of the motor car have met with failure, in spite of plans announced at the time of election. In many countries as well as my own, national port planning faces similar problems to that of the motor car mentioned above. Logically, one can argue that in very many countries, certainly within the EU, there are too many ports. The obvious conclusion of such an argument is that there are ports that should be closed, but as a port closure would invariably mean job losses and the running down of a whole community with the consequent unpopularity of the politicians concerned, such a motion as port closure seldom appears on any political agenda.

EU PORT AND TRANSPORT POLICY

Trade handled by EU sea ports:

1980	1.8 Billion Tonnes
1993	2.3 Billion Tonnes
2000	2.6 Billion Tonnes
2010	3.4 Billion Tonnes (estimated)

In 1994, 1164.2 million tons, or 75.4% of the total trade between the EU members and third countries, and 208.3 million tonnes, or 29% of the trade between the Member States trade, was carried by sea. There is also some 224 million tonnes of national coastwise traffic.

Policy

In 1993 the Trans-European Transport Network (TEN) Policy entered into force. This treaty commits the Community to contribute to the establishment of Trans-European networks in the areas of transport, telecommunications and energy infrastructures. One common area of interest seems to be to get goods off the road and onto the railways. Such investment if not carefully handled could promote greater advantages for some ports rather than others.

The current CTP (Common Transport Policy) basis was laid down in 1992 when the Commission issued a White Paper addressing the general aims and framework within the Policy.

Main EU policy proposals

1. Improvement and modernisation of port infrastructure and inclusion in the Trans-European transport network. The European Investment Bank (EIB) has been a major contributor supporting investment in port infrastructure. To benefit from an EU loan or grant the project should cover:-
2. (a) Improvements in access to the port from land, sea or inland waterway. (b) Improvement inside the port area.
3. Creation of a competitive playing field. There is, however, difficulty in coming to an agreement about which forms of

state aid should be permitted, not least because national policies differ significantly, particularly as regards the division of costs between the public sector, the private operator and the user.

4. Advance of Research & Development for ports. Article 103f of the Maastricht Treaty states that the EU objectives are to strengthen the scientific and technological basis of Community industries such as optimising berthing/unberthing procedures and cargo-handling procedures. One of the central EU concepts is the support of several projects aiming at the creation of a European maritime information highway (MARIS). Much of this work is co-ordinated through the European Sea Ports Organisation (ESPO) which was set up in 1993. In 1994 the Federation of European Port Operators (FEPORT) was established.

5. Support in setting up an enhanced dialogue between all partners to address relevant problems. The most popular areas for agreement between ports seems to lie in harmonising pollution prevention rules and Port State Control implementation. It is interesting to note that in a research project undertaken in 1982 the port industries' perception of an all-embracing European ports policy was that it was "extremely unattractive".

RELATIONSHIP BETWEEN PORT AND STATE (OR AREA AUTHORITY)

The State will almost certainly exercise control over:

(a) National transport policy—location of roads, rails, bridges, tunnels, canals, etc.
(b) Location of major industries.
(c) Customs and immigration.
(d) Safety requirements and minimum conditions for workers.
(e) Environmental and aesthetic factors.

The State may probably be concerned with:

(a) Free-port areas.
(b) Port investment and development plans.
(c) Security.

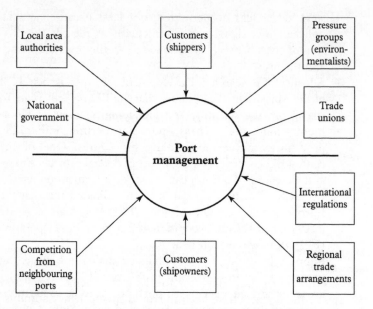

Figure 21: Constraining influences on port management.

The State may possibly decide to be involved with:

(a) Port pricing policy.
(b) Pilotage control and pricing.
(c) Dredging and navigational aids.

A common policy on the degree and extent to which a state exercises control over its ports is difficult to implement because for one thing the UK and Japan have perhaps an excess of port locations, all of which cannot be allowed to develop. On the other hand, many continental countries with only limited access to the sea will not experience this problem.

Regional Trading Areas, such as the EU, with many ports may wish to have a central policy on such issues as pricing and subsidies to avoid "unfair competition" between its ports.

Goals and objectives of ports

What is the port management trying to achieve—maximum profit for the port, for the locality or for the country? Perhaps it is trying to maximise cargo throughput or minimise its costs or help with local employment. It may be attempting to achieve a compromise of most of these, as all the external constraining groups will be putting pressure on the port management to satisfy their needs.

A further associated problem is that, because so many groups and interests are involved in port activities, port management and administration tends to become too large, complex and unwieldy.

Constraining influences on port management

Figure 21 (opposite) indicates that port management operates under a great many tight constraints of which a considerable number will be mandatory. The port's relationship with the state will of necessity be a close one regardless of the type of ownership adopted.

PORT OWNERSHIP

As mentioned in Chapter Five, the Editor of *Port Development International* seems to have summed up in 1992 a general worldwide attitude when he wrote "for too long the inefficiencies and excesses of the dockers have been mirrored by top-heavy administrations—over-manned, under-talented and equally obdurate to change". The general trend worldwide in Europe, China, Africa, Asia, etc., is to decentralise direct government control and to place the port on a more commercial footing.

See the table on page 96 comparing the ownership of the different activities within ports and the arguments for increased private sector participation in the port industry.

PORT AND STATE FINANCIAL ASSISTANCE

As noted several times in this book the UK ports have long been amongst the most expensive in Europe. The British National Ports Council, however, back in 1969 produced a survey which concluded that many continental countries such as Germany, Belgium, Netherlands and France offer extensive subsidies to their ports. In fact, the report suggested that if British ports received the same level of financial aid as their continental competitors they could be amongst the cheapest ports in Europe. (Note the National Ports Council was abolished in 1981 but the literature and surveys this body completed were amongst some of the best documentary work on British ports.) In the late 1980s the British Ports Federation produced a further document showing how it perceived its competitors in north-western Europe to receive considerable financial aid, particularly in the area of infrastructure developments.

State Aid remains a controversial issue. A Commission Document "General Study on State Aid in the Port Sector" (DOC.VII/103/89) stated that support from public authorities for port infrastructure should not in principle be considered as state aid within the terms of article 92 paragraph 1. However, recent statements by some Commission representatives indicate that there might be a change in attitude. For instance it was stated in the EC Commission in 1995 in Barcelona that "The general premise is that ports should operate on a commercial basis. The all-inclusive costs of port installations, including capital costs, in principle should be recovered through the port fees". The Commission also stated in 1995 that "State Aid must not allow a port to reduce tariffs in order to undercut the tariffs of its competitors".

The subject does, however, become very complex, not so much because of its nature but because of how the problem is perceived and defined by each of the participants. For instance, all ports in north-west Europe will be emphatic that they get no subsidies but they will assure you that their competitors do. This does not reflect on their honesty but rather on what they would perceive as a subsidy. For instance, lack of charges on a country's motorways might be considered a subsidy by a port in another country faced with significant motorway charges for its cargo distribution.

"A level playing field" for port facilities as regards competition

A British Ports Federation view

Continental European governments are subsidising both the operating and investment costs of their major ports. This results in these ports being able to keep their port charges at an artificially low level, so causing distortions to competition, e.g.:

— The finances of the port and the city of Hamburg are merged together. The port is capitalised and financed by the city. The Federal Government pays for the dredging of the Lower Elbe.
— Rotterdam—local and central government have, in the past, funded all berth developments and the local authority,

which owns the port, finances construction, dredging and maintenance of berths.

It is, however, impossible to determine the actual level of Government financial aid given to any port in virtually any country, due to the lack of clear unambiguous detailed data for all port activities.

Antwerp v Rotterdam (as reported in *Lloyd's List*, 21 March 1997)

Antwerp authorities were reported to be complaining to Dutch authorities controlling the mouth of the Scheldt concerning delays in licensing the necessary dredging. At the same time there were those within the port of Rotterdam who were concerned about problems freight trains from Rotterdam seemed to be experiencing in passing through Belgium.

Bremen v Rotterdam (as reported in *Lloyd's List*, 7 April 1997)

The head of Bremen's Association of Port Users was reported as saying "... with unfair policies the Dutch try to achieve their goal to maintain Rotterdam as the European leading port". One specific example that was cited concerned subsidised block trains from Rotterdam into its vast European hinterland.

Rotterdam v Amsterdam (as reported in *Lloyd's List*, 24 May 1999)

ECT & Rotterdam Short Sea Terminals (RST) are to lodge a complaint with the European commissioners if the city of Amsterdam goes ahead with its plan to fund a new container terminal for the US company Ceres

PORT PRICING

Port costs are important as some 50% of ocean transportation costs can be made up of port costs. Ports pricing policy is one which national authorities usually monitor, as do regional authorities such as the EU. With the advent of intermodalism which has brought growing competition between ports, the analysis of port pricing policy has become a popular study for academics. In practice, however, I suspect that the majority of ports, like supermarkets, watch their major competitors and try not to charge more.

Different approaches to port pricing

(1) Governed by market forces:
    (a) Aim to maximise revenue; or
    (b) Aim to maximise users—undercut the competition.
    Note: The extent of utilisation is of crucial importance to port tariff policy.
(2) Aim to generate economic and other benefits—e.g. encourage movement of vital commodities.
(3) Cost-based:
    (a) To cover all costs—capital, dredging, etc.;
    (b) To cover operating costs;
    (c) Using a government or other cost based formula, i.e. Freas Formula (USA 1950), Rochdale (UK 1970);
    (d) As a percentage of users total costs.
(4) Perpetuating an historically inherited system, pragmatically adjusted as required!
    Note: If the Port does not cover all its costs by charges to customers—where does the balance come from?

Who sets the rates?

(a) The government
(b) The local area authority
(c) The port
Note: Even in the privatised situation the port may not be allowed a free hand in setting its tariffs as most governments are concerned about "unfair competition".

Methodology

(As suggested by Dowd and Fleming in *Maritime Policy and Management*, 1994, vol. 21.)

Step 1: Establish the benchmark price by calculating:

(a) The historical costs of providing the service or facility;
(b) The imputed cost—the unreimbursed and often unrecorded benefits provided by an outside entity (e.g. fire, police, computer, etc.);
(c) The return on investments for both land and equipment;

(d) The sensitivity analysis—as (a), (b) and (c) will often require assumptions, this will indicate the degree of accuracy required.

Step 2: External examination or reality check:

(a) competition;
(b) important customers;
(c) political pressures;
(d) goals of the port.

Step 3: Negotiation and acceptance

Elements in the pricing system

(1) Should there be a global charge or an individual complex tariff system?
(2) Consideration of the time element
(3) On what unit is the user charged—GT, NT, length, amount of cargo handled, etc.?

Note: Time as a cost to the shipowner should be considered, e.g. a shipowner with high costs will pay for fast service and vice versa

Tariff structures

Port tariff nomenclature can vary considerably between ports both nationally and internationally. As one of its last creative acts before its demise, the National Ports Council published a suggestion as to how it might be standardised.

The National Ports Council Proposed Standard Nomenclature of Main Port Charges:

(1) *Conservancy Charge*—this charge is made for the upkeep of the approach channel and waterways. (On most of continental Europe this charge is met by the taxpayer.)
(2) *Dock Charge*—to cover the cost of locks, other entrance charges and berth charge.
(3) *Wharfage*—dues paid by the cargo for passing over dock estate.
(4) *Handling Charge*—in most cases this will be the largest single item.
(5) *Storage Charge*—if the cargo is not collected within a specified time.
(6) *Passenger Charge*.

(7) *Other Charges* for services and facilities offered. For instance, in the UK and some other countries, Light Dues are charged to cover the cost of navigational aids and in Scandinavian countries extra charges are levied for use of an ice breaker.

With the advent of containers there have been further moves to simplify these charges. For instance, at some ports, container ship operators are charged a standard rate per container, laden or empty, which is inclusive of dock and conservancy charges, port rates and all normal handling charges from the time of receipt or discharge until the time of shipment or loading to land transport. In short, the first five of the above charges are made as a single charge.

In India a Tariff Authority was established in mid April 1997 and, according to an article in *Lloyd's List* in April 1998, this body will use tariffs to attempt to divert old ships and slower cheaper cargoes to the country's minor ports.

An example of how port costs can be allocated in different countries is the payment of dredging in the USA. Under the 1986 Act of Congress a fee of 0.125% (1993) of value is charged on cargo loaded/unloaded to fund maintenance of dredging. In 1991 $700 million was collected.

The EU in its Green Paper on Sea Ports of December 1997 says "... that port infrastructure should be priced in such a way that users should bear the real costs of the port services and facilities that they consume".

The Green Paper identifies three types of payment systems:

1. Those related to the provision of services and facilities to enable a ship to enter safely and use the port.
2. Those for specific services or supplies rendered.
3. Rents or charges for the use of land or equipment.

For infrastructure charges three possible approaches are also identified:

1. Average cost pricing (this would guarantee full cost recovery).
2. Charging for operating costs only.
3. Marginal cost pricing.

CHAPTER SEVEN

BERTHS AND TERMINALS

Number of berths required in a port—terminal productivity definitions—how to reduce waiting time—land productivity—berth size, type and lay-out—equipment and terminal layout—cruise ship terminals—dry bulk terminals—tanker terminals—berth maintenance—alternatives to formal port systems—port logistics and distriparks.

THE NUMBER OF BERTHS REQUIRED IN A PORT

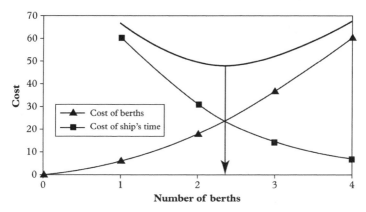

Figure 22: Optimum of berths required in a port.

Ideally, the ship operator would like to see empty berths to ensure that there are no delays for his ship when it arrives. The port operator on the other hand would like to reduce his capital outlay, and have only one berth with a queue of ships, so that the berth is always in use and earning. From the practical point of view however, it will be to the advantage of both of them to keep the total

131

costs to a minimum. Hence for any given conditions it is theoretically possible to determine the optimum number of berths. The optimum shown in the graph on page 131 is an optimum for the total
costs and would only be true in a situation where the ship and the
port were part of an integrated cost structure, as for example where
an oil company owns both ships and port. In practice, it is seldom
easy to establish the given conditions as ports suffer from the old
transport problem of peaks—that is, one day the port is empty and
the next there is a queue waiting. Further, as there is now usually
competition between ports, many have adopted the dictum that "the
berth must wait for the ship not the ship for the berth".

The problem can be analysed quantitatively in different ways:

(1) The application of queuing theory. This is a rather dated
method today. It was evolved between 1910 and 1920 by
the Danish statistician Erlang for queuing problems at
telephone exchanges. The same theory can be used wher-
ever a queuing situation occurs. It has severe limitations
for a modern port, as it assumes ships arrive in a random
fashion, whereas in most ports liner ships arrive to fixed
schedules, as do many other ships. Also, some ships on
certain trades may arrive in "waves" due to seasonal or
other demand considerations. Queuing theory also assumes
that all berths are interchangeable and it can only cope
with individual berths—it cannot cope with a long berth
which might take, say, three large ships or four small ones.
It assumes the queue is on a first come, first service basis,
and does not allow for priority or queuing systems.

(2) Simulations are a sound method and have few of the
problems posed by queuing theory. There are two types:

(a) Computer simulations. These can be expensive as a
good one needs to be tailor-made for the port. Depending on the cost, some assumptions will have to be made.

(b) Physical manual simulations. These have the advantage that they are simple, cheap and everyone under-
stands them.

(3) Analysis of arrival and departure data on a well-organised
spreadsheet. The same spreadsheet of data can do a great
deal more than simply analyse the queuing problem. It
can also analyse many of the other significant port opera-

tional problems. This also has the advantage that the software will be available to most port managers and most have the ability to use it.

Terminal productivity definitions

Berth Occupancy Ratio is the ratio obtained by dividing the time a berth has been occupied by the time a berth is available during a considered period of time (a week, month or year).

I.e.: Berth Occupancy Ratio = $Ts/8760$ (8760 is the number of hours in a year.)

Service Time (Ts) is the period of time during which a vessel is berthed in a port whether the ship works or not. The service time will therefore include working and non-working periods.

Waiting Time (Wq) is the time a ship is waiting for an available berth.

Waiting Ratio = Wq/Ts

Dwell Time is the time spent by the container in the port. It will depend on many factors such as status (FCL, LCL, Empties etc.), customs procedures, communications efficiency between the parties concerned, the port's pricing policy on this matter, etc.

The expression Berth Utilisation may also be used and this will be defined as:

Berth Utilisation = Ts/Possible Working days in Period (say 300 days per year)

Number of berths

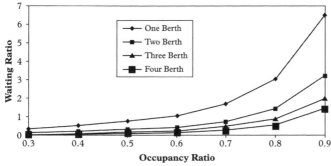

Figure 23: Relationship between berth occupancy ratio and waiting ratio.

Figure 23 (on page 133), based on Erlang's ideas, indicates that the *waiting ratio increases* quite dramatically as the *number of berths decreases*.

For a general-purpose berth an occupancy ratio of around 0.7 could be considered about right. If the ratio is too large the port is facing the serious possibility of congestion. On the other hand if the ratio is too small the management could face the criticism of over-investment.

Takel, in his book *Industrial Port Development*, noted that in 1970 the South Wales Ports had an average Berth Utilisation factor of 0.46 or 46% and that Le Havre considered its Berth Utilisation Factor of 67% too high and promptly decided to build six extra berths, which it estimated would bring the berth utilisation factor down to around 57%.

How to reduce waiting time

Obviously, to reduce waiting time port management has a choice of three options:

1. Increase the number of berths.
2. Increase the working time at the berths.
3. Increase the terminal cargo-handling productivity.

As an example, consider a port which has an annual traffic throughput of 400,000 tonnes at three berths. The port works 300 days per year and on average handles 500 tons per ship/day. The port has however a congestion or queuing problem of keeping ships waiting—last year there was a waiting time of around 1,400–1,500 hours. The table opposite indicates how changing either the number of berths or the handling rates or the working time can reduce the waiting time.

No. of Berths	Waiting Time	Handling Rates	Waiting Time	Working Days	Waiting Time
3	1,400	500	1,400	298	1,400
		520	1,200	306	1,200
		536	1,000	315	1,000
		555	800	325	800
		574	600	336	600
		596	400	348	400
4	200	640	200		200
5	0		0		0

The number of berths required in a port depends of course on many factors such as demand, type and size of ship, etc. If the terminal is of the dedicated type such as those belonging to an oil company or ferry service, then the demand or ship arrival sequence can usually be anticipated with some degree of accuracy, at least in the short term. On the other hand, for a common user multi-purpose berth the port management can rely only on tentative projections and has to make allowances for the cyclical nature of the demand. To make this allowance it would be normal, having determined what the average demand would be, to increase it by a "peaking factor" of say 20%–30 %.

Although the factors involved are fairly obvious, the sensitivity of the results to these factors are not always appreciated. For instance, using either queuing theory or simulations, the previous table shows that, for example in a terminal with three berths which had a waiting time of 58 days, this waiting time could be reduced to eight days with four berths or zero delays with five berths.

However, new berths and the necessary superstructure do not come cheaply, and management should analyse all the possible options in the search for the optimum solution. For instance, in the above example the three-berth terminal could have reduced the waiting time by increasing its cargo-handling productivity. Increasing its daily cargo-handling rate by around 50% would have had a similar effect on waiting time as constructing two new berths.

Land productivity at leading container terminals

Recent research has indicated that land productivity, that is the number of containers stowed per hectare on the terminal, varies in different regions. Typical figures for many Asian ports show a storage capacity of 230–470 TEUs/ha, European ports 180–300 TEUs/ha, while North American ports tend to show a capacity of 160 TEUs/ha. The author of this study indicates that the variation may be due to the availability and price of land, the speed of growth and the degree of port competition leading to over-capacity. Whether a high or low figure is a good thing is debatable and much will depend on the economics of the container terminal operation in the different regions. A high figure means that less land is required but almost certainly also means that containers must be stacked higher. High stacking of containers will probably mean more unproductive lifting and moving of containers, as when trucks appear at the terminal to pick up the import containers. Therefore one would expect high land productivity when labour is cheap and land is expensive.

Quantity of equipment

To ensure the smooth operation of a terminal the amount and number of equipment may be critical. For example, consider the cycle time for lorries at a container terminal arriving to pick up an import container.

Number of straddle carriers	15	20	25	30
Lorries through the model	18,018	23,984	23,981	23,983
Mean cycle time in minutes	544.34	16.42	16.39	16.32
In-gate queue length	1,047	4	4	4

Source: S. Bonsall—unpublished Ph.D. Thesis.

Note that for the conditions on this model terminal, having only 15 straddle carriers produced chaos whereas having more than 20 made little difference to the smooth running of the terminal. The improvement in productivity is not a linear improvement that gradually increases with the amount of equipment but that there are critical points below which smooth efficient operation becomes almost impossible.

Public user v private dedicated terminals

If demand for terminals is uncorrelated it will probably be in everyone's interest for the port to develop well equipped public user terminals rather than a string of under-utilised private dedicated terminals.

BERTH SIZE AND LAYOUT

As mentioned in Chapter Two, 1960s dock transit sheds were about 500ft × 120ft, and were now built with high roofs to accommodate fork lift trucks which could stack high, easily and cheaply.

In 1922 a typical long pier system (1000ft long) might have had transit sheds partly owned by city and partly private. The sheds were 120 feet wide and 900 feet long, with two floors—upper for incoming, lower for outgoing. Note: London and Liverpool had more space for cranes due to their dock system. The New York piers were too narrow for cranes and the port also had water-depth

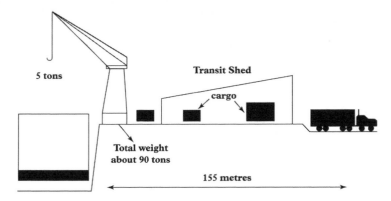

Figure 24: Conventional breakbulk general cargo berth.

problems. It had to dredge a 40 feet channel in 1922 to cope with new large liners. New York had no railway system like other US ports.

In 1924 Albert Dock had transit sheds 120 ft wide, 300–350ft long, double storey and single storey. It also had special cold stores for meat cargoes with mechanical lowering conveyors.

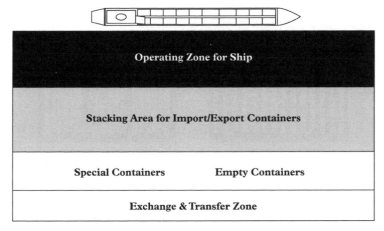

Figure 25: General layout of a container terminal.

When considering the basic layout of a container terminal the operational problems have to be considered, therefore the actual layout of a terminal will depend on the equipment used. For instance, on a container terminal, the layout and optimum shape and size would depend on whether a yard had a gantry crane system, a straddle carrier system, a front-end loader system or tractor/chassis system was used.

Systems Features	Tractor/Chassis System	Straddle Carrier	Yard Gantry Crane System	Front-end Loader System
Land utilisation	Very poor 185 TEU/hectare	Good 385 TEU/hectare	Very good 750 TEU/hectare	Poor 275 TEU/hectare
Terminal development costs	Very low: high quality surfacing not necessary	Medium: hard-wearing surface needed	High: high load-bearing surface needed for crane wheels	High: Heavy wear on terminal surface
Equipment cost	High: large number of chassis required	Moderate: six straddle carriers per ship/shore crane	High	Moderate: cost effective for low throughputs
Equipment maintenance cost	Low	High	Low	Medium
Manning levels 2 crane operation	High: 28 men but low skill required	Low: 22 men High skill required	High: 29 men Medium high skill required	Medium: 26 men Medium skill requirement
Operating factors	Good accessibility. Simple terminal organisation	High flexibility Good stacking	Good land use. Scope for automation	Versatile equipment

Source:　UNCTAD, *Improving Port Performance—Container Terminal Development.*

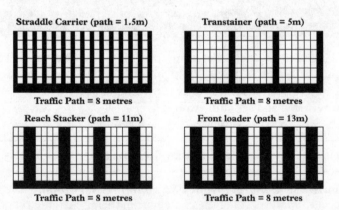

The path is the distance between the rows

Figure 26: Traffic Paths.

As each type of system has its own manoeuvring and stacking characteristics, the number of containers allowable in a row and the minimum distance between the rows becomes critical. The preceding sketch shows the basic layout patterns for the most popular types of systems.

Estimating land required for container stacking area

Annual Throughput	Ty	
Daily Requirement	Dr	$Dr = Ty/365$
Dwell Time	Dt	Expressed in days or fractions of days
Peaking factor	Pf	An allowance for peak conditions. Often assumed to be 0.75

TEU ground areas = $15.25m^2$

Stacking Area	TGS	Twenty feet ground slots
Stacking Height	Sh	

$TGS = (15.25 \times Dr \times Dt)/Pf/Sh$

Global Yard Area/Total TGS Area = **e**

Total Container Stacking Area in m^2 = Total TGS Area $\times$ **e**

Approximate **e** factors for:

Straddle Carriers	e = 1.8
Transtainer	e = 1.3
Front Loaders	e = 3.9
Reach Stacker	e = 2.3

The optimum solution for a specific port will depend on how the specific variables for that port constrain the final choice, for instance is there land available. For many ports it is less than ideal. Then again, has a large unskilled labour force with a long traditional working culture been inherited, or is there an opportunity to open up a new terminal and select the work-force?

Container shuffling

An inevitable expense incurred by the most efficient terminal is the necessity of having to shuffle the containers within the stacks. Statistical analysis would indicate that a typical terminal could expect to shuffle 21% of the containers in the discharging (import) stacks, 9% of the containers in the loading (export) stacks and some 17% of the containers in the transit stacks.

Types of berth
Ro/Ro berth

This is usually one of the simplest types of berths to construct. Apart from the loading ramp which may need to be reasonably sophisticated if the berth experiences a significant tidal range, little expensive civil engineering is required because the loading weight per unit area is usually quite low. Further, there are usually few constraints on design other than one would expect to find in a car park. As a car park its position does not of necessity have to be adjacent to the ship (though it very often is because if port labour is being used to drive the cargo aboard, it reduces the logistical problem of uniting drivers with their Ro/Ro cargo).

Many Ro/Ro berths will have a *linkspan* to unite the ship and berth. These are similar to mobile bridges connecting the quay to the ship. Their length must be sufficient to avoid the steep slopes, which are incompatible with freight traffic. A slope of 13 to 14% is considered maximum for road vehicles and 3 to 4% for railway vehicles. The main part of the linkspan is a pontoon on which a superstructure may be built containing access lanes and ramps. It may also be fitted with automooring devices, which act on the bollards on the vessel thus eliminating mooring ropes. The linkspan in Gothenburg is also fitted with bunker facilities and water tanks with pumps. It also has facilities for the collection of sewage and bilge waste.

Passenger berth

A passenger berth needs virtually the same requirements as an airport, i.e. tickets and information, toilets, cafeterias, shops, disabled access, security. If it is international, there will need to be customs and immigration facilities. Also, as at an airport, there should be a covered and easy form of access from the terminal onto the vehicle.

Cruise ship terminals

The leading cruise ship port at the moment is generally considered to be Miami, which reflects the importance of the USA home market to cruising and the relative nearness of the Caribbean.

The table on page 141 gives an indication of cruise port usage and restrictions in the Baltic Region.

A Floating Cruise Terminal for London opened in 2004. It can handle 600 passengers per hour.

Port	No. Visits 1995	Max. Draft	Restrictions
Copenhagen	240	10.0	None
Bergen	170	11.5	None
Tallin	150	9.0	270m length
Helsinki	135	10.0	280m length
Southampton	128	12.0	None
Stockholm	125	9.4	300m length
St Petersburg	120	9.0	None
Visby	120	8.0	None
Amsterdam	90	9.7	400m length, locks
Tilbury	71	10.0	None

Source: *Seatrade Review*, March 1995.

Dry bulk carrier berth

Large bulkers require deep water, large powerful cranes and conveyor belts for stacking the cargo. A large flat stacking area is required. Facilities for barge transhipment are also often a feature. Dust is nearly always a problem with dry bulk cargo and where there are strong prevailing winds this may give rise to environmental pollution.

Ship/shore liaison at bulk carrier terminals

In 1998 the results of an international survey covering 1,000 reports from ships and terminals were published. The reports covered 222 terminals in 46 different countries. Many of the reports contained adverse comments on some aspects of loading and discharging. Both ships and terminals experienced problems. For example, a common complaint from the ships was "loaded us too fast and we had to leave with our ballast on board", while many terminals reported "poor communications with the ship, lack of interest from the crew who were often asleep during the cargo work". It was also noted that a number of ships did not seem to use cargo plans at all, they would simply arrive at the terminal and say "We want 50,000 tons; fill her up"!

Most of the problems reported by ships and terminals related to the breakdown of communications and mutual understanding. Some 30% of ship reports considered the terminal interface unsatisfactory and that frequently there was no terminal representative on site with authority to accept responsibility or take decisions. On the other hand a principal factor reported by loading terminals was the slow discharge of ship's ballast, which is not surprising considering the numbers of ageing bulkers still trading.

Recommendations

— The IMO Draft Code of Practice for the Safe Loading and Unloading of Bulk Carriers, as approved by the 20th Assembly, should be complied with by both ship and terminal.
— Cargo loading rate never to exceed the agreed figure and any deviation from this figure to be agreed in writing and appended to the agreed loading plan.
— Terminals should sign and accept the IMO approved ship/shore checklist.

Some leading dry bulk terminals in 2003				
Name	*Country*	*Mn Tonnes*	*Main cargo*	*Import/Export*
Qinhuangdao	China	101.2	Coal	E
Hay Point Services	Australia	74.7	Coal	E
Newcastle	Australia	71.5	Coal	E
Richards Bay	S Africa	68.9	Coal	E
Port of Gladstone	Australia	38.2	Coal	E
EMO Rotterdam	Netherland	24.7	Coal	I
Taichung	Taiwan	17.2	Coal	E
Duluth	USA	16.3	Coal	E
Port of Virginia	USA	14.8	Coal	E
Paradip	India	13.2	Coal	E
Port Hedland	Australia	76.6	Iron Ore	E
Port of Tubaro	Brazil	75.9	Iron Ore	E
Dampier	Australia	74.1	Iron Ore	E
Itaqui	Brazil	64.9	Iron Ore	E
EMO Rotterdam	Netherland	38.0	Iron Ore	I
Saldanha	S. Africa	26.2	Iron Ore	E

Source: ISL Port Data Base 2004.

This table illustrates that major dry bulk terminals deal mainly with coal and iron ore, though many of them do also handle other bulks. Also as expected, with the exception of Rotterdam, these high capacity specialised terminals are export terminals.

Tanker berth

Tanker berths are often built onto jetties, as modern large tankers need deep water. In most cases they do need to be jetties and not solid piers, which would in most cases encourage siltation. This does however make them relatively fragile structures, so great care and patience is necessary when berthing. When some of the jetties at Milford Haven were built they were over 3,000 feet long. The 1970 cost for such a jetty was over £5 million.

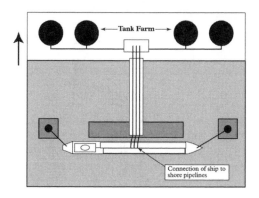

Figure 27: Tanker berth.

The connection of the ship's pipelines to the shore pipelines is obviously a weak link in the oil transfer and they have to be flexible enough to allow for ship movement at the berth.

Because of the economies of using large tankers, capacious storage space near the berth is necessary. At a loading berth the shore tanks are usually higher than the ship so that the oil can flow into the tanker under the force of gravity. This is safer than pumping, as it avoids the risk of a build-up in pressure should the tanker close a valve and impede the flow of oil.

To avoid any secondary transport of crude oil, the position of a tanker terminal and a refinery is usually a common project.

Associated with an oil terminal one would expect oil-reception facilities and environmental protection equipment against oil spills such as "booms", etc.

OCIMF—the Oil Companies International Marine Forum—lays down clear guidelines concerning safety and good operating practices for tanker terminals.

Comprehensive information on all the world's tanker terminals is available on disc compiled by *Fairplay*. This contains all the up-to-the-minute data required by tanker brokers and tanker operators such as berth length and depth of water alongside, tidal rise, BCM (bow to centre of manifolds), reception facilities, etc.

General cargo and containers need to be handled on and off the ship from an area alongside the ship, whereas oil could be pumped to or from the ship by pipeline to a tank which could, if necessary, be placed miles away.

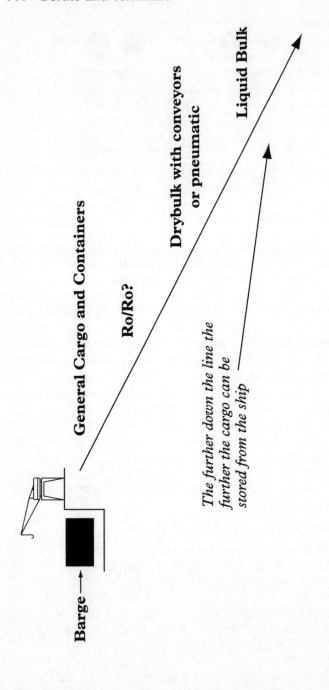

Figure 28: *Distance from ship/shore interface to storage.*

Berth maintenance

It is axiomatic that the higher the degree of sophistication of the equipment and automation on the berth, the greater will be the necessity of achieving a high level of maintenance. Safety and maintenance are obviously linked, and in cases of port ownership, such as landlord ports, where the landlord is responsible for the infrastructure and the terminal operator for the superstructure, there have been known to be fringe areas where the responsibility for maintenance was not clear. In the early days of straddle carriers they tended to incorporate a great deal of hydraulics. These hydraulic parts needed a very high level of maintenance and in spite of this covered much of the terminal with oil, which considerably reduced safety levels in wet weather. Then there is the question of who pays when the superstructure damages the infrastructure. Further, in times of cost-cutting, routine maintenance tends to be one of the first costs to be cut.

ALTERNATIVES TO FORMAL PORT SYSTEMS

For general cargo

Possibly most ports at some stage in their development have loaded and discharged to ships moored at anchor or to buoys with the use of barges. Although such a method reduces the port's capital investment in deepwater terminals the cargo handling tends to be slow, involves extra handling and is more prone to be more susceptible to bad weather. Further, as the cargo-handling into barges usually has to be done by ship's gear each lift would normally be limited to around 5 tons or less. There are exceptions to this and Hong Kong has shown that containers of all weights and sizes can be easily handled by their purpose-built heavy-lift barges.

A modern development of this which is in use for bulk cargoes and sometimes referred to as logistic outsourcing, is the floating terminal. For example, as reported in *Lloyd's List* in October 1998, the port of Bahrain, uses a self-unloading Panamax vessel, the *Bulk Gulf*, which lightens the 170,000 Capesize vessels laden with iron ore pellets some 40 nm out at sea. The *Bulk Gulf* is fitted with four cranes, which guarantees fast operation and reliability. The choice between floating terminal or floating crane tends to be dependent on the various constraints involved, e.g. whether shallow barges are necessary, the volume of throughput, the average weather profile, etc. Floating terminals will usually work out more economical with higher volumes of cargo throughput. Another advantage of such a floating terminal is that they do not necessarily have to be a capital investment but could be chartered in on a variety of contracts for short or long periods.

Theoretically, barge-carrying ships such as the Lash system could dispense with much of the traditional general cargo port set-up. In theory the ship could steam round in circles dropping off "floating containers" and collecting others while passing. It has also been suggested that heavy-lift helicopters could load and discharge the ship while it was steaming along the coast!

Bulk (Oil)

In the post Second World War era with tanker size and oil demand increasing, loading and discharging offshore in deeper water developed. In the early days the tankers were moored fore and aft to buoys and the oil pipeline hauled off the sea bed. In 1958 the concept of single point mooring (SPM) and single buoy mooring (SBM) were developed. These methods allow the tanker to take the line of least resistance to the forces of wind, wave and current by being able to weathervane around the mooring point. This was a big improvement on the previous method as the mooring of the tanker was much faster and as it reduces the stresses from wind, wave and current, and makes it safer over a wider range of severe weather conditions. ELSBM means Exposed Location SBM. Such systems, although a cheaper option than developing terminals to handle large tankers, still cost money. It was reported in *Asia Hub* in November 1998 that it is proposed to establish an SPM 45 km west of Karachi at a cost of US$40 million.

LOOP (Louisiana Offshore Oil Port) is a deep-water oil port located approximately 30.4 km offshore. It consists of three SPMs and a pumping platform complex, which pumps the oil ashore. At this "port" there are no port charges, immigration or customs. However, bunkering, stores and crew changes can be arranged if required.

There are now numerous SBMs and SPMs all over the world though they probably peaked in the early 1980s. (In 1983 there were about 250. In 1998 there were around 180 ports that had

SBM or SPM facilities.) Since then many of their functions have been taken over by Floating Storage Terminals and Floating Production, Storage and Offloading Units.

Floating Storage Terminals (FSOs) have been in operation since 1972 and FPSOs (Floating Production, Storage and Offloading Units or "floaters") are now becoming increasingly popular and more versatile. One of the first FPSOs was a tanker converted for use at the Shell's Castellon field in offshore Spain in 1977. Dead-weight tonnage of "floaters" ranges from 52,000 to 285,000.

With the growth of offshore oil fields and their development there has grown up a sophisticated technology associated with floaters. For instance, in 1998 we were told that in the North Sea there were five submerged turret loading (STL) systems in operation. In this system a buoy is moored to the seabed. The buoy is pulled into and secured in a mating cone in the bottom of the floater, thus mooring the vessel and establishing a means of oil transfer.

In 1971 the first SBM for loading iron ore in slurry form was installed at Waipip in New Zealand. It was situated one and a half miles offshore and could load at 1,000 tons per hour.

The Keiyo Sea Berth is a huge floating man-made-islet designed for the handling of oil, 470 metres long and 54 metres wide. It lies seven kilometres offshore from Sodegaura in Chiba-ken, north-east of Tokyo. The Keiyo Sea Berth is linked to four oil refineries and handles 25 million kilolitres of oil per year. More than 100 oil tankers use the Sea Berth facility during the course of a year.

Legal considerations for offshore terminals

The legal implications for offshore terminals, floating terminals, floating cranes, etc., can be very complex, depending on the factors and the national legal system involved. Is the asset, for example, to be operated in international or territorial waters. Will the equipment be categorised as a vessel which would involve all the expensive considerations of registration, manning, etc.?

PORT LOGISTICS

As major gateways for maritime trade, many ports are taking advantage of their strategic position in the logistic chain by offering numerous additional value-added services. These not only add value to the cargo they handle but can also greatly increase the prosperity of the port. They can include not only the traditional port storage facilities but may also include setting up such services as distribution and market preparation centres.

Distribution centres

These have been coyly named *distriparks* by some ports, to include a collection of distribution centres. Inland Clearance Depots (ICDs) or Container Freight Stations (CFSs) have been part of the transport scene since the beginning of containerisation where they act as consolidating or receiving stations for Less than Container Load (LCL) shippers and consignees. Many of these CFSs were located well out of the port in an attempt to avoid restrictions required by some dock labour unions and to be better placed as regards road and rail connections.

The Distribution Centre is, however, a vastly more sophisticated concept. Apart from simply stripping the container the goods may be prepared directly for the customer For example, goods may be combined with others, repackaged or reassembled and prepared for different markets or brand-named outlets. In the case of the port of Blyth on the east coast of the UK, it is estimated that only about 20% of the arriving containers drive straight out of the port, the rest goes into one or other of the port facilities for unpacking, storage, repackaging or stacking onto pallets for onward distribution. These distribution centres could be in the port but owned privately, or owned by the port, or owned by the port but located outside of the port. In many cases if a free port area exists they would be located within the free port to avoid capital being tied up in excise duty.

The limitations of the potential of a distribution centre are only those of the decision makers in charge and the ability with which they apply logistic theory, marketing and the latest information technology to the problem. It would be a mistake, and it is a mistake often observed on the part of management in general, for a port simply to copy the activities adopted by some of the leaders in this development such as Bremen or Rotterdam. A port must exploit the conditions, culture and practices which exist in its own region.

CHAPTER EIGHT

CARGO AND CARGO-HANDLING

Definitions—stowage factors—pre-shipment planning, stowage plan and on-board stowage—ship stresses and stability—developments in cargo-handling and terminal operation—benchmarking for quality standards—cargo positioning and stowage on the terminal—facts concerning the container—equipment development and definitions—purchase, maintenance and control of equipment—safety of labour and cargo—cargo security—warehouse technology.

BASIC DEFINITIONS FOR CARGO-STOWAGE ON THE SHIP

Estivage (Fr.) packing closely—a mode of stowage by pressing or screwing cargo into the hold by means of machinery (American and Mediterranean).

Stevedore from the Spanish estibador—packer. The term stevedore is fairly universal but its precise meaning can vary from port to port. In London it used to mean the person employed on the ship to stow the cargo. In the UK and in some other countries the term is no longer officially used and the term docker is preferred as it reflects the current view that those engaged in cargo-handling should be flexible and be prepared to undertake any activity on the terminal.

Stevedoring. Joseph Conrad in his *Mirror of the Sea* writes of his experience at the end of the nineteenth century: "Stevedoring, which had been a skilled labour, is fast becoming a labour without the skill. The modern steamship with her many holds is not loaded within the sailor-like meaning of the word. She is filled up. Her cargo is not stowed in any sense; it is simply dumped in her through

149

six hatchways, more or less, by twelve winches or so, with clatter and hurry and racket and heat, in a cloud of steam and a mess of coal-dust. As long as you can keep her propeller under water and take care, say, not to fling down barrels of oil on top of bales of silk, or deposit an iron bridge girder of five tons or so upon a bed of coffee bags, you have done about all in the way of duty that the cry for prompt dispatch will allow you to do." This observation is interesting as in essence one has heard the same criticism from every chief officer over at least the last century reflecting on how cargo used to be stowed.

Dunnage is anything used to protect the cargo. There are two basic types of dunnage:

(1) Permanent dunnage, which may take the form of battens of wood, fixed to the side of the ship to allow air to circulate and to keep the cargo off the cool sides of the ship, where condensation could take place.

   The bottom of the hold may also be covered with wood to reduce the risk of damage to both ship and cargo from any impact as the cargo is loaded, to assist ventilation and to prevent contamination from any liquids that drain down to the bottom of the hold or leak through from the bunkers in the double bottoms.

(2) Non-permanent dunnage which for the most part consists of planks of soft wood but could be anything which is used to assist ventilation and drainage, and stop the cargo moving, chafing, etc. This dunnage must of course be paid for, and for cargoes requiring large quantities it can form a sizeable expenditure.

Angle of repose is the angle between the horizontal plane and the cone slope when bulk cargo is emptied in to the ship's hold. Obviously the smaller the angle of repose, the greater the tendency the cargo has to flow. It is recommended that when the angle of repose is less than 35 degrees the cargo needs trimming (levelling out) and perhaps precautions need to be taken against the cargo shifting.

Stowage factor. The stowage factor of any commodity is the number of cubic feet (cubic metres) which a ton (tonne) of that commodity will occupy in stowage. This figure should include an allowance for broken stowage, e.g.:

Commodity	ft³/ton	m³/tonne	Angle of repose
Pig Iron	11.31	0.36	
Iron Ore	11–17	0.31–0.47	30–75
Bauxite	20–32	0.56–0.89	28–55
Scrap	20–40	0.56–1.11	45
Sand	11–28	0.5–0.98	30–52
Salt	29–40	0.81–1.12	30–45
Cement	23–29	0.67–1.00	8–90
Sulphur	27–36	0.74	35–40
Coal	40–55	0.79–1.53	30–65
Water	36	1.0	0
Wheat bulk	47–49	1.31–1.37	25
Wheat bags	52–54	1.45–1.5	
Urea	47	1.17–1.56	28–45
Pet. coke	48–55	1.25–1.67	33–42
Canned goods	55–60	1.53–1.61	
Wood chips	110–160	3.07–4.46	45
Esparto grass	190	4.0	
Cork	200	5.57	

1 cubic metre per tonne = 35.8 ft³ per ton.   1 cubic metre per ton = 35.3 ft³ per tonne.

The purpose of the preceding table of stowage factors is to show the range from the heaviest types of cargo (pig iron) to one of the lightest (cork). Water has been included as it is the dividing commodity. Those heavier are considered *deadweight* cargo, that is they put the ship down to her loadline marks without filling the holds. Those lighter are sometimes classified as *measurement* cargoes, that is, they fill the holds but the ship is not down to her loadline marks. Dead-weight cargoes usually pay on weight while measurement cargoes usually pay on volume.

Broken stowage. Space which is lost to cargo because of the shape of the cargo, packaging, dunnage, shape of compartment, pillars, etc. For example, one of the effects of palletisation is to increase broken stowage.

Therefore, to find the space required by any consignment the weight of the cargo is multiplied by the stowage factor or conversely the space divided by the stowage factor will give the weight that might be put in that space.

However, there are other factors that have to be considered. For example, a 20-foot container has about 32 cubic metres but the amount of pig iron you could load into it is not 32/ 0.31(the SF of pig iron). This would give you an answer of over 100 tons, which you might physically be able to put into the container, but an ISO TEU is constructed to take only 20 tons. There are various other legal weight limits, such as axle weights for road vehicles, etc., which will limit, say, the amount of pig iron you can actually put into the container, as well as the problem of *broken stowage*.

PRE-SHIPMENT PLANNING, THE STOWAGE PLAN AND ON-BOARD STOWAGE

Traditionally this has always been the ship's concern but over the last couple of decades there has been a growing tendency for the stevedores and terminal operators to become involved. Further, since the advent of containers, most container terminals will have facilities and the know-how in a depot for stuffing and stripping containers to service LCL shippers. This pre-shipment planning is important not only for the ship stowage but also to plan the disposition of the cargo on the terminal.

The stowage plan may well have to be flexible as some containers may be late arriving and errors will be made in the movement of containers through the terminal. An example quoted in *Lloyd's List* in August 1998 for a large container ship loading in the Far East, indicated that around 10% changes in the stowage plan were necessary, mostly in the latter stages of loading. Such last-minute changes can cause serious problems for the ship's officers as the stability of container ships needs to be carefully checked and the ballast adjusted for any changes in top weight.

CARGO POSITIONING AND STOWAGE ON THE TERMINAL

Traditionally for the cargo ship, a fairly universal operation had developed. At the loading berth the export cargo for the ship was assembled in the transit shed with the cargo for each hold in the ship prepared longitudinally and laterally in the shed. The ship's chief officer and the foreman stevedore could discuss the fine tuning and the system adjusted as the cargo was loaded in 2–5 ton units over the following days and often weeks that the operation took.

With containerisation the same basic problem exists but the volumes of cargo passing through the terminal per day have greatly increased, say by 10 to 20 times. This increase in speed and volume requires a better-regulated systems approach by the terminal management to avoid chaos, which in the past could be avoided by an experienced shed foreman using his common sense.

One of the major problems facing a large container terminal's management is reducing unproductive and expensive container moves within the terminal. This is quite complex, as for instance export containers have to be sorted by:

(a) the ship;
(b) the port of discharge;
(c) the type of container, e.g. TEU, FEU, Reefer etc.;
(d) the weight of the container into heavy, medium or light;
(e) dangerous cargo.

To avoid cargo arriving too early at the terminal, say more than a week in advance, the terminal should have a well organised "calling forward" routine with the shipper and consider a pricing policy that deters delivery too early.

For import cargo, consignees must be encouraged to collect their cargo quickly and in developing countries, documentation and currency (payment) problems often add to the logistic ones. Where space is limited containers have to be stacked high and with a random arrival of consignees to collect their containers; this is an area where unproductive moves and delays can easily occur. For a large busy terminal this control is probably only possible by a computerised system with a good software package.

SHIP STRESSES AND STABILITY

Hogging and sagging

On long ships, such as very large tankers and bulk carriers, those responsible for loading the ship have to take care to avoid straining the vessel's hull. If too much weight is placed amidships the vessel will sag. As the vessel cannot submerge her loadline mark amidships she will not be able to load her full cargo.

If excess weight is placed at the ends of the ship and not enough in the middle the vessel may hog. If a vessel in such a condition were loaded with a full deadweight cargo, her loadline marks amidships would indicate she could carry more cargo. In the "bad old days" it is said that this was done deliberately.

With large modern vessels this distortion can be metres rather than centimetres. Apart from the obvious strain on the hull and the problems already mentioned it might also increase the draft, which is often critical for large ships getting in and out of port.

Ships are fairly flexible structures and the bending may not do much permanent harm. If bent severely, however, the ship may become permanently distorted which is undesirable from many points of view. To help ship's officers and those responsible for making the necessary calculations to avoid this bending they must of course be supplied with the necessary information, gadgets and calculators. Any such longitudinal stresses will be aggravated by the vessel *pitching* when end-on to the waves.

Stability

With smaller general-cargo ships the problem of hogging and sagging is not so likely to be serious but that of stability can well be.

Ship stability can be defined as the *ability of the ship to return to the upright* when slightly inclined. Instability can result from too much top weight or conversely too little bottom weight. For the sake of argument, consider all the weight of the ship and cargo to act at a single point G (the centre of gravity) and the upward force of buoyancy to act at a single point B (the centre of buoyancy). Unless the cargo shifts, the point G will be fixed as the vessel rolls. The point B on the other hand will move out to the side as the vessel heels over. The point where the upward force of buoyancy cuts the centre line of the ship is known as the metacentre M. M can be considered stationary for small angles of *heel*.

Note the difference between *heel* and *list*. The vessel is said to list when inclined because of an excess of weight on one side so the centre of gravity (G) is no longer on the centre line. A vessel heels when inclined by an external force such as wind and waves.

Figure 29 (opposite) shows a cross-section of a ship inclined by external forces.

Without going into the mechanics of the situation, it can be seen that as long as M is above G the vessel is stable, i.e. returns to the upright.

If the cargo was loaded or bottom weight, such as bunkers used, so that G moves up above M it can be seen that the ship becomes unstable. Should by chance G and M coincide, the vessel's stability is neutral and the ship just lolls over at any angle she is moved to.

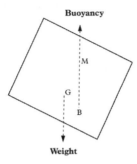

Figure 29:   Cross section of a ship inclined by external forces.

The ship's GM, known as the *metacentric height,* is therefore a measure of the ship's stability.

The completion of loading of the ship with a safe GM is a prime consideration to the ship's officer and others responsible for stowing the cargo. With large modern container ships the loading plan, of which the stability is an element, will often form part of the terminal service.

An empirical formula connecting GM and the ship's period of roll T (T is the time it takes to roll from starboard to port and back to starboard again) is

$$GM = (0.8 \text{ Beam}/T)^2 \text{ or } T = 0.8 \text{ Beam}/(GM)^{0.5}$$

From this it can be seen that if GM is small the period of roll becomes large and the vessel is said to be *tender.*

As GM becomes larger the period of roll becomes smaller and the vessel is eventually said to be *stiff,* that is, the period of roll becomes excessively fast.

With fast vicious rolling the cargo is more likely to shift, the ship to strain herself and the crew to be thoroughly uncomfortable. (The 1986 IUMI Conference noted the dangers of deck cargoes of logs shifting if the GM was too large.) There is also a greater possibility of "isochronous" rolling, i.e. the ship's rolling getting into phase with the passing waves and resulting in increased rolling amplitude.

For example, assume a vessel of 23 metres beam with a GM of 0.08 metres, 0.6 metres and 5 metres respectively. Then:

$T = (0.08 \times 23)/(.08)^{0.5} = 65$ seconds
$T = (0.08 \times 23)/(0.6)^{0.5} = 23.8$ seconds (about right)
$T = (0.08 \times 23)/(5)^{0.5} = 8.2$ seconds (too fast)

It can be seen that in this case a GM of about 0.6 metres would be a good level of stability to aim for when loading the cargo, as 65 seconds would indicate that the vessel is verging on instability and at 8.5 seconds the "accelerations" would be dangerous.

To reduce the amplitude of rolling there are various expensive devices such as fins which can be projected out of the side of the ship under water. They are automatically tilted as the sea tries to push the vessel over and the vessel remains upright. Another method is to use liquid in tanks and cause it to flow quickly from one side of the ship to the other thus cancelling out the tendency to roll caused by the sea.

Another danger to stability is "slack tanks", that is, if liquids are allowed to surge from side to side across the vessel while it is rolling. This causes a virtual rise of G with a consequent reduction in stability. In tanks designed to take liquids, wash-plates and bulkheads are constructed to reduce this hazard but it can be overlooked at such times for instance as fire-fighting, when water is free to move across the decks. This is also one of the major problems for Ro/Ro vessels should water get into the car decks

DEVELOPMENTS IN CARGO-HANDLING AND TERMINAL OPERATION

		The key stages
Element	*Description*	*Changes*
1	Cargo to port	Cargo to ship—to warehouse—to transit shed—to container stack.
2	Cargo checked	Less handling—larger units—less checking.
3	Cargo made into set	The size of the set depended on the amount that could be placed on hand truck in one derrick cycle. For decades this size remained about 30 cwt until the introduction of the container.
4	Set moved to ship	See 1. Even with the container the crane/ship transfer is perhaps the most critical feature of the cycle.
5	Set hoisted aboard	Perhaps the one unchanging element except with Ro/Ro.
6	Cargo moved horizontally in ship	As H.A.C. increases this decreases. With dedicated container tonnage this element disappears.
7	Cargo stowage	With breakbulk cargo this is a highly individual packing skill which still exists in stuffing containers but no longer on the ship.

Historical changes in cargo-handling

Mechanisation

The dates and modes of operation given in the following section are merely indications of the methods that could be found employed in many major ports about that time. The descriptions are largely based on London. Until 1908 London was really a collection of private unregulated terminals, so that at any one time the practices adopted at one terminal or dock were often quite different to those practised at other terminals in the vicinity. However, the importance of establishing precisely when things happened is not so important as identifying why the changes occurred.

While the barrel remained the basic unit there was less need for mechanical help. Nowadays it is often forgotten what a splendid transport unit the barrel was. Even the larger ones, like the tun, could be rolled easily and safely along any flat surface by one man with perfect control.

1800–1850

This period also saw the introduction of powered mechanical handling, with the first major application being in the bulk handling of coal. In 1813 coaling equipment (coal drops) replaced pack animals when in 1813 Whitehaven introduced a system for tipping coal from iron wagons. A similar system was adopted in the Tyne (500–600 wagonloads a day) a few years later.

In 1846 William Armstrong in his native Newcastle constructed the first hydraulic crane that actually worked. This was so successful that he formed the Newcastle Cranage Company. Orders were received from Liverpool, Glasgow, Birkenhead and Grimsby, and by 1858 Armstrong had sold 1,200 cranes and hoists. Electrically powered cranes were slowly introduced at the end of the century, though many hydraulic systems were still in use a century later.

Steam cranes were also introduced; for example, by 1850 Hartlepool had three powerful steam cranes in operation.

Mechanisation was implemented only at the newer bigger terminals and ran in parallel with the older manual systems. For instance, the Henry Mayhew Treadmill crane with six to eight men treading, could lift up to one ton 27 feet high. It had a wheel 16 feet in diameter, was 8–9 feet wide and it could manage 40 cycles an hour. There were still a few treadmill cranes in use in the Port of London in 1909.

Lloyd's List 250th Anniversary Special Supplement, which came out on 17 April 1984, had the following short description of coal jumpers, "who discharged the thousands of colliers which brought coal from the Northeast to London. The coal in the ship's holds was shovelled into large baskets which were hauled up to a chute which discharged into a lighter or barge alongside. The weight of the basket was such that to lift it the coal jumpers had to do just what their name described—jump, on the end of a lifting rope, on to a staging slung alongside the ship's hull. Only this powerful snatch would get the heavy basket of coal topside to be swayed down the chute. Then they clambered back aboard to do it again … and again."

1850–1900 *(see also Chapter Two)*

An observation from the Factory and Workshop Annual Report in 1899:

"… Two characteristic methods of loading are:
  (a) By hoisting the packages of goods direct from the quay and depositing them in the ship's hold (in one operation) by means of cranes, which either stand on the quay or are built on to the warehouse or sheds near the quay edge.
  (b) By first hauling the packages up an inclined plane or "stage" from the quay edge to a temporary platform, built on the deck at the side of the hatchway and then lowering the goods into the hold by the steamer's own winches. When the vessel is sufficiently low in the water the packages may be wheeled on trucks or trolleys along planks from the quay to the ship, or to the temporary platform over the hatchway…alternatively a floating crane might be used…

In some docks the goods before or after loading are conveyed into sheds called transit sheds…. For loading coal two systems are in use … one is at Staiths or what is known as the 'drop' system. Here the wagons of coal are lifted bodily and swung over the ship's hold and then tipped. Wagons intended for this method of coaling must be provided with hinged ends doors or bottoms … Bunkering may be done by employing men to carry baskets of coal on board. Otherwise baskets, tubs (sometimes with drop bottoms) or buckets…. Hoisting Machinery: hand windlass (only on the smallest sailing vessels); steam cranes found chiefly on coasting vessels; steam winch which may be used with a derrick pole or without it."

Development of mechanisation in cargo-handling

This growth in demand was met with increased dock building and increased mechanisation. In 1855 the Victoria Docks were opened. This was the first dock expressly built for steamships and the first London dock to incorporate hydraulic machinery supplied by Sir William Armstrong.

The following table gives an indication of when some significant changes took place:

Year	Details
1852	First steam screw collier in London discharged with steam winches. By the early 1870s the power-driven winch was beginning to have a considerable impact on methods of cargo handling.
1888	Hand trucks for goods from ship to shed considered the most unskilled of dock labour. As 30 cwt (1.5 tons) was the average amount of goods that could be moved to or from the crane by the hand trucks in 2 to 3 minutes (a typical crane cycle time) this became the standard lift for the crane.
1890	Union Purchase introduced on the W. Coast of America. This was made possible by ships including derrick posts (king posts), mast tables and cross trees.
1900	576 hydraulic quay cranes in use in London but not fully utilised.
1900	Electric cranes first used in London Docks replacing hydraulic cranes.

Bulk cargoes, mainly coal and grain, continued to improve their mechanised systems and their productivity, e.g.:

1859	Gravity Staith for loading rail coal wagons into ships on Tyne 420 tph.
1870	Mechanisation for handling grain introduced.
1880	Average loading speed for bulk was around 1000 tons per day for developed countries.
1888	Grabs mentioned for discharge of grain in London as alternative to grain elevator.
1890	2–4 ton grabs introduced and discharge speeds around 500 tpd were achieved—reducing costs to a third over shovels and tubs. By 1909 Hulett unloaders with 15-ton grabs could discharge around 12,000 tons in single shift.
1899	Appendix 12 of the Factories and Workshops Annual Report for 1899 says: "cargoes of grain in bulk are often discharged direct into granaries arranged on the docks near to the quay side. For this work mechanical elevators or pneumatic suction elevators by engines either in the granary or placed temporarily on the ship's deck for that purpose. With such apparatus there is very little manual work needed as the machine deposits the grain on mechanical conveyors in the granaries, one or two machines taking the place of a large staff of porters."

Much of this new era of mechanisation seems to have passed the sailing ships by, and they continued to load and discharge at berths making few concessions to the new developments available. This is illustrated by the following extracts from diaries and memoirs written during this period. This is from the diary of an apprentice on a small brigantine written in 1877 (part published in *Port of London Magazine*, Winter 1977): "The weather cleared off and it was on a hot day that we hauled alongside (SW Dock London) to load. The bags of grain were sent down a shoot from the upper warehouse to the deck of the vessel. I stood on the pitch, which had been made by the first bags sent down, and I received them from the man on the deck. I had a cotton hook in one hand to fix into the bags, placing my other arm round them on the pitch in such a manner that the men in the hold could take them on their backs and stow them at each end."

Henri Kummerman writing in the *Fairplay Centenary Issue*, 19 May 1983, about the period 1880 said: "Many of the sailing ships relied entirely on manual cargo-handling, with only a simple block and tackle on the lower yard with another over the hatch, worked by a hand winch—though horses, donkeys or mules sometimes provided the muscle power. A few of the larger sailing ships were equipped with a donkey boiler on deck and one or two steam winches which could be used not only for cargo-handling but also for working the anchor windlass and pumps. Nevertheless, time spent in port remained much longer than for steamship—typically 40 days versus 10 days."

Direct benefits for cargo handling from mechanisation during this period seemed to be a matter of reducing labour content and costs rather than increasing productivity. This is probably true for the smaller ship with small hatch openings. However, cargo-handling speeds during the latter part of the nineteenth century are full of paradoxes, as it seemed to be a period when the "hustler" could achieve extremely high speeds. One can, for instance, find figures for some ships, particularly mail ships, which achieved breakbulk cargo-handling load/discharge speeds rarely if ever bettered in any later period. For example, in evidence given to the Select Committee on Sweating in 1888 one ship was described as discharging 3,400 tons of bagged wheat in London in 22 hours, which gives 38.6 tons per hatch per hour. Another vessel, the *Hawarde Castle*, discharged 200 tons in 14 hours (48 men) which gives 35.7 tons per hatch per hour.

1900–1970

During this period there were few dramatic developments in cargo-handling techniques. The typical cargo ship increased only slightly in size, and the cargo-handling equipment and techniques were refined. With the onset of containerisation in the 1960s, considerable efforts were made to improve the productivity of the breakbulk general cargo handling by the use of pallets and pre-slinging, etc., and the introduction of hybrid crane/derricks. It remained a very labour-intensive activity.

Date	Details
1913	Hamburg best-equipped port in world. New York one of worst, but by despatch New York was best as the labour force worked at high speed all hours.
1921	King George V dock in London opened. It was equipped with four 3-ton electric cranes per berth.
1922	Hamburg had cranes every 100ft in new basin.
1924	Harwich to Zeebrugge Ro/Ro Train ferry.
1924	Liverpool heavy lift Mammoth crane had a SWL of 200 tons.
1935	Specialised ore-discharging plant installed in Rotterdam.
1960	Velle, Hallen type derricks introduced on ships. They could perform much like cranes.

1964 1964	System	Hook cycle time	Cycles per hour	Load size	tph
	Crane	87.2 secs	41.2	3.0 tons	123.8
	Union Pur.	66.5 secs	54.1	1.1 tons	59.5

Many working in smaller ports around the world will probably still be able to relate to the breakbulk cargo handling figures shown for 1964.

1970 to the present

By 1970 the split of cargo into bulk cargo and containerised cargo was well established through much of the world. This not only dramatically increased cargo-handling speeds but also drastically reduced port labour requirements.

By the early 1990s we see the development of virtually completely automated terminals, such as the ECT terminal at Rotterdam and at Thamesport at London, where the cargo is transferred from shore to ship by machine. Bulk liquid terminals have long been operated by a single controller and dry bulk terminals are now also operated by a minimum number of personnel.

Dry bulk cargoes can be handled as a continuous process by pouring the cargo into the ship and discharged using continuous unloaders, such as bucket conveyors or conveyor spirals, feeding a conveyor belt system on the terminal. Grain has been sucked out for over a century. Slurry is a term for a mixture of small solid particles in liquid (often seawater). Although coal had been transported in slurry form by pipeline for some time, its use for loading ships with coal and iron ore did not seem to start until the 1970s. Further developments in handling commodities "like liquids" were also pursued as in blowing cement through pipes. Alternatively, dry bulks can be discharged by grabs and large modern grabs can grab in excess of 50 tonnes a bite and have a cycle time of less than one minute. The advantage of grabs is that they are very versatile and can be used for virtually any dry bulk cargo. Most of the continuous unloaders are cargo specific.

Benchmarking quality standards

One of the major developments in transporting cargo over the last few years has been the increasingly high specifications required by many shippers, particularly as regards foodstuffs, and the precise and often expensive equipment available to measure contamination. For instance sulphur dust blown over half a mile from one terminal in a port to another terminal loading soya beans would have probably gone unnoticed a decade or so ago but in 1996 it caused the soya cargo to be condemned. This new quality analysis equipment, which can be very expensive, allows a new level of benchmarking for quality standards required by ports for their cargo handling and storage.

CONTAINERS

Growth of containerisation at some leading ports (in % of general cargo)			
Port	*1992*	*1995*	*2000*
Singapore	86.7	91	93.1
Long Beach	93.2	96.9	96.6
Busan	91	98	98.2
Rotterdam	66.3	67.4	77.6
Antwerp	43.4	50.9	64.8
Hamburg	77.6	84.6	92.9
Oakland	90.2	97.5	99.1
Bremen	63.6	73.4	80.2

Globally containerised cargo accounted for around 54% of worldwide trade in general cargo in 2000. It had been 48% in 1995 and

37% in 1990. As can be seen in the table on page 162, some of the leading container ports are gradually verging onto the 100% level for containerised general cargo.

Stuffing containers

In general the same principles of stowage and the same problems of carriage exist for cargo loaded into a container as for cargo loaded directly into a ship's hold. The advantages of loading into a container are that it can be done under cover in relative comfort and safety and if there are any delays these need not necessarily involve the ship that will carry them. Further, as there are a variety of ships for certain types of cargo, i.e. refrigerated cargo and fruit, so there exist a variety of containers.

All containers have security points set into the floor, doorway and corner posts, but, in addition, the majority has arrangements of securing points in the sidewalls. The floor of the container is usually covered with wood (dunnage).

Facts concerning containers

Technically, containers are governed by ISO (the International Standards Organisation) and the CSC (Container Safety Convention).

In 1968 ISO defined a container as an "Article of Transport Equipment" which:

— is of permanent character;
— is intermodal;
— is easily handled;
— is easily filled and empties;
— has an internal volume greater than one cubic metre.

An ISO container has therefore standard size, standard strength and *standard lifting facilities*. It is this latter point which to my mind is the really significant factor which differentiates the present container revolution from previous attempts at putting things into standard sized units

The CSC (Container Safety Convention) was set up by IMO in September 1977. The need for this was probably that by 1977 many containers had been around for several years and that accidents were starting to happen. Container doors were falling off, bottoms falling out during lifts, etc. In 1984 the CSC safety plate came into force. This is a plate fitted to the container door, showing its initial approval and plating and when it was last surveyed. Under the CSC, containers have to be regularly surveyed in a similar manner to ships.

The life expectancy of a container depends on many factors but on average is about eight years. However, on average one of those years will be spent out of service for repairs.

Container ownership	Percentage share
Carriers	53
Lessors	47
Length	
20ft	48
40ft	50
Height	
8ft	3
8ft 6in	89 (33m^3)
9ft 6in	7
Cladding	
Steel	87
Aluminium	11
GRP	1

In 2002 producing country of the world's containers
China produced 87%
Other Asia 6%
Europe 6%
Others 1%

Fleets of leased specialised containers in 2002 (in thousand TEU's)
High cube reefers 190
Open tops and open sides 140
Reefers 130
Tanks 10

The top five leasing companies control about 75% of the containers available for leasing. This is not surprising as a container leasing company must virtually of necessity have a large international operation. A typical rental rate for a standard teu in 2000 was US$0.75 per day.

Standard containers (all lengths) amount to over 5 million or about 87% of the total.

Tank containers are available for the carriage of various bulk liquid cargoes. The tanks are supported within standard ISO steel frames and are equipped with hatches to allow access for cleaning. Some are fitted with heating facilities and may also be suitable for the carriage of hazardous cargo.

World Container Production 2002		Average price for a container in 2001	
Type	*Numbers (million TEUs)*	*Type*	*Price in US$*
Dry Freight	1.3	TEU	1,450
Reefer & Specials	0.3	FEU	2,300
		Reefer TEU	14,500
		Reefer FEU	19,500

The problem of empty containers

In 1997 the ports of the world handled 134 million loaded TEUs and 33 million empty TEUs. This means that of the total number of containers moved throughout the world some 20% were empty. This percentage figure has been constant for some time and is predicted to continue well into the future. In 2003 the global percentage of empty containers being moved across the oceans was estimated to be 16%.

Gang size

Gang size depends on: type of commodity, type and design of ship, type of equipment available, local working practices and union agreements.

As the table in Chapter Nine concerning labour clearly shows, the gang size working in the hatch on a breakbulk vessel has remained remarkably constant over the last century and, in most countries, that is somewhere between 10 and 15 persons. It is in the reduction in the shore gang from around 80 men in 1880 to zero at an advanced container terminal in the 1990s that one sees the most dramatic shrinkage in labour requirements.

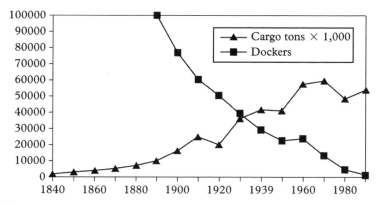

Figure 30: London—cargo tons v dockers.

This graph shows that the reduction in labour per ton of cargo has been a fairly constant feature of port cargo handling over the last century. It did not occur only with the advent of containers.

EQUIPMENT

Lifting and cargo-handling equipment has developed its own jargon and technical vocabulary and although most port managers are familiar with the basic shipping terms, many find difficulty conversing at the same technical level on lifting gear. The following section has been included to help those with such difficulties.

Cranes

A machine for raising and lowering heavy weights. In its usual form it consists of a vertical post capable of rotating on its vertical axis, a projecting arm or jib over which passes a rope or chain from which the weight is suspended, and a barrel round which the chain or rope is wound.

Crane and derrick definitions

(Based on British Standards Glossary of terms used in materials handling.) See Figure 31 (opposite).

1991 UNCTAD/Ship/494(9) Notes on cranes

Multipurpose heavy lift cranes have capacities ranging from 25 to 40 tons. They are usually rigged to handle heavy loads and containers with a main hook, and lighter unitised loads with an auxiliary hook. They handle bulk cargo with a grab, and sheet steel and the like with an electro-magnet.

Maximum reach: although 1,500-TEU container ships have a beam of only 31m, a small increase is desirable to enable the crane to handle 13 rows of containers (Panamax beam), which requires a reach of 32.5m from the edge of the wharf.

A *mobile crane* is specifically designed for port use and is different from the self-propelled crane or crane mounted on a road vehicle. Mobile cranes are of great use in multipurpose terminals since they can be used to load and unload ships and also to handle heavy loads in the terminal cargo-handling areas. On the other hand, their initial and maintenance costs are twice those of conventional cranes and positioning takes time.

Crane requirements

In 1985 Rotterdam had 284 cranes, 32 container cranes, 18 floating cranes, 13 floating derricks, 18 floating elevators, 15 ramps and

Luffing or derricking	Angular movement of the crane in a vertical plane.
Hoisting	The motion of lifting or lowering of the load in a vertical direction.
Level luffing	A luffing motion during which the load is automatically kept at a constant height.
Slewing	Rotary motion of crane about its vertical axis.
Spotting	The ability of the crane or derrick to lower or lift the cargo precisely from or on to the spot required.
Travelling	Crane able to move along the berth, i.e. mobile. Older cranes had to be moved by hand and the movement over even short distances entailed the loss of considerable time. Nearly all modern quay cranes are self-travelling.
Cargo runner	Wire by which the cargo is hoisted or lowered.
Spreader	Frame attached to cargo runner and designed to engage with the corner fittings of the container, or frame for unitised cargo.
Swing defeater	Microcomputer aid to prevent the load swinging.
Topping	Lifting a crane jib or derrick to the required angle.
Union Purchase	Also called married gear or in America burtoning. In this rig the derricks are used in pairs. One derrick is positioned with its head over the hold while the other derrick is fixed with its head over the ship's side (the outboard or yardarm derrick).
House Fall	Works similarly to Union Purchase except the outboard derrick is replaced by a runner worked by a shore winch through a block attached usually to the transit shed.

Dockside or wharf full portal crane (left) and semi-portal crane (right). (Cranes shown fitted with simple jibs)

Dockside bridge grabbing crane (left). A Scotch derrick crane— a part slewing king post (right)

Gantry Crane—its precise spotting and long outreach make it an ideal container crane*

*First Container Crane built in 1958. 1982 first second trolley crane. Some constructed in 2002 had an outreach over 50 metres, lift height of 40 metres with a SWL of 77 tonnes (weight 1,500 tons with a total height of 120 metres).

Crane fitted with quadrilateral jib. Heavier than a simple jib and costs about 10% more but greatly facilitates the rapid handling of heavy loads such as coiled steel since the load and the pulley at the end of the jib travel horizontally, thus reducing oscillation of the load.

Figure 31: Types of cranes.

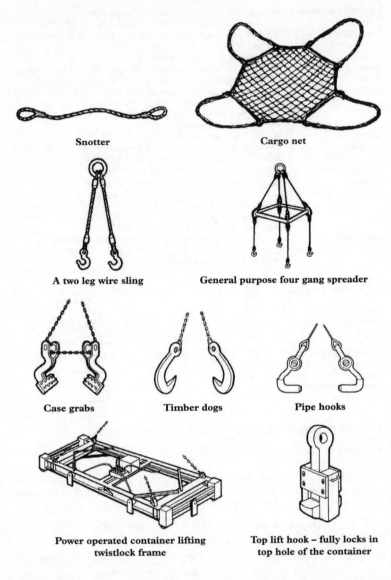

Snotter

Cargo net

A two leg wire sling

General purpose four gang spreader

Case grabs

Timber dogs

Pipe hooks

Power operated container lifting
twistlock frame

Top lift hook – fully locks in
top hole of the container

Courtesy Coubro Scrutton

*Figure 32: Some of the many varieties of cargo gear
available from a specialist stevedore supplier.*

and 46 tugs. In 1992 a sample containing several major ports gave
the following average figures:

(a) Berth Length/ Number of Cranes = 350 metres where v/l
    capacity<1500 TEUs

(b) Berth Length/ Number of Cranes = 130 metres where v/l
    capacity>1500 TEUs

Cost of cranes and equipment	
Cost in US$	*Equipment*
100,000	Tug Master and three trailers (1990 UNCTAD/Ship/494(9)
600,000	12 ton crane (1990 UNCTAD/Ship/494(9)
600,000	Straddle Carrier (1990 UNCTAD/Ship/494(9)
900,000	16–20 ton crane (1990 UNCTAD/Ship/494(9)
1,750,000	Multipurpose crane (1990 UNCTAD/Ship/494(9)
2,250,000	Mobile crane (1990 UNCTAD/Ship/494(9)

Handling equipment development	
Date	*Details—lifting—transporting—stacking*
1888	Hand trucks for goods from ship to shed, considered the most unskilled of dock labour.
1908	Electric conveyor used to move bales of jute from ship to transit shed.
1920	1920—1930 introduction of conveyors for coal and bananas.
1922	Electric truck for meat cargoes.
1930	Forklift trucks in use in US.
1940	Straddle carriers in use in USA.
1951	ICHCA formed.

1991 UNCTAD/Ship/494(9) Notes on equipment

Three types of trailer are used to move containers in a terminal.

(1) Low platform trailers, which are best suited to Ro/Ro
    operation. Over long distances the low speed due to small
    wheels is a handicap, as is the need to secure the goose-
    neck coupling with chains. They have the advantage of
    being able to be stacked when empty.

(2) Normal height trailers—similar to those for road use but
    simpler and sturdier, with no suspension or extra con-
    nections.

(3) Hydraulic lift trailers—which have the advantage over the
    other two types of not needing a machine to load them. A
    hydraulic lift raises the cargo but cannot be used for stacking.

Machine	Capacity m²/TEU	TEU/ Hectare	Manning Level for 2 crane Op.	World Total 1998
FLT and SLT	60	275	26 Medium skill	
RSC	30			
STC and MPC	25	385	22 High skill	2,987
RTG and RMG	25	750	29 Medium Skill	3,687
Tractor /chassis		180	28 Low skill	

FLT (Front Lift Truck): the workhorse of the multipurpose berth as it can both lift and carry cargo. Can vary in lifting capacity from two to 40 tons.

SLT (Side Lift Truck): has capabilities similar to the FLT but less versatile.

Carrier Truck: self-propelled and capable of stacking up to three containers.

RSC (Reach Stacker Crane): performs similar functions to those of FLTs and SLTs and can stack containers in blocks of four rows, four containers high.

MPC (Mobile Portal Crane): can perform the functions of an FLT, an RSC and the straddle carrier. Its purchase price and maintenance costs are between those of an FLT and a straddle carrier

STC (Straddle Carrier): It offers high flexibility but the purchase price and maintenance costs are high. Also the load imposed on the pavement is heavy. Earlier hydraulic models in the seventies were notoriously unreliable, and the oil leaks on the pavement made the surface very slippery. Six STCs were considered necessary to feed each ship-shore crane.

RTG and RMG (Rubber Tyred and Rail Mounted Gantries): highly specialised pieces of equipment with high stacking capability. Well adapted to highly organised operations. Rarely seen on multi-purpose terminals. Low maintenance costs.

Stacking Density for containers by these machines is given in m²/TEU.

TEU/Hectare: measure of land utilisation.

Equipment purchase, maintenance and control

Purchase, maintenance and control are not separate issues. For instance the purchase price and maintenance cost should be considered as one cost when considering the purchase of new equipment. The new price should not be the main argument. Rather *life cycle costing* or the initial cost plus the lifetime maintenance cost should be the figure considered when comparing the merits of different equipment. Experience has shown that lifting equipment does require a high level of maintenance and in the early days of straddle carriers it was not unknown, even at sophisticated terminals, for 50% of the vehicles to be out of action. Modern straddle carriers are considerably more reliable but a high standard of scheduled maintenance is necessary.

It is fairly obvious that good maintenance avoids delays and therefore saves money. It reduces accidents and the subsequent claims and litigation. It will also almost certainly prolong the life of the vehicle. To achieve a high level of maintenance requires a high level of training, which should be regarded as an investment rather than a questionable cost. One port in a developing country did a cost benefit analysis concerning training costs in this area and discovered that for every dollar invested the port saved five dollars in lost revenue.

A well-organised procedure to ensure adequate spare parts are kept in stock is important, as surveys of ports, particularly in developing countries, have shown that delays have too frequently been caused by the lack of spare parts. The delay in obtaining the parts was often not an engineering problem or a transport problem but permission to spend the foreign currency problem.

There are also differing opinions as to who should control the equipment. Should the equipment be in the control of the engineers who supply it to the cargo handlers as required, or should it be under the control of the cargo handlers who call on the service of the engineers when maintenance is required?

A great deal of modern cargo handling equipment is sold with a data communications and diagnostic system linking the equipment directly to the manufacturer's service headquarters. Early warning signs can therefore be analysed and possible faults predicted before they develop into cost and time-consuming breakdowns.

SAFETY OF CARGO OPERATIONS

Dockers' safety

Up until the middle of the nineteenth century, safety was very much the individual's own problem, but about that time public concern brought in the start of legislation which has developed into one of modern management's major nightmares concerning liabilities towards employees. The Employers' Liability Act had come in around the 1850s. This introduction of liability to employees was one of the reasons for the introduction of P & I Clubs at around the same time. By the end of the century in London, married dockers off sick were paid 8 shillings a week and single men 5 shillings a week. A case was cited where one man seriously injured was given £125 compensation to set up a shop.

Safety development

Year	Details
1888	E & W India Docks reported one fatal accident and 104 other accidents.
1932	**ILO Convention 32.** Convention Concerning the Protection against Accidents of Workers Employed in Loading or Unloading Ships.
1934	British Docks Regulations based on ILO Convention 32.
1950	52 fatal and 5970 total accidents in UK ports.
1960	38 fatal and 7130 total accidents in UK ports.
1976	UK—26 reportable injuries per 100.
1979	**ILO Convention 152.** Health and Safety in Dock Work, e.g. safety hats, high visibility clothing etc.
1988	UK Docks Regulations—based on ILO Convention 152.
1992	The **Ports' Safety Organisation (PSO)** was set up to carry on the health and safety services to the ports of Britain and Ireland, formerly provided by the British Ports' Federation. Membership: 82 ports and port companies. Represents the industry in discussions with government departments. Collates statistics.
1993	UK—six reportable injuries per 100 whereas 26 per 100 in 1976.
1994	UK ports have 43 full-time safety officers whereas in 1966 there were only two.
1999	The IMO introduced recommendations on safety of personnel during container securing operations in a MSC Circular. These recommendations have been found necessary due to a number of fatal accidents involving falls from the top of containers during securing and unsecuring operations.

The UK Health and Safety Commission publication, *Safety in docks—Docks Regulations 1988 and Guidance,* is quite a comprehensive document covering planning, lighting, access, emergencies, hatches, ramps and car decks, driving, vehicles, lifting plant and its use—examination and marking, record keeping of safety equipment, protective clothing, etc. Appendix 1 of the document lists over 50 separate items of legislation relevant to health and safety in dock operations. This publication is a Code of Practice which has been prepared following discussions between the Confederation of British Industry, the Trades Union Congress, other Government

Departments and the Health and Safety Executive.

Codes of safe practice for lifting equipment are produced by ICHCA, Lloyd's Register of Shipping and the Chain Testers' Association.

On UK registered ships it is usual for the chief officer to keep the Chain Register, which is a comprehensive record of all tests made to the ship's lifting equipment. In some ports of the world the stevedores' union may wish to inspect such records before using the ship's gear.

Dangerous cargo

The IMDG code and other codes as indicated in Chapter Four, do give specific detail as to any particular requirements needed in the handling of dangerous cargoes.

Safety of cargo

Safety of cargo through ports is, however, seldom covered or mentioned by the ports for obvious reasons. Global average statistics are produced and published by the major P & I clubs which do provide some guidance as regards a norm. For instance, the UK P & I club shows that for the years 1987–1990 the averages for major cargo claims (i.e. claim, over 100,000 USD) are:

— 23% due to bad stowage
— 8% due to bad handling
— 2% due to fraud
— 1% failure to collect cargo

CARGO SECURITY

Theft

Another problem which has always faced transport terminals is security from theft. In 1798 in the Port of London theft had reached epidemic proportions, so the Thames River Police were instituted, and they were in fact the first police force in the country. P. Colquhoun in his *Treatise on the Commerce and Police of the Thames* (1800) estimated that of the 36,000 men working in the port, a quarter were given to plunder and pilfering: "and ever hovering in their punts and bum-boats were the professionals: 100 river pirates; 200 night plunderers of barges; 200 'light-horsemen'

—night plunderers of ships; 550 receivers and 200 mudlarks scavenged greedily along the shore."

Transport terminals where valuable goods are stored have always been obvious targets for criminal elements in society and this problem is often reflected in the architecture of cargo terminals. The early London Docks were built adjacent to the Tower of London and did not look out of place with their high walls and defended entrances.

With the advent of containerisation and the mass movement of high value goods, theft has become an even greater problem. At the port of New York at the present time, losses are estimated to be in the region of a billion dollars a year and as experience shows that less that 50% of losses are reported, the actual figure may well be much higher. On a world-wide level, cargo crime in 1999 cost the transport industry between $30 bn–$50 bn.

One of the problems in this area facing port management is that to increase security may well involve a reduction in productivity, increased delays and increased costs.

If the port is a free port then there will be the added problem of customs security.

Drug control

Lloyd's List in April 1997 stated that the USA calls for greater international co-operation in regard to drug smuggling in containers. The British Ports' Association and HM Customs and Excise have a co-operation pact which protects against offences involving the use of port transport and cargo-handling facilities.

Because of the heavy fines imposed on shipowners if drugs are discovered in any containers carried on that ship, shipowners have been known to withdraw their services entirely from the load port. If the shipowner concerned is a major international carrier the loss of such a customer could be catastrophic for the port.

Warehouse technology

Much new technology is available for warehouse operation. Among the most important developments are automatic stacking and retrieving devices, computerised cargo locator systems, narrow aisle automated pallet movers, deep shelf conveyors. This increase in productivity in the warehouse and transit shed is of course a vital part of the total berth cargo throughput.

CHAPTER NINE

PORT LABOUR

Labour development—how dockers were employed—how dockers were paid—unions—numbers employed—labour split—gang size—labour versus technology—tonnage and labour—technological change and improved operation—how labour is managed—training.

LABOUR DEVELOPMENT

To understand the tensions that have traditionally existed between management and labour within most dock systems it is necessary to see how labour practices have developed in ports. Unions have long memories, particularly in industries that draw their labour from a closed community and sons follow fathers into the same sphere of activities. In the late 1960s the author remembers overhearing a bitter discussion among London stevedores which made frequent pointed references to the "dockers' tanner" strike. I assumed from the conversation that this had happened only months previously and was astonished to learn that this struggle had taken place in 1889.

As most ports since, say 1800, have had basically the same labour problems, the same general pattern of development can be recognised almost universally. It is important that management considers this development as traditionally management has not been drawn from labour but has entered from other areas of commerce and industry and many of the mistakes made by management has been their lack of understanding of labour's perception of the problem.

Around 1800

Cargoes were usually loaded and discharged on and off the ship by the crew, though the Master or agent could employ extra labour if

175

they needed or wished to. The cargo would be handled manually, though tackle often seems to have been used to lift the cargo vertically out of the hold to the ship's deck. It is however interesting to note that John Pudney in his book, *London Docks*, observes that towards the end of the 1700s the London watermen opposed the use of cranes. These would of course be hand-operated cranes since hydraulic and steam cranes were still in their theoretical or experimental stage.

However, although this had not been a dynamic period of changes for ports, efforts were beginning to improve port facilities. For instance, in 1780 the Hull Dock Company developed a 2-horse power operated dredger capable of shifting 22 tons per hour.

1800–1850

In 1802 the West India Dock was the first enclosed dock in London as compared to a riverside wharf. These enclosed docks, which were appearing in the ports of the world, were run by companies which were able to bring in a new level of organisation into the dockside procedure. Many of them started to organise the labour so the modern idea of dockers could be said to start around this period. In Liverpool, for instance, the dock committee took steps to introduce a system of master porterage and appointment was regularised. Before that consignees went down to collect their own goods.

Mechanisation was only at the newer bigger terminals and ran in parallel with the older manual systems. This is the same as a modern port which will have sophisticated container terminals with older terminals still dealing with breakbulk vessels.

1850–1900

One of the greatest problems facing employers of labour in ports is the short-term fluctuation in demand, i.e. ship arrivals. These fluctuations were worse in days of sail when adverse winds could hold ships off the port for days or even weeks. Records for four consecutive weeks in 1861 at London show the ship arrivals to be 42, 131, 209 and 21. With fluctuations like these it is not surprising that employers sought refuge in casual labour. There were, however, some permanent men in London, and the casual employees seemed to have been split into a preferred group who were selected first, and then the rest. There were also many specialised groups of porters, of which deal porters and corn porters seemed to have been at the top of the heap.

In 1872 the first Dockers' Union was established in the UK, though in the early days only a relatively small percentage of the labour force seems to have joined. Among the Unions' first improvements to the working conditions was to put an end to the 12-hour day and to introduce the eight- or nine-hour day. However, one still reads accounts of men working incredibly long hours.

In 1888 the Select Committee on Sweating give the following information: gang size for 5,000 GRT ship is ten per hold; with four holds there would be 40 dockers in total on the ship but 300 men on quay. For mail ships there would be perhaps 60 dockers on the ship, as they wanted a faster discharge. There was a clear distinction between shipboard workers and those working ashore, probably due to the days when ships discharged at anchor into barges. Working hours were 8 a.m. to 6 p.m. 1 March to 31 October and from 7 a.m. to 5 p.m. for the rest of year. This seemed to be considered an eight-hour working day. Men were paid 5d (£0.02) an hour, 6d (£0.025) for overtime. For steamships, especially mail ships, the gang would work 22–24 hours continuously (the same gang).

In 1889 there was the great strike of "the dockers' tanner" which started on 14 August and ended on 16 September. Although it was not a very long strike it was very bitter and soured docker-management relations for over a century. Following the strike there were moves to improve labour conditions. A, B and C men were introduced (see "How dockers were employed" on page 179), as were paid holidays, sick pay and a pension at 70. (In 1911 pensions were £0.25 a week.)

In 1888 the *Report from the Select Committee on Sweating* gives a comprehensive insight into the operational working of the London Docks for that moment of time, with employers, union officials and dock workers being cross-examined as regards the working practices of the moment. Most seem to take mechanisation (cranes) for granted in the docks (though not on the smaller river wharves) and some made wistful comments about how good it was 15 or so years ago before the cranes brought unemployment and lower wages into the docks. Comments were also made concerning the growth in the number of steam tugs which had done much to even out the ship arrivals hitherto so dependent on the wind to manoeuvre upriver. The growth in the numbers of steamships was also noted, as well as the fact that they were nearly all geared and needed little extra equipment to work cargo. Sailing vessels, on the other hand, were seldom at berths with cranes and would often need a barge with a portable steam winch and boiler. Many were questioned as to the numbers working in the dock and answers varied from 200,000 down to about 30,000. Tillett, the Union Official, reckoned about 100,000. The difficulty in arriving at a correct figure is caused by casual labour where virtually anyone who could make it to the call could be employed. Different people included and excluded different groups. Many, for reasons I do not understand, excluded deal and corn porters. The wages in London were reckoned to be lower than most other ports due to the over-supply of labour. In Bristol, for instance, the average weekly wage was reckoned to be 13s compared to London of 7s. However, it was suggested that 16 years before, the average weekly wage was 25s.

Labour developments between 1900 and 1920

Date	Details
1912	London Dock Strike, 10 weeks—ended 24th July
1919	Until 1920 Saturday was a normal working day—now a half-day. ILO formed.
1920	Dockers' wage comparable at last to workers in other industries.
1930	1930s: low wages caused by depression prevented modernisation.
1933	Dispute reported in BIMCO Journal concerning disputes in Canada on the use of ship's winchmen with shore stevedores. NB: This argument recurred in 1990s.
1934	UK Stevedores' National Agreement—stevedores' pay cut 3.75%.
1941	National Dock Labour Board set up and put on a permanent basis in 1947. See next table.

Post Second World War

Date	Details
1962	Number of piecework rates in London reduced from 4,300 to 240. See section on How Dockers were Paid.
1967	As a result of Lord Devlin's Report, what was known as Devlin Stage 1 was introduced in the UK. As a result of this, casual labour was abolished and dockers guaranteed a weekly wage, though this was paid to them via the Docks' Board. In 1970 Devlin Stage 2 was introduced. This meant each man worked for a specific employer and many restrictive practices were removed. One immediate effect was to reduce the number of employers of dock labour (400 employers prior to 1967—after 1967 only a few remained). New York decasualised in 1954, New Zealand 1965, Sweden 1967, Dublin 1971.
1967	Eight-week strike in London mainly concerning the introduction of container technology.
1970	25% drop in productivity in London after Devlin Stage 2 introduced. This was because the financial incentive offered by piecework rates was replaced by a fixed weekly wage.

HOW DOCKERS WERE EMPLOYED

Ports have always suffered from the major transport problems of "peaks". In the days of sail an off-port wind could hold a queue of ships outside the port. Then when the wind changed they would all arrive together. For instance, as mentioned previously, in four consecutive weeks in 1861 at London, the number of ship arrivals were 42, 131, 209 and 21. At this time stevedoring was very labour-intensive, so to arrange a supply of labour to meet this fluctuating demand, the obvious solution was to look to casual labour. This seems to have been the solution adopted almost universally. It remained the pattern until the late 1960s when social expectations, strong unions, increased technology and reduced labour requirements saw a swing to permanent employment. Casual labour in practice did, however, come in a variety of forms. In some places and periods it was literally thrown open to anyone who appeared at the agreed hiring station.

The introduction of steam tugs in the early part of the nineteenth century obviously improved the situation concerning the effect of wind on peaks, but fluctuations in the supply and demand for various commodities throughout the year has meant that peaks in ship arrivals have remained a problem in port labour management.

Although casual labour was the norm there were many interesting and intricate local variations which varied from dock to dock and country to country. In London there were in the nineteenth century many accepted pools of casual labour, such as the A, B and C registers of workers which designated employers' preference. That is, A men were first choice, etc. Other groups existed for specific cargoes such as corn porters, timber porters, coal porters, etc. The actual building of docks and the formation of dock companies in the early part of the nineteenth century also made a radical difference. While ships handled their cargo in the river or at a riverside wharf it was largely the problem of the Master or receiver to use the crew or find labour to handle the cargo. When the dock companies were formed, many of them gradually took over the task of arranging the cargo handling labour and devised various schemes. Some had a small nucleus of "permanents" followed by various "preference groups" who would get the first options when work was being offered.

In the UK this casual system ran into problems during the Second World War when conscription was introduced for men who were not permanently employed in certain "important" jobs. To overcome this the National Dock Labour Board was set up in 1941. It drew up a Register of Dockworkers and only registered dock-workers could be employed. This Register was put on a permanent basis after the war in 1947 but only applied to scheme ports (large ports in 1947). This in turn created its own problems because ports like Felixstowe, which grew rapidly after 1947, enjoyed certain labour advantages denied to their competitors. Further, because of the high labour costs and restrictive practices associated with scheme ports, many shipowners preferred the non-scheme ports. Therefore, post-war UK saw a resurgence of the smaller ports and a decline of the larger ones. This Register continued right up to 1989 when it was discontinued during a period of anti-Union legislation to prepare the way for privatisation of UK ports.

Because of labour unrest in the Port of London the Devlin Inquiry was set up in the early 1960s. The outcome of this was that in 1967, under "Devlin Stage 1", casual labour was abolished and the dockers received a guaranteed weekly wage—though this was paid to them via the Docks' Board. It is also worth noting that at this time the specific terms such as stevedore, lumper, etc., were abolished and the all-embracing term of docker was to be used to cover all cargo-handling personnel. The idea was to have one flex-ible labour force and not specific groups of people each with their own restrictive practices. In 1970 in London "Devlin Stage 2" was introduced, which meant that each docker now worked for a specific employer. However, if the docker's employer went out of business, which many did in the new circumstances, the docker was not out of work. He was simply returned to the Board who reallo-cated him among the remaining employers. The docker was in effect guaranteed a job for life—that is, until the Board was dis-banded in 1989.

Therefore, in the UK, the docker's employment had gone from a very precarious *ad hoc* casual arrangement to a protected period of guaranteed wages and conditions, and then to relatively unpro-tected "permanent" employment under "market force" conditions. However, in October 2004 the EU introduced a new package on port service legislation, which would, if enacted, break the monop-oly of dockers to handle cargo. Such legislation would allow the ship's crew, or such personnel as determined by the shipowner, to handle the cargo.

HOW DOCKERS WERE PAID

Piecework or time rates

The obvious and traditional way of paying casual workers is by piecework or by the amount of work done. For many occupations this may be satisfactory. However, for cargo-handling serious problems arose. With the development of Unions, "rates for the job" were negotiated but every cargo and even a variation of the same type of cargo becomes a different job. In London by the 1960s this rates system had become very complex with many thousands of rates being involved. This led to many sudden "wildcat" strikes as the boarding gang of dockers viewed the cargo down the hold and reckoned that a better rate was needed and work stopped until a satisfactory new rate was negotiated.

The variety of rates involved in discharging general cargo also meant that calculating payment for the docker was complicated.

A further problem arose for a shipowner with "low rate" cargoes on his ship, because in periods of high demand he might well find difficulty in finding dockers willing to discharge/load his ship when the reward for working on other ships was significantly higher.

In some ports, particularly in developing countries when dockers are desperate for money, safety can become a secondary issue as men struggle to make a living wage. Even in London there was evidence to indicate that many young dockers with large financial commitments worked too hard and were "worn out" by their mid-thirties.

It is, perhaps, therefore not surprising that when Devlin Stage 2 was introduced in London in 1970 nearly all wanted to end the piecework system and opted for a fixed weekly wage. However, also not surprisingly, productivity dropped 25% without the spur of financial incentive.

Now most UK ports have a fixed-wage system combined with an incentive bonus system, which is hopefully not too complicated in its application. Perhaps the design and monitoring of this incentive bonus system should be one of the jobs to which labour management should give high priority.

Dockers' pay

Dockers' basic rates of pay in GBP per day	
Year	London
1840	0.18
1880	0.21
1920	0.80
1960	1.60
1993	60.00

The casual system and the high supply of labour meant that during the nineteenth century dockers in London were not well paid in comparison with other workers. By 1920 the docker's wage was comparable with that of workers in other industries. By 1960 they were the highest paid "blue collar" workers in the country. These relatively high rates of pay were particularly prevalent at this time in the USA and Australia, which was why these were the two countries where containerisation was first introduced. These relatively high rates for dockers compared with other workers was also the cause of the long-running dispute in many countries as to who should stuff and strip containers—highly paid dockers or lower paid workers from other unions.

Dockers' monthly wage rates in US$ 1992 (ITF Review)		
Country	Average Monthly Wage	% Higher than National Average
Argentina	847	
Australia	1,572	35
Belgium	2,243	25
Germany	2,280	
Spain	1,980	
UK	2,540	23
India	145	
Japan	2,366	3
Korea	1,200	
Portugal		50
Sweden		6

UNIONS

As already mentioned, the first dockers' union in the UK was formed in 1872, but in the early days fear of victimisation seems to have kept the membership down to a relatively small percentage of the total.

The great strike for "the dockers' tanner", although not a victory for the Unions, did make the workers realise their strength, and the employers knew they had to improve conditions, such as some degree of permanency, paid holidays, sick pay, pension at 70, etc.

Where the UK differs from some other countries is in the number of unions. British industry in general, not just the docks, has been bedevilled by squabbles between the unions safeguarding their member "differentials", interests and group perks.

As can be deduced from the tables showing the relative high salaries for dockers, these unions have been powerful and largely successful, though during the 1980s over much of the world there seems to have been a general reduction in this power. This is perhaps partly due to a changing political and social climate and partly due to the changing nature of transport itself. Intermodalism allows competition not only between ports themselves but also between different modes of transport. Dockers in the UK can no longer hold the country to ransom. The workers on the Channel Tunnel have now probably more power.

The table in Chapter Ten (see page 197) does show how serious the strike situation was in post-war UK during the 1950s and 1960s compared with other industries. The sharp rise in 1970 following the introduction of containers and container working practices is very noticeable

ITF and ILO

In 1896, as a result of a series of serious strikes in Europe, the International Federation of Ship, Dock and River Workers was formed. This led to the formation of the International Transport Workers' Federation in 1898. Although the ITF does not seem to have played a great part in the development of port labour it has, over the last couple of decades, successfully called on port labour to "black" various ships (usually of a flag of convenience), to bring pressure on shipowners on matters concerning crews' wages and conditions.

In 1919 the International Labour Organisation (ILO) was formed, and ultimately provided a voice within the United Nations relating to the rights, social conditions and employment of port workers worldwide.

Working hours

Until 1920 in the UK, Saturday was a normal working day in ports. It then became a half-day and remained so for the next 50 years until the ports adopted a five-day working week. Most ports, particularly container and bulk terminals, will of course now work 24 hours a day seven days a week. However, the establishment of the official working hours is an important element in the formula for working out aspects of laytime and dockers' overtime rates.

NUMBERS EMPLOYED

Labour split

For different cargo types		
Year	*Port*	*Details*
1985	Rotterdam	10,303 dock workers 43.0% work with breakbulk general cargo 24.7% work with container cargo 19.0% work with bulk cargo 13.3% work with grain cargo

For different work grades		
Year	*Port*	*Details*
1992	All Ports UK	31,487 persons working in UK Ports (only 8% women) 37.4 % Cargo handlers 8.6 % Managers 54.0 % Others

The above table does indicate that now that the numbers of cargo-handling personnel has been reduced, the "others" group is becoming relatively larger.

Gang size

Gang size depends on type of commodity, type and design of ship, type of equipment available, local working practices and union agreements.

Date	Gang Size		
	Components		*Total*
1880	Ship's Gang—BB Cargo	10–15	
	Shore Gang—BB Cargo	70–80	80–95
1990	Ship's Gang—BB Cargo	12	
	Shore Gang—BB Cargo	16	28 (tph say 20)
	Ship's Gang—Container Basic	8	
	Shore Gang—Container Basic	9	17 (tph say 216)
	Ship's Gang—Container Advanced	1	
	Shore Gang—Container Advanced	0	1 (tph say 276)

Typical gang size per crane on an Australian container terminal per shift = 10–13—made up of 2 crane drivers, 3–5 straddle carrier drivers, 1–4 general hands, foremen 1–3, 1 clerk (1999 Research Paper).

In Tilbury, Singapore, Port Klang the figures would be smaller—for instance only 1 crane driver. In Australia about 80–89% of the stevedores were permanent employees.

Reduction in labour due to technological change and improved operation

Numbers employed in cargo-handling in port or country (tons per man per year)						
Year	London	Antwerp	New York	Rotterdam	Cochin	Singapore
1890	100,000 (16.5)					
1900	76,500 (26)					
1910	60,000					
1920	52,000 (81)					
1930	39,000 (118)					
1939	29,000 (1,400)					
1950	22,237					
1960	23,484		31,000			
1970	13,280	15,000 (4,800)	19,500 (2,780)	12,000 (15,000)	3,100	3,000
1980	4,429	9,539 (8,000)	10,000 (4,900)	10,000 (25,000)		
1990	900-Tilbury	7,633 (9,600)		8,130 (35,000)		
1995	258-Tilbury	6,643		6,455		

The table above shows a steady decrease in the labour force over the years at virtually all ports even though cargo throughput has been rising steadily (Note: the tons per man per year ratio seems to be remarkably consistent at 6% growth per year.)

The figures shown before 1970 shows that this decrease due to technological change and more efficient operational practices did not just start with containerisation but has been a steady ongoing progress.

It can be argued that the reduction in dock labour requirement, since the introduction of the container, could be misleading. It is true that the dock labour requirements have been dramatically reduced but the containers have to be stuffed and stripped and this takes labour. Even in a sophisticated high tech country, for example Sweden, it takes on average three persons 20 minutes to stuff a container and a similar sort of figure to strip one. That is, it takes around one man-hour to fill a container and the same to empty it. Therefore, to empty and fill the 6,000 boxes on a large container ship takes some 12,000 person hours. Labour is therefore still needed though not necessarily on the terminal, and as far as one can see, this requirement will need to be met for some time in the future. One hears relatively little of automated container stuffing equipment.

In some aspects containers will increase labour requirements. Containers have to be built, surveyed regularly, cleaned and maintained. Containers get lost and have to be found even though there are sophisticated computer packages and operators who record their every movement.

LABOUR v TECHNOLOGY

Comparison of tonnage and labour figures for the Port of London (1925–1975)

(The figures for tonnage throughput exclude petroleum cargoes.)

If technology replaces one link in the cargo-handling chain then the effect on the cargo-handling throughput will be only to reduce the labour content and perhaps cost. It will not increase cargo-handling speed unless the link being replaced is the slowest link.

For the cargo-handling speed to be significantly increased the whole logistic system needs to be analysed and new technology and methods applied where they will be most effective.

From 1840 to 1970 technological impact on cargo handling in ports was largely in replacing activities requiring high labour content. The effect of the container was not just the new gadgets but that it forced all concerned in the movement of goods to re-evaluate the system, not just in the ports but throughout the whole transport chain.

Vacuvators and grabs seem to have been introduced into many large ports by the 1890s but the carriage of grain in bulk was still only a relatively small percentage of the total, even though this

Tons per man per year		
Year (Source Wilson—Dockers)	Numbers employed in UK Ports	Tons per man per year (tons mn)
1921	125,000	296 (37)
1924	118,000	567 (67)
1929	110,000	608 (67)
1931	111,000	466 (52)
1935	104,000	593 (62)
1938	100,000	669 (67)
1947	78,458	655 (52)
1950	75,265	796 (60)
1955	80,674	897 (72)
1960	72,550	1,290 (94)
1965	65,128	1,550 (101)
1970	46,912	2,580 (121)
1973	32,000	
1976	31,062	
1981	21,022	
1982	15,000	

technology made the discharge from the ship faster and cheaper. However, as the shipments were still in small quantities and arrived at the port of loading in bags and the distribution at the port of discharge was in bags, any advantage gained in the ship-handling speed and cost would be lost in the effort of de-bagging and re-bagging.

The North American Great Lakes ports trading in grain and many other cargoes have, since the end of the last century, often led the way in ship technology and cargo-handling technology and enjoyed the benefit of higher cargo-handling speeds. However, until the St Lawrence Seaway opened in 1959 it was a closed system and did not suffer from the constraints imposed by international trading.

See Figure 30 on page 165, showing the reduction in the number of London dockers against the increase of cargo handled.

HOW LABOUR IS MANAGED

With casual labour and simple equipment, labour management's main problems were obtaining labour contracts with shipowners if there was competition from other stevedoring companies, and negotiating handling rates and conditions with the union. With permanent employment come all the growing problems associated with any employer of labour.

The tradition of casual labour has meant that in the UK and in many other countries, labour management has tended to be confrontational. In the past relatively few of the "workers" have wished, or been invited to cross the labour divide into management. However in most ports, old attitudes are changing fast, encouraged by the privatisation and the general revolution in port administration that has happened almost universally in the last decade.

Perhaps one of the greatest differences between developed and undeveloped countries is in the hierarchical pyramid for decision-making. In developing countries virtually all decisions are referred upwards whereas in ports in developed countries, many of the basic decisions are left to the gang to decide for themselves.

Safety and security

Dockers' safety

See Chapter Eight.

Training

Until the 1950s it was assumed that the individual would ensure that he was trained for the job he was hired for and as the work was mainly labour-intensive the level of skill required was, for much of the work, fairly low. Since the 1950s dock work has become rapidly more mechanised and sophisticated, requiring skilled operation and maintenance. Today training is not just a good idea, it is a sound investment, and particularly, as in most ports, a multi-skilled work force is required.

CHAPTER TEN

TIME IN PORT AND SPEED OF CARGO HANDLING

Port time and cargo handling—speeds for different vessel types, general cargoes, containers, bulk cargoes, tankers—general operational delays— strikes—port time other than berth time—weather delays—congestion— compensation—port productivity—basic data a port should collect— safety of cargo.

Minimising the time a ship spends in port will now be virtually every port manager's priority. This priority increases as ships grow in size and capital intensity and ports face increasing competition for customers.

TURNAROUND TIME IN DAYS FOR SAILING VESSELS 1863–1912

The figures in the table on page 190 were derived from taking random samples from back copies of *Lloyd's List*, which gave the vessels' arrival and departure dates.

The table suggests that all sailing vessels showed an improvement in the turnaround time between 1878 and 1890. This improvement was sustained in the final period only for the largest vessels or those ports which still catered largely for sailing vessels. In ports catering for the new steam vessels the sailing ships were probably relegated to the older areas and given lower priority as regards cargo-handling. This probably also indicates that the larger sailing vessels were in more secure trade routes, i.e. they could still find cargoes. The smaller vessels were less capable of finding ports with ready cargoes—hence their longer time in port.

In his book *British Merchant Shipping*, published in 1922, Clement Jones quotes Edward Arnold and Co. who estimated that at that time a ship spent half its life in port, though the table indicates that on the Australia trade around the early twenties, the percentage time spent in port was nearer 40%.

Size	1863–1877	1878–1890	1891–1912
250–499	25.6	21	29.1
500–999	29.7	24.2	25.1
1000–1499	38.7	30.5	31.3
1500 +	50.5	32.3	21.9
Specific ports			
Liverpool	24.1	23.2	26.1
London	25.8	25.8	26.4
New York	21.3	18.6	31.9
Antwerp	30.6	24.3	21.2
Rio de Janeiro	27.7	25.2	20.3
Bombay	29.2	26.1	24.7
Melbourne	35.8	34.3	31.6

GENERAL CARGO

Typical dry cargo power driven breakbulk vessels on Europe to Australia run 1870–1970)							
Year	dwt	Speed	Daily consumption	Voyage time	Port time	% of voyage	Tons pd per hatch
1870	2,970	7	17.4	232	88	38	46
1890	4,530	9	23	257	144	56	54
1910	9,496	11	40	237	145	61	64
1930	11,719	12	31	229	144	63	69
1950	13,066	13	20	217	143	66	90
1970	15,473	15	24	213	145	68	107

What is interesting in this table is the virtually constant total port time of around 140 days from 1870–1970. It would seem to indicate that this was the upper limit of port time that the shipowner considered tolerable. As the cargo-handling speed increased, as shown by the tons per day per hatch, the size of the ship increased. The thesis that the maximum economic size of ship is largely governed by the port time which in turn is a factor of cargo-handling speed, is borne out by the fact that as soon as containerisation was introduced, with its higher cargo-handling speeds, cargo ship size increased dramatically.

The daily fuel consumption shown is also remarkably constant, in spite of the increase in ship size and speed. Although the economics of ship speed has many factors, port time is an important one, as it is quite easy to demonstrate that with a high proportion of port time relatively little effect is made on voyage time by adjusting ship speed.

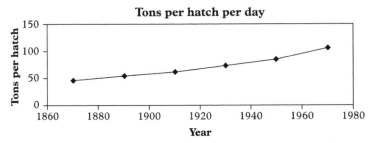

Figure 33: Gross average speed of cargo handling per hatch for the entire stay in port.

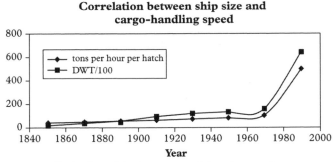

Figure 34: Relationship between ship size and cargo handling speed.

Figure 34 shows the relationship between ship size and cargo-handling speed. The samples taken have been for ships carrying general cargo between Europe and the Far East (including Australia). As can be seen there is almost perfect correlation.

The interesting question is, which is the cause and which the effect?

1965 conventional breakbulk

A Clan Line General Cargo-handling Survey made in 1965 (an internal survey done by their own R and D department) concluded that on average:

— Handling speed per hatch was 10–40 tons per hour.
— Loading speed on average was about half discharge speed.
— Cranes were about twice as fast as derricks.

1965 is a good year to benchmark conventional breakbulk cargo handling speed, as new ideas of unitisation were being tried and conventional breakbulk probably reached the peak of its efficiency at this point. The sailing ship, a century earlier, only reached its optimum efficiency just before it was eclipsed by the steamship.

Year	Some examples of general cargo-handling speeds
1876	London 1,100 tons sugar in 23 days 55 tpd (**tpd = tons per day**)
1880	Discharge of 50 tpd considered poor. Belfast offered discharge rates of 60 tpd in winter, 80 tpd in summer, but capable of 330 tpd if right financial inducements were offered.
1888	3,400 tons wheat discharged in London in 22 hours, which gives 38.6 tons per hatch per hour. *Hawarde Castle* discharges 200 tons in 14 hours (48 men) which gives 35.7 tons per hatch.
1888	Sailing ship had to give shippers three days notice before working cargo but steamships had to give only one. Mail ships would however commence work immediately. Steamships worked faster than sail, where there was little overtime. Docks were more highly mechanised than river wharves so they worked faster but required less labour per ton handled.
1924	Paper to the NE Coast Marine Engineers estimates speed of cargo work 800–1,600 tpd.
1928	Chamber of Shipping *Annual Report*: Sydney 550 tpd, S. Australia 430 tpd.
1929	Lagos—electric cranes 600 tons per day.
1939	Average lay time in UK ports 17 days—1951 20 days.
1945	London—1500 tpd for discharging bagged sugar.
1969	NPC Port Progress Report gives the following comparison for tons of cargo handled per man per hour on the terminal—Container 30, palletised 4.5, conventional 1.7.
1978	UNCTAD report gives the following figures. Deep sea ships 700 tpd, short sea routes 500 tpd, palletised and preslung 900 tpd, forest products 1,500 tpd, bundled iron and steel 2,000 tpd.
1982	Typical 18–25 tons per gang hour (tpgh) Bremen and Hamburg 14–22 tpgh, New York 12–18 tpgh, Karachi 2–18 tpgh, Valparaiso 14–18 tpgh.

CONTAINERS

Containers loading/discharge speed are virtually the same.

Speed in boxes per hour per crane = 10 -50 (average 30 for good port). For large mother ships at a container centre port, 80 moves per hours should be expected.

Examples 1998			
Port	*Country*	*Boxes per ship hour*	*Boxes per crane hour*
Juwaharial	India		15
Colombo	Sri Lanka	20–24	26
Singapore		69	36

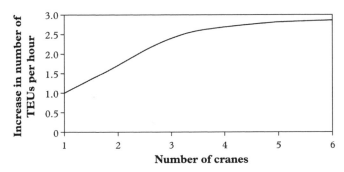

Figure 35: If using several cranes to load and discharge.

BULK CARGOES

The table on page 194 illustrates that the cargo handling technology for bulk cargo has been constantly changing and improving with very significant improvements in cargo handling speeds, unlike breakbulk cargo where cargo handling has shown little change.

1987 Bulk cargo-handling speeds (tons per hour)

Sample of 50 load ports and 50 discharge ports selected at random from the BIMCO Journal 1987			
Commodity	*Average of sample*		*Best of sample*
	Load	*Discharge*	
Grain	167	108	316
Ore	618	482	1705
Coal	678	352	1342
Phosphates	183	120	340
Scrap	96	49.5	174

As one might anticipate, the higher figures are for ore and coal which are the two main dry bulk cargoes shipped in large quantities from specialised terminals. Therefore one would expect a greater capital investment in the handling equipment.

Date	Some examples of bulk cargo-handling speed
1813	Coaling equipment (coal drops). Coal first to mechanise replacing pack animals in 1813. Whitehaven had an inclined plane for iron wagons. Similar system in Tyne (500–600 wagon loads a day).
1835	Darlington coal drop could load a wagon load (4 tons) into a ship in 2 minutes (120 tph).
1880	Average loading speed for bulk cargo was 1000 tpd in developed countries.
1890	2–4 ton grabs introduced allowing 500 tpd to be achieved. This simple development reduced costs to a third compared with shovels and tubs.
1897	Grain loading in USA 700 tph.
1910	Loading rates of 2,000 tpd commonplace for coal and ore. 5000 tpd possible.
1910	Transporter introduced at Rotterdam. This was a wide bridge structure spanning several rail tracks reaching 140ft overside.
1912	In Surrey Docks pneumatic or bucket elevators were capable of lifting, delivering and weighing 200 tons of grain per hour. 1903 Millwall had two floating pneumatic elevators that could handle 500 tph.
1912	Continuous self-unloading lakers for ore carriage.
1924	Coal discharge speeds of 500–600 tph were typical.
1930	Typical chartering figures for coal: 7000 tons allowed three weeks laytime for loading and discharging.
1934	Baltimore could load 240,000 bushels of grain per hour. At Narvik ore trains 60 ft above berth could load a vessel in two hours. Norfolk, Virginia could load 1,500 tph. For bulk ports a week more or less should be sufficient but some ports exceed that time. For coal discharge rates of 500–1,500 tph cover the majority of ports.
1939	Ore loaded by spouts—little trimming required—very fast.
1939	Great Lake ore-carriers could discharge at 2,500 tph and some were self-unloaders. Lifting magnets capable of lifting up to 20 tons.
1949	Coal could be loaded at Hampton Roads at a speed of 2,500 tpd.
1954	Coal could be discharged at Rotterdam at 3,000 tpd.
1955	Typical chartering figures for coal—15,000 tons were allowed 1.5 weeks laytime for loading and discharging.
1966	Typical chartering figures: coal—25,000-dwt 6 days laytime all purposes.
1970	Average loading speed for bulk cargo was 2,300 tpd in developed countries.
1970	Australia—for ships loading bulk the average time in port was 9.7 days, time prior to loading 2.8 days; time spent loading 6.5 days—average speed of loading 3865 tpd.
1989	Antwerp bulk (ore, coal, etc.) 2,500 tph discharge. Grain elevators 400 tph.
1992	Hamburg 34.9 million tons bulk cargo—45.5% liquid and pumped, 15.5 % suction cargo, 39% grabbed.

For all bulks in sample:

— Mean loading speed 365 tph
— Mean discharge speed 218 tph

Correlation between loading speed and cargo dwt is 0.85. Correlation between discharging speed and cargo dwt is 0.78.

These correlation figures indicate that larger vessels go to larger ports where the cargo-handling speed is faster.

UNCTAD Port Development gives the following

Ship loaders	1000-7000 tph
Grabs	180-2000 tph
Slurry	6000-8000 tph
Pneumatic	200 tph
Bucket elevators	1000-5000 tph

N.B. Weighing accuracy between 1% and 2%.

Scale loading speed

Some specialised bulk cargo terminals, such as Richards Bay, have a loading scale which gives the expected metric tonnes loaded per weather working day. Such a scale rate may be used when chartering the vessel to determine the laytime.

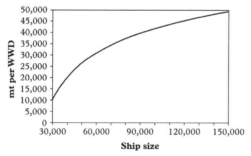

Figure 36: Scale loading speed for Richards Bay.

TANKERS

There are 72 hours allowed for Load + Discharge time. See the *New Worldscale Book*.

As tankers are handling liquids, which can be easily pumped, very fast handling speeds are possible. This is one of the reasons why tankers were the first ship types to grow in size after the Second World War. Virtually all tankers are allowed the same port time because larger tankers have larger pipelines and larger pumps and so can handle the cargo proportionally faster. As a simple rule of thumb, a tanker can be estimated to have a maximum pumping speed per hour of 10% of her deadweight tonnage. This does not mean that a tanker can discharge in ten hours since time has to be allowed for the more viscous oils to drain. Hence the discharge time is usually slightly longer than loading time. However, prior to 1950 when 10,000 dwt could be considered to be the typical tanker, 200 tph could be considered to be a typical cargo-handling figure.

GENERAL OPERATIONAL DELAYS

The table below summarises the causes of operational delays at a general cargo berth over a one-week period in 1990.

Delay caused	Man hours lost
Absenteeism	170
Late starts	110
Non-availability of cargo	76
Extended meal breaks	70
Shifting quayside cranes	55
Bad weather	40
Equipment breakdown	25

STRIKES

The word "strike" appeared in English in its more aggressive sense in the thirteenth century, but it was not until the mid-eighteenth century that it was applied to the withdrawal of labour. This use was first recorded in 1768 and is thought to have derived from the specific use of the word strike in the sense of "to pack up and go", as in the nautical expression "to strike sail".

The next table shows what a serious problem strikes were in the UK ports in the three decades following the Second World War, much worse than was experienced throughout the rest of British industry. It reached a climax, as one might have expected, at the end of the sixties when containerisation was introduced and labour requirements were being savagely reduced. However, by 1989 when Margaret Thatcher's government finally abolished the dock workers' registration scheme set up in 1941, the labour situation seems to have stabilised and the UK ports have now one of the best strike-free records in Europe.

Year	No. of stoppages in UK Ports	Days lost per 1,000 employed	Days lost per 1,000 empl. all industries
1947	77	1,687	N/A
1950	63 (av. 50–54)	3,162	90
1955	93 (av. 55–59)	4,602	270
1960	113(av. 60–64)	3,180	138.5
1965	224 (av. 65–69)	3,929	169
1970	374	13,986	475

The following table indicates the countries whose ports have been worst affected by strikes over the last couple of decades.

Port delays caused by strikes—countries most affected					
(Strike Club figures for) 1981–1985)		(Strike Club figures for 1993/94)		Strike Club Figures for 1996/97 approx.	
Country	*%*	*Country*	*%*	*Country*	*%*
Australia	26,5	Korea	27.6	Korea	40
UK	25.4	Brazil	18.7	Brazil	15
Portugal	8.9	Canada	18.1	Australia	8
Canada	7.1	Australia	14.2	New Caledonia	7.5
Nigeria	5.4	India	5.7	Spain	4.5
France	5.0	Nigeria	2.5	India	3.5

Source: Shipowners Mutual Strike Insurance Association (founded 1956).

As the following table shows, not all port strikes are caused by the stevedores, in fact over 50% of delays caused by labour problems can be seen to arise from among the other groups of workers connected with the port.

Port delays caused by strikes 1993/94	
Incidence by type of workforce	*%*
Stevedores	47.5
Other port workers	23.7
Factory and other workforce	9.0
Land transport workers	7.3
Customs officers	7.3
Pilot and tug crews	2.3

PORT TIME OTHER THAN BERTH TIME

The *National Ports Council Report 1978* states that for UK ports "port time is 6.5% longer than berth time". However, if all the ships which loaded or discharged at Bombay are considered for the years 1983–1987 the average excess of port time over berth time was about 40 %. However, it would be only fair to state that the situation in Bombay has greatly improved since then. In 1992 at Singapore the average containership wait for berth was 2.3 hours.

Ship catastrophe

The global probability of a delay or problem due to a mechanical failure, collision, contact damage, fire, etc., has been estimated at 0.00012 per day. (Analysis of one month's casualty data reported in *Lloyd's List* in the mid-seventies.)

Pilotage and mooring time

This will obviously vary for each port depending on the length of pilotage, tide, currents, weather, locks, etc. The following table shows the pilotage times for large powerful vessels arriving and leaving 18 randomly selected ports on the world's major trade routes.

Pilotage time	
(Hours)	*No. of Ports*
0	0
0.5	4
1	5
2	2
3	2
4	2
5	1
8	1
22	1

Of these pilotage movements, more than 80% were under four hours.

Weather delays

The weather can affect port time in several ways. Gales and fog can reduce or halt movement within a port. Gales may also prevent cargo handling at berths with large cranes, as at container terminals, and at exposed berths. It can be one of the few causes of stoppages at a tanker terminal. With some cargoes, particularly the traditional general cargoes and bulk cargoes, such as sugar, rain can stop all cargo working.

Climates do of course vary widely between ports throughout the world, and at any one port the climate will vary with the seasons. However, by consulting the Admiralty Pilot Books and the Admiralty Seasonal Climatological Charts for 16 major ports positioned evenly over the major trade routes, the following conclusions should give some indication of the meteorological problems to be expected in port over the course of one year's world-wide trading.

Weather type	Range in days per annum when phenomenon is experienced	% Time (Average for all 16 ports)
Gales	0–30	5%
Fog	0–45	1%
Rain	0–169	5%

PORT DELAYS (CONGESTION)

Port congestion arises when port capacity is insufficient to cope with the traffic arriving at the port. It is not a new problem and can occur at any port if there is a sudden upsurge in demand or hold-up in the port such as a strike. After the oil price rise in 1973 many of the OPEC countries spent their increased revenues on extra imports which caused severe congestion in many cases. In 1976, for example, ships carrying cement to Nigeria were waiting over 200 days at Apapa/Lagos.

A conference of experts organised by UNCTAD in April 1976 gave the following table for the average waiting time for thirty ports which are regularly subject to port congestion:

Year	Average days delay
1971	2.2
1972	2.3
1973	4.0
1974	4.8
1975	14.3
1976	40.4

Extending the table for the average delay at the 30 worst ports following 1976, from the port data given in *Lloyd's List,* gives:

1979	17.5
1983	8.9
1986	4.5
1998	3.7
2004	5.3

The above extension to the table shows that the problem has declined but still flares up from time to time, as in 2004 due to the surprising growth in demand at this time. During the autumn of 2004 at many of the world's leading ports, such Los Angeles, Long Beach, New Orleans, Felixstowe, etc., ships were experiencing several days delay, though at many ports the management preferred to simply say that they were very busy.

Note: In October 2002 a port strike on the West Coast of USA also caused problems. *Lloyd's List* reported: "The 200 or so ships anchored off the coasts of California, Oregon and Washington are carrying enough freight to fill more than 650,000 tractor trailers."

It is very important to identify clearly the cause of the delay. If, for instance, the delay was caused by slow customs clearance but this was not recognised and new berths were built, then it would only aggravate the situation.

Because of the severe nature of some of the congestion in the early 1970s, UNCTAD in 1975 set up a small group to analyse the situation. BIMCO, who were represented on the UNCTAD working group, summarised the 10 major causes of congestion in one of their 1976 Bulletins as follows, and although about 30 years old the summary is still valid:

1. Planning

   (a) Investment in new berths without ensuring that back-up areas, port access and operating capabilities such as trained manpower, cargo-handling equipment and warehousing space (either within or outside the port area) are able to service these new berths.
   (b) Inadequacy of inland transport, both in capacity and efficiency, in relation to trucks, wagons, highways and port access routes.
   (c) Late completion of port and transport development projects, so that expected capacity is not available on time.
   (d) Failure to keep traffic forecasts updated to reflect changes in the pace of major economic developments.
   (e) Improvements by rebuilding wharves without providing for the accommodation of expanding traffic volumes during construction.
   (f) Failure of port management and planning authorities to make adequate plans in time for port developments.

(g) Inflexibility in development plans to allow later changes in modes of traffic flows.

(h) Low appeal of port and shipping problems in the public mind, leading to lesser priorities being accorded to port investment.

(i) Political and social interference which bear on the decision-making processes.

2. Management

(a) Lack of continuity in senior port management positions.

(b) Senior port management chosen without regard for the qualifications required by the job and the adequate provision for upgrading knowledge.

(c) Too little training for other staff, particularly of the middle management and operating levels.

(d) Lack of direct authority of management to effect remedial actions.

3. Labour

(a) Poor labour relations, leading to inefficient restrictive practices.

(b) Problems caused by too much or too little labour, according to circumstances.

(c) Inefficient deployment of labour.

(d) Failure to adapt working practices to local circumstances, such as the climate.

(e) Lack of training of dockworkers, especially in the use of sophisticated equipment.

4. Co-ordination

(a) Lack of co-operation between different private and governmental organisations working in the port area.

(b) Inadequate consultation between the port authority and users of the port in respect of operations and development.

5. Traffic

(a) Irregular traffic due to erratic import and export policies, especially with regard to bulk purchasing and the granting of import licences.

(b) Short-term traffic variations due to unrationalised shipping schedules, leading to ship bunching.

(c) Too many ships operating on certain routes and consequently calling for small tonnages and making inefficient use of berths.

(d) Inefficient distribution of cargo between hatches thus preventing intensive working of the ship.

(e) Cargo stowed at port of loading without regard to efficiency of discharge.

(f) Forms of packaging and cargo presentation unsuitable for efficient handling at the port.

(g) Consignees without adequate financial resources or physical facilities to take cargo.

(h) Ships spending longer than necessary at berth for reasons such as slack in their schedules.

6. Operations

(a) Inappropriate policies which lead to transit facilities being used for long-term storage where space is inadequate, thus reducing berth throughput.

(b) Lack of inland or port warehousing facilities, causing cargo to remain too long in the port transit facilities.

(c) Necessity of handling bulk cargoes at general cargo berths.

(d) Lack of reserve capacity to deal with recurring surges of demands placed on ports.

(e) Pilferage and smuggling resulting in tight controls which impede a free and efficient movement.

(f) Lack of finance for modern handling equipment.

(g) Inefficient mix of handling equipment due to circumstances beyond the control of port management.

7. Maintenance

Inadequate maintenance policies which result in a high proportion of equipment being out of service due to:

(a) Absence of preventative and running maintenance.

(b) Lack of qualified maintenance personnel.

(c) Lack of adequate stocks of spare parts.

(d) Insufficient standardisation of equipment types.

8. Clearance Procedures and Documentation

(a) Late arriving documents.

(b) Faulty documents.

(c) Outmoded documentation requirements and processing methods.

(d) Outmoded clearance facilities for vessel and cargo.

(e) Importers allowed to order shipments without sufficient funds to take delivery on arrival.

9. Dynamic Effects

(a) Changes in ship types, especially on an experimental basis, with inadequate prior consultation, leading to temporary inefficiency.

(b) Teething troubles with new cargo-handling methods.

(c) Emergency diversion and transhipment of cargo destined for another port, which can bring temporary peaks in quantities of cargoes, which a port has to handle.

(d) Periods of exceptionally bad weather.

10. Function and Location of the Port

(a) Impossibility of improving back-up land accesses in ports because adjacent lands have been occupied by urban developments.

(b) Activities carried out in the port area, not related directly to cargo handling, which may conflict with higher port throughput. (For instance, customs' controls inspection procedures, etc.).

(c) Special difficulties which may occur with traffic of landlocked countries.

(d) Dislocation of traffic by decisions of neighbouring countries if ports are serving a regional trade.

In the long term the cure for congestion is of course to rectify the cause. In the short term there are however some immediate alternatives that can be tried:

(1) Use other ports nearby.

(2) Use different types of ships. For instance, Ro/Ro ships have helped considerably to reduce congestion at some ports in the last few years.

(3) Use alternative transport systems such as air.

(4) Pass immediate legislation to implement better control on the flow of traffic entering the country.

Compensation if the agreed time in port is exceeded

In tramp ship chartering the charterer has to compensate the shipowner if the time in port (laytime) exceeds an agreed limit. This compensation is known as demurrage and is meant to reflect what the ship could be earning per day if not held up in port. The charterparty will nearly always also contain clauses as to which delays or stoppages should be excluded or exempted when calculating how much laytime was used.

In liner shipping, the shipowner has traditionally had to bear virtually all the costs of a port visit. However, in the last few years we have seen some ports prepared to indemnify the shipowner if the port stay is prolonged beyond an agreed limit.

PORT PRODUCTIVITY

Productivity

To a great extent most attempts to improve port productivity reduce either the time the ship spends in port or reduce costs without seriously affecting the time the ship spends in port. To know whether the level of productivity in a port is acceptable the port has to be able to compare its activities against certain standard benchmarks achieved by its competitors.

As regards productivity, one of the most commonly used statistics is the *Berth Occupancy Ratio* (see Chapter Seven, especially page 133). This is the ratio obtained by dividing the time a berth or group of berths has been occupied by the time the berth (or group of berths) is available during a considered period of time (week, month or year). However, as a useful comparable statistic it is of limited value. There are many reasons for this but the two main ones are:

(1) In many terminals with a long quay wall there is no determined number of berths.

(2) The time actually measured varies from port to port. Some ports will use the Service Time, which is usually the total actual time the vessel is berthed, while other ports may consider only the working time.

Another variation of this statistic is the *Berth Utilisation Ratio* = Occupancy time/Working time.

It would seem better to consider one or all of the following:

— For each crane or "cargo-handling gateway" measure the number of boxes moved per crane in both the total ship time on the berth and the working ship time on the berth. This gives a gross and net productivity level.

— The number of people employed on the terminal concerned with cargo handling can also be measured, as can the equipment (e.g. straddle carriers, fork lifts, etc.). Therefore, the annual number of boxes per person and per piece of equipment per annum can be measured.

— The ratio of berth length to the number of cranes is a useful indicator.

— Dwell time of a container on the terminal is important but not too easy to measure to get a meaningful result. However, the time for a driver arriving at the gate to drop/pick up cargo and return back through the gate is measurable and a useful indicator. Also the length of time per day the gate is in operation can be determined.

— Further delays lost by strikes should be recorded—say, average days lost per month over the last five years. These are recorded by the various strike P & I clubs that exist— also in *Lloyd's List*. Time waiting for a berth should also be recorded.

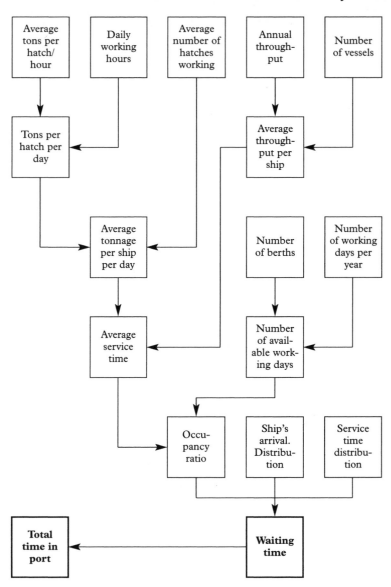

Figure 37: Basic data a port should collect.

Examples of different ways of establishing benchmarks

In most cases the following statistics are calculated as averages of random samples of at least 50 ports taken on a worldwide basis. Where no figures are given this indicates that research in that area is not complete. Note that port productivity may fall off sharply as maximum capacity is approached.

(1) (a) Berth Length/ Number of Cranes = 350 metres where vessel capacity < 1500 TEUs

     (b) Berth Length/ Number of Cranes = 130 metres where vessel capacity > 1500 TEUs

(2) Total working time on berth / Total time on berth. There is no average for this but a higher figure indicates higher productivity.

(3) Number of TEUs/Terminal Area in sq. metres. This seems to vary between 0.53 and 2.1

(4) Average vehicle turnaround time on the terminal when receiving/delivering containers. For an efficient port the average should lie between about 20-30 minutes

(5) Number of boxes moved per person per year on the terminal: no average yet available but one million boxes per person is a *good* ratio.

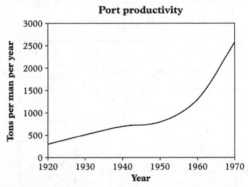

Port productivity

Figure 38: Port productivity.

Figure 38 shows that productivity was relatively stagnant from around 1930 to 1960. From the 1960s, unitisation in its various forms, the increasing use of specialist ships and the carriage of cargo in bulk, has encouraged large increases in port productivity.

This latter increase in productivity is of course well known. What is not so well appreciated is the steady increase in productivity over the previous 150 years.

Safety of cargo—an important element in port efficiency and productivity

Safety of cargo through ports is seldom covered or mentioned by the ports for obvious reasons. Global average statistics are produced and published by the major P & I clubs which do provide some guidance as regards a norm. For instance, as mentioned in Chapter Eight, the UK P&I club shows that for the years 1987–1990 the average for major cargo claims (i.e. claim over 100,000 USD) are:

— 23% due to bad stowage
— 8% due to bad handling
— 2% due to fraud
— 1% failure to collect cargo.

The following are suggested comparable safety statistics which could be collected—perhaps as average figures over five years:

— Percentage of cargo value lost through cargo damage over five years.
— Percentage of boxes handled which is damaged.
— Percentage of cargo lost or stolen.
— Percentage number of port workers who suffer from industrial injuries.

The above data is all recorded by different organisations and could be found by any diligent researcher.

CHAPTER ELEVEN

PORT COSTS, PRICES
AND REVENUE

*How much does a port cost—development of port costs—shipowners'
major costs—total port charges—average port disbursements—cargo-
handling costs—stevedoring rates—typical port revenue and expenditure—port pricing—who sets the prices—costs and cost centres—port
finance and profitability.*

Where relevant or considered useful, costs and prices have been
given throughout the book. The aim of this chapter is to take a brief
look at ports as a whole and analyse how some of the more important costs and prices have changed and developed, especially where
they have been catalysts for change.

HOW MUCH DOES A PORT COST?

This is of course an impossible question to answer in general as
every port is different, unlike ships where one can generalise.
Average prices for Panamax bulkers or VLCCs, for example, are frequently given in the maritime press. Further, ports are rarely sold on
the open market. However, on 18 December 1997 *Lloyd's List* gave
details of the sale of Thamesport, basically a container terminal developed in the late 1980s on an old BP oil terminal at the Isle of
Grain. In 1997 Thamesport forecast a throughput of 240,000 TEUs,
which was a healthy increase on the 180,000 TEUs handled in 1996.
The reported price paid for Thamesport at the end of 1997 was
£112 million ($186 million) which was a large increase on the
£52.45 million paid for it in 1995 when the port was in financial
difficulties, being unable to service its £100 million debt.

In 1997 Thamesport was technically one of the most advanced
ports in the world from an automated cargo-handling point of view

and being on the site of an oil terminal it has good deep-water facilities and space to expand. Further, as Felixstowe (its major competitor) bought Thamesport, the new owners will control just under 50% of the UK container market. Those trying to estimate a model for port value from these details should bear in mind what is in fact the port's biggest problem, its poor road and rail connections.

A similar development that was reported in *Lloyd's List* on 12 January 1998 was that at Taranto in southern Italy. At this port the large container ship company Evergreen were proposing to invest in a new dedicated container terminal, to be developed at what had been a dry bulk terminal. The new terminal would consist of a 2,100 metre long pier with 16 post panamax cranes and a depth alongside of 14.5 metres, though further dredging was being considered. For this terminal Evergreen were proposing to invest $50 million with the Italian government adding a further $11 million.

On 22 January 1998, *Lloyd's List* reported that Antwerp was to go ahead with a planned construction programme that would double the container-handling capacity at the port from 2.5 million TEUs to over 5 million. The estimated cost of the proposed quay construction was about $109 million while the expected dredging costs were to be around $22 million. The Belgian government will finance 60 % of the project.

In September 2002, *Lloyd's List* reported that the proposed new container terminal at Dibden Bay at Southampton would cost around US$ 1 billion. However, the fact that in 2004 the port lost the planning permission battle against the environmentalists does not invalidate the estimate.

DEVELOPMENT OF PORT COSTS

Figure 39 on page 211 (aggregated figures for several ports) and the table below (London figures) indicate that at the beginning of the period shown, the non cargo-handling costs were higher than the cargo-handling costs. In fact, this was the case until the 1950s, when stevedoring labour throughout much of the developed world started to become expensive. During the 1960s the cargo handling costs rose dramatically, and for liner shipowners became their largest cost. Hence one can argue that it was management's desire to reduce this cost that brought about the introduction of bulk

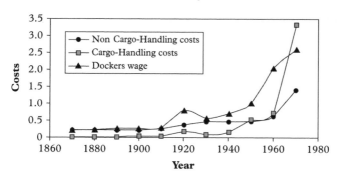

Figure 39: Development of port costs.

Costs in Pounds Sterling			
	Non cargo-handling £ per NRT	Loading costs per ton (London)	Stevedores' daily wage
Year	*Non Cargo-handling costs*	*Cargo-handling costs*	*Dockers' wage*
1870	0.20	0.03	0.21
1890	0.20	0.03	0.25
1910	0.25	0.05	0.29
1930	0.46	0.09	0.56
1950	0.50	0.52	1.00
1970	1.42	3.33	2.60
1990	1.25**	6.08*	

Source: Author's M.Phil.
* Based on £90 per container (world average) with an average load of 15 tonnes.
** World average for dry cargo vessels.

cargoes in the fifties and unitisation in the sixties and seventies. This argument is strengthened when one considers that containerisation first appeared in countries where the stevedoring costs were the highest, i.e. USA and Australia.

The graph and table also make clear that, as expected, dockers' wages and cargo-handling costs were highly correlated throughout this period. However, now that containerisation has made cargo-handling a capital-intensive operation rather than a labour-intensive one, this correlation no longer exists.

The table on page 212 shows how much more expensive cargo handling was in Australia compared with the UK. Presumably during this period Australian stevedores were better paid than their British counterparts

Australia cargo-handling costs

Year	Cargo-handling per ton of cargo (£ per ton)	
1922	0.89	In and Out
1930	1.04	In and Out
1935	0.94	In and Out
1939	1.07	In and Out

Source: Paper by Dr K. Trace.

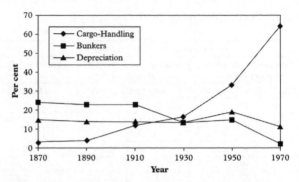

Figure 40: Shipowners' major costs expressed as a percentage.

As shown in Figure 40 above, cargo-handling throughout this period changed from being one of the shipowners' lowest costs to being, after 1950, a rapidly escalating one. In fact by 1960 on the UK/Australia liner trade virtually 50% of the freight earned by the shipowner for carrying the cargo on this route was being used simply to lift the cargo on and off the ship. On shorter routes the percentage would of course have been much higher.

TOTAL PORT CHARGES

As can be seen in the next table, UK average port costs for shipowners are 67% higher than the continental costs and this basic difference in costs persists to the present day. The light dues are often blamed for this difference but the table shows that in 1923 all the costs at the continental ports are lower except tallying.

Comparison between average costs at UK ports and continental ports 1923				
Cost type	Av. costs in £s UK ports	Av. cost per ton in pence	Av. costs in £s continental ports	Av. cost per ton in pence
Pilotage	172.71	0.60	152.48	0.52
Towage	270.11	0.92	153.09	0.52
Dock and Harbour Dues	926.02	3.5	334.05	1.13
Light Dues	137.58	0.47	Nil	Nil
Discharging	2,618.48	8.9	1,574	5.4
Tallying	238.53	0.81	376.48	1.27
Total	4363.43	15.2	2,611.43	8.85

The following table shows some costs for 1933/34. This indicates that Rotterdam and Leghorn are still very much cheaper than London, though New York costs are at a similar level.

BIMCO Journal 1933/34 £1=$4.93				
Port	Cargo x dwt	Time in port	Cost of discharging 1 ton in $	Total port costs per net ton
Bordeaux	Groundnuts 1526	9 days	0.67	
Antwerp	Peanuts 1383		0.53	
Rotterdam	Fruit 161	1.5 days	0.54	0.61
New York	Rye 6491	10.5 days	0.61	1.52
Leghorn	Coal 2803	5 days	0.138	0.33
Philadelphia	Chrome ore 2712	4 days	0.65	
London	General fruit		0.61	1.55

Cranage and winchmen were usually charged as an extra cost per day. BIMCO also reported on a case where the Master checked the labour present and claimed the labour bill should have been £30 not £80. Receivers refused to reduce the price and said it was the normal practice. Half the cost of weighing cargo was debited to the shipowner. There was little evidence of FIO contracts. These seem to have come in around the Second World War.

According to a report made for the National Ports Council in 1969, many continental countries such as Germany, Belgium, Netherlands and France do offer very extensive subsidies to their ports. Even though this was some time ago, British ports are still convinced that their continental rivals do receive considerable "financial aid" in some form or other. However, it is very difficult to prove or establish that one port is helped more or needs more help than another.

These continental ports are competing for a very large continental hinterland and the ports in this case can be tremendous foreign currency earners. These possibilities do not really apply to ports in the UK, though London has undoubtedly lost trade to Rotterdam with its lower charges. Note that the National Ports Council is now defunct but the literature and surveys this body completed were amongst some of the best documentary work on British ports.

Examples of port and canal charges in US$—from *Lloyd's Shipping Economist*						
	20,000 dwt		60,000 dwt		250,000 dwt	
	1985	*1992*	*1985*	*1992*	*1985*	*1992*
Rotterdam	17,000	34,000	39,000	76,000	125,000	248,000
Ras Tanura	4,000	3,000	8,000	7,000	25,000	26,000
Yokohama	12,000	16,000	24,000	31,000	56,0000	85,000
Panama Canal loaded	21,200	49,100	49,000	68,000	too large	
Suez Canal ballast	×	71,000	52,000	114,000	139,000	295,000
Suez Canal loaded	56,000	84,000	65,000	135,000	only part loaded	

The table above compares port charges for different sizes of vessels in 1985 and 1992. As one would perhaps expect, the costs at a large oil port like Ras Tanura are less than at a large general port such as Rotterdam though it is interesting to note that, according to these figures, Rotterdam is expensive when compared with Yokohama.

The table below is a good example of how port charges can vary from port to port and country to country within Europe for the same ship with the same cargo, e.g. a 64,500 dwt Panamax vessel having a draft of 13.25 metres and a length overall of 225 metres (*Lloyd's List*, 1988).

Country/Port	Port Charges US$	Country/Port	Port Charges US$
Yugoslavia	65,000	Italy	30,000
Rotterdam	50,000	France	85,000
Finland	150,000	Southampton	150,000
Lisbon	12,500		

The above table again shows UK ports as among the most expensive.

Estimated cost of port call for a typical 5,500 teu vessel in US$ in 2000				
	Antwerp	*Amsterdam*	*Rotterdam*	*Hamburg*
Harbour Dues	10,125	7,487	22,381	12,762
Harbour Towage	6,209	9,986	8,481	18,171
Mooring/unmooring	2,576	4,471	2,785	2,489
Pilotage	7,516	8,369	9,578	19,689
VTS dues	416	1,272	1,272	0
Reporting	89	197	328	107
Sea Police dues	288	0	0	0
Total	27,219	31,782	44,825	53,227

Source: Amsterdam Port Authority.

AVERAGE PORT DISBURSEMENTS
(NON CARGO-HANDLING)

All port non cargo-handling disbursements—Charges per Net Ton (NT) in US$:

Dry cargo vessels: Average 2 US$ per NT, SD 1.5 (Ship-handling made up 57% of total).

Tankers: Average 1.5 USD per NT, SD 0.97 (Ship-handling made up 55.5% of total).

The statistics above were calculated as averages of random samples of at least 50 ports taken on a world-wide basis (SD = standard deviation).

These costs are usually made up of three groups:

— *Agency costs*. These costs are usually based on a scale of charges agreed by some appropriate national organisation. The fee charged will depend on the nature and scale of the work involved.

— *Harbour dues*. This is primarily the rental charged for the use of the terminal. A random sample from 120 ports world-wide showed for dry-cargo ships an average of 0.186 per NT with a standard deviation of 0.47, while for tankers the average was 0.0618 per NT with a standard deviation of 0.19.

— *Ship-handling charges* made up of Pilotage, Boatmen and Tugs. From the same sample of ports the average for dry-cargo ships was 0.707 per NT with a standard deviation of 0.77 while for tankers the average was 0.5963 per NT with a standard deviation of 0.63.

There are other charges by some ports, in the UK for instance charges are levied for the maintenance of lights, navigational aids and dredging.

CARGO-HANDLING COSTS

Place	Commodity		Charge
	Total terminal cargo-handling charges (1864)		
Glasgow	Pig iron—per ton	(Loading)L	£0.04
Glasgow	Coal—loaded and trimmed per ton	L	£0.07
Glasgow	Barrels—ale, flour, etc.	L	£0.01
Glasgow	Heavy machinery lifted with crane	L	£0.15
Glasgow	Bags—oats and flour	L	£0.01
New York	Pig iron, guano, saltpetre per ton	(Discharge) D	$0.50
New York	Light goods per ton	D	$0.30
New York	Heavy goods per ton	D	$0.44
New York	Coffee per bag	D	$0.03
New York	Ballast per ton	L or D	$0.45
New York	Coal per ton	L	$0.50

This table gives some typical cargo charges per bag or ton as indicated for the latter part of the last century.

Total Terminal Handling Charges (THC)

Average total terminal charges per TEU (sample of some 100 ports in 1993) were US$136.8 having a standard deviation of 56.5.
Source: 1993 WMU student research.

A survey published in *Lloyd's List* in 1997 indicated that many Caribbean ports were too expensive, charging 200–400 US$ per TEU, when compared with most Latin American ports which charged only 150 US$ per TEU.

In 1998 the conference, THC for Hong Kong to Europe, USA & Australia, found that the charge was $267 per TEU.

A report published in 2001 suggested a charge of $80 as a competitive price in the Mediterranean for a transhipment box in a port such as Gioia Tauro.

Typical terminal charges for loading/discharging specific cargo as indicated are as follows:

— per ton of grain 2–7 US$
— per ton of pig iron 5–15 US$
— per ton of coal 2.5–10 US$

— per ton of general 3–20 US$
— per car loaded—around 19 US$
— per ton of paper pulp—around 10 US$

International benchmarking of container stevedoring

"Prices and productivity at Australian box terminals generally improved against their overseas counterparts between 1997 and 2002", according to a new report by the Productivity Commission.

The commission's report, *International Benchmarking of Container Stevedoring*, shows that major Australian container ports in 2002 are now cheaper "rather than more expensive as used to be the case" than Los Angeles.

On the US East Coast trades, Philadelphia has moved from rating equally with Australian ports to being more expensive.

Both Los Angeles and Philadelphia are considerably more expensive than Australia on reefer handling, a trend repeated around the world.

In Europe, Australian ports have moved from being more costly in 1997 to being on a pricing par with Hamburg and Tilbury, and they are cheaper than both for reefers.

Australian reefer charges are much lower than the south-east Asian ports of Singapore and Port Klang. For dry cargo, however, Singapore remains cheaper "though not by as much as 1997".

The price gap with Port Klang, however, has opened considerably.

Australian terminals are still much more expensive than Busan, and cheaper than the neighbouring northeast Asian port of Nagoya, though the gap has closed since 1997. The cost of handling reefers at Busan and Nagoya is much higher than in Australia.

The commission says that some of the gains are a result of more 40ft equipment being handled in Australia, which reduces the per-20ft cost rating.

The shift in exchange rates also had a major impact on the cost comparison with US ports, accounting for half of the increase of Los Angeles over Australian ports. But even allowing for the dollar factor, the price gap in Australia's favour is still considerable. The gains in crane productivity on overseas counterparts were marked, but not as impressive as the gains in cost.

A sample survey of net crane rate at Sydney showed the port closing the gap on Los Angeles, Philadelphia, Hamburg, Nagoya and Busan.

However, Sydney pulled ahead of only one port in the period, Tilbury. Singapore and Port Klang actually increased their lead of 1997.

TYPICAL PORT REVENUE AND EXPENDITURE

Revenues for Rotterdam 1990		Revenues for Singapore 1990	
Port dues	62%	Container handling	54.0%
Rental income	33%	Cargo-handling	10.0%
Other	5%	Marine services	12.3%
Total	100%	Commercial services	11.7%
Source of expenditure for Rotterdam 1990		Sundry services	12.0%
		Total	100%
Personnel	13.6%	**Source of expenditure for Singapore 1990**	
Port maintenance	10.0%		
Other maintenance	10.1%	Authority	89.4%
Depreciation	29.2%	Subsidiaries	11.6%
Interest	33.8%	Total	100%
Other	3.3%		
Total	100%		

The table above gives a percentage breakdown of the expenditures and revenues for the ports of Singapore and Rotterdam. The differences in the lists reflect the differences between the port authorities on the matter of port ownership.

PORT PRICING

See also Chapter Six.

Who sets prices?

(a) The state or regional authority

This has often been the case to avoid unfair competition between ports. An alternative is where the state does not set the price but requires its ports to seek its permission before making any price changes.

(b) The port

The question of port charges has become more significant since the advent of intermodalism has increased the competitive potential between ports.

Lord Rochdale in his report on British Ports (1962) stated:

"There has been a tendency, not only in this country, to treat various branches of the transport industry as some form of public service to which, for one reason or the other, sound financial principles need not be applied. As far as major ports are concerned, we entirely reject the concept of public service in so far as this might be held to limit the responsibility for conducting their financial affairs on the basis of sound economic and accounting principles. In other words we see no reason why the major ports should not be treated for this purpose as commercial undertakings."

For a long period most of the ports in north-west Europe have looked enviously at each other convinced that their competitors all enjoy substantial financial subsidies which makes a mockery of the concept of fair competition. As already mentioned, in 1969 the British National Ports Council produced a report which indicated that many continental countries such as Germany, Belgium, the Netherlands and France all offered extensive subsidies to their ports. When charged with this unfair practice all the ports in these countries strenuously deny such help and claim the situation is totally otherwise. The disparity in the assessment seems to lie in the interpretation of what constitutes financial assistance. In 1969, for example, the Port of Hamburg and the City of Hamburg were treated as one in such matters as street lighting and road maintenance, so who could say if the port was being subsidised in this area? Communities also differ as to their perception as to who should pick up the bill for costs such as dredging, navigation marks, ice breaking, policing, etc. However, in a European Ports' Study by Hulse and Speel as reported in *Lloyd's List* on 20 February 1986, UK ports charge 60% more due to investment, maintenance costs and light dues which their continental competitors can leave to governmental finances. Note: dredging is usually a relatively high cost. For instance in 1962 the dredging cost per ton of cargo in London was 3d (1.25 pence).

COSTS AND COST CENTRES

Charges on ship				
Type of charge	*Nature of charge*	*Charging base*	*Possible units*	*Charging system*
Conservancy	Dredging and charting approaches	Size and trade	Draft, GT	Flat rate per size group per visit
Port dues	Utilisation of maritime facilities	Size and type of ship	GT or length	Flat rate for groups of unit chosen
Pilotage	For piloting	Draft or GT	Idem	As above
Towage	For towing ship	Size and time	GT	Rate per hour
Berthing	For line handling	GT	GT	Flat rate per unit
Berth occupancy	Occupation	Size, type, time	GT or length per day	Flat rate for berth type per day

Charges on cargo				
Type of charge	*Nature of charge*	*Charging base*	*Possible units*	*Charging system*
Dues on cargo	Utilisation of cargo facilities and services	Weights and type of cargo	metric ton	Flat rate per ton of cargo type
Cargo-handling on ship	Moving cargo from hold to quay	Weight and type of packaging	metric ton	Flat rate per ton of cargo type
Cargo-handling on quay	Moving cargo from quay to shed	Weight and type of packaging	metric ton	Flat rate per ton of cargo type
Storage	Use of transit shed	Weight, volume time in shed	metric ton × days	Increasing rate per ton per day
Warehousing	Use of space	Weight, volume time in shed	metric ton × days	Flat rate per ton per week

The above table is based on the UNCTAD Report on Port Pricing and is part of a widespread attempt to get some uniformity into the system. Many ports may for their own specific problems wish to adjust the charging system. For instance, a port with very little spare berth space may charge for its berth occupancy by the hour rather than the day.

A variation on the attempt to standardise port charges was made by the (British) National Ports Council. As the Council is now defunct, its proposals to simplify and standardise port charges never progressed to their logical conclusion. However, these proposals sowed the seeds for change and there have been many moves to simplify the charges. With the advent of containers there have been further moves to simplify these charges. For instance, at some ports, container ship operators are charged a standard rate per container, laden or empty, which is inclusive of dock and conservancy charges, port rates and all normal handling charges from the time of receipt or discharge until the time of shipment or loading to land transport.

PORT FINANCE AND PROFITABILITY

A port's profitability is not a direct reflection of management efficiency but more of market forces. If the port management is efficient however, it will respond quickly to changes in prevailing market conditions. Different accounting methods, different tax requirements and concessions in different countries, and the very varying elements of financial assistance that are offered make most forms of comparative financial analysis of dubious value. However, since the Second World War most ports do seem to have moved in general from being a financial liability to being a profitable commercial activity.

CHAPTER TWELVE

PORT ENVIRONMENTAL MATTERS—SUSTAINABLE DEVELOPMENT

Port environmental matters—sustainable development—the organisations concerned and their involvement—causes of port environmental pollution—port and harbour related pollution types, sources and environmental effects—policies for sustainable development in a port—emergency plans, personnel and training.

THE ORGANISATIONS, CONVENTIONS AND REPORTS

UNCTAD—Sustainable Development For Ports (Report, 25 October 1993).

IMO—Convention on the Prevention of Marine Pollution by Dumping of Wastes and Other Matter (London Dumping Convention—in force since 1975).

– MARPOL 73/78 in force since 1983.

– SOLAS 74/78 in force since 1980.

Oil Pollution Preparedness, Response and Co-operation (OPRC 90) in force since 1990—makes it mandatory for ports to have oil pollution plans co-ordinated within a national contingency arrangement. Since maritime casualties can seriously affect ports, shipping conventions may also apply.

UNCED—UN Conference on Environment and Development in 1992—Agenda 21 of the Rio Conference. This recommends assessment of environmental impact in project planning, port reception facilities, contingency plans for oil and chemical spills, systematic recording of the state of the marine environment.

IAPH—(International Association of Ports and Harbours) has established a subcommittee on Port, Ship, Safety and Environment and Construction—COPSSEC. IAPH has also prepared a draft charter on environmental policy for ports.

PIANC—Permanent International Association of Navigation Congress now includes environmental issues on its agenda.

World Bank—Technical Paper No. 126/1990, Environmental Considerations for Port and Harbour Development.

ESCAP—Assessment of the Environmental Impact of Port Development 1993.

ICS—International Chamber of Shipping.

INTERTANKO—International Association of Independent Tanker Owners.

ISGOTT—International Safety Guide for Oil Tankers and Terminals.

OCIMF—Oil Companies International Marine Forum.

SIGTTO—Society of International Gas Tankers and Terminal Operators.

ESPO—European Sea Ports Organisation (published September 2003) updates to Code of Practice including 10 commandments for managing green objectives.

THE BASIC ARGUMENT

The use of maritime transport throughout the world is necessarily of interest to those who must consider the possible consequences of the transportation of cargoes potentially harmful to the environment. It is also of interest because of the potential for harm to the environment from investments in maritime transport infrastructure and superstructure.

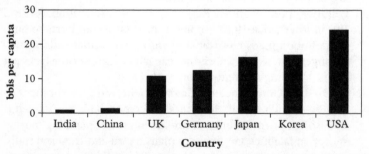

Figure 41: Comparison of oil consumption per person around the world.

Those concerned with global environmental issues often look with grave concern at a future in 20 years time where population levels are greatly increased compared to the present day. Trends in energy consumption, if projected over the next 20 years for the increasing global population, give cause for alarm because of the greater stress that will be placed on non-renewable resources. Other potential effects—such as global warming, sea-level rise, and depletion of the ozone layer—can result from the burning of these fuel resources. While these two issues are not the only causes for environmental alarm when looking at the future, they are both major factors with which the world must deal. (Figure 42, below, is a possible projection for 2025).

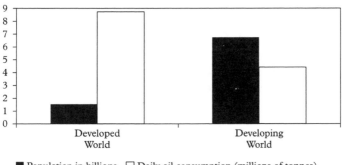

■ Population in billions   □ Daily oil consumption (millions of tonnes)

Figure 42: Global population and oil consumption in 2025 (estimated).

This suggests an increase in total daily consumption of crude oil from 10 million tonnes to roughly 13 million tonnes. If, however, the consumption for the developing world is adjusted based on the per capita consumption of the developed world, then one could expect an increase in total daily consumption of crude oil from 10 million tonnes to roughly 50 million tonnes

From this one example it is clear that the environmental problems will grow rather than diminish as societies develop.

At the same time, these two issues hold great promise for those whose primary concern is the movement of the world's raw materials, processed materials and manufactured goods. At present it is estimated that 80% of the goods of the world are moved by maritime transport. The huge increase in population holds within it the potential for a steadily and rapidly increasing consumer base, and the greater consumption of fuel sources portends the need for distribution systems that are able to handle significantly greater quantities with capability for delivery to an increasing number of locations. While an evaluation of potential consequences suggests that consumption of products and energy cannot increase in direct proportion to the population without incurring devastating effects upon the global environment, there can be no doubt that the world will for many years face a need for the transport of steadily increasing quantities of material to new and more remote locations. This portends a steady increase in the number, and/or size, of vessels that will be engaged in moving these goods.

As the existing global transportation system expands to meet this growing transport demand, we must anticipate the threats that this holds for the global environment. Already busy ports will expand to accommodate the increased cargo throughput. New ports will be developed where in the past there was only a waterway. Needs to accommodate the efficient movement of goods will require the use of previously undeveloped land, or the transformation of existing land uses in the vicinity of modal connection nodes. Extension of distribution systems to reach new locations at greater distances into the hinterlands and expansion of existing distribution systems to accommodate an increased flow of materials will subject areas to new or greater risks from the hazards of products being transported and to the emission effects of the transport vehicles.

All of this is not to suggest that this anticipated development in maritime transport will be bad environmentally and therefore should not take place, but one must emphasise the point that with this anticipated significant development will come a significant threat to the environment. The global transportation system will expand in response to the anticipated levels of economic development and the challenge will be to find a way to accommodate this expansion in an environmentally sustainable manner.

Modal movement of daily global crude oil demand (10 million tonnes per day in 1993)
Maritime mode = 59.99%
Other transport modes = 40.00%
Spillage in maritime mode = 0.01%

Since the international carriage of freight continues to move in increasing volumes through effectively linked intermodal systems, much of the coming increased transport demand can be expected to be accommodated by well planned intermodal transport systems. How the world's intermodal systems grow to accept this demand, when viewed in the macro sense, will have a tremendous global environmental impact. Yet, there will be no single government entity that will oversee this growth and thus, no single entity to examine the global environmental impact. The environmental interests of the world will be safeguarded only if each of the governments, and each of the administrations, organisations and companies involved in this development, take local actions that are in harmony with global thinking. The very fact that effective intermodal freight movement requires careful planning bodes well for the global environment—if, as a part of that planning, principles for achieving sustainable development are incorporated.

There is a great challenge here for those who will be involved with the design and operation of the maritime transport systems needed to support this increased demand. In countries with developing economies, the need for economic development will continue to foster a tendency to favour development at the expense of, and sometimes without a thought for, the environmental considerations. In countries with developed economies, the possibility of gaining a larger share of the export and transport market will provide similar pressures to ignore or downplay environmental consequences despite a growing environmental awareness of the populace.

The greatest proportion of population increases will come within countries characterised as having developing economies. This means that the new market that must be supplied with freight will lie largely in regions that previously have not been subjected to the environmental degradation that so often accompanies the industrialisation process. These are regions which, because of past industrialisation practices in countries with developed economies, have taken on an even greater significance in maintaining the ecological balance of the world. The development here will come and, in fairness to those who live in these regions, should come. But, it must be sustainable development.

The greatest capability of providing the goods, and the means of transport, to this emerging market lies within the countries with developed economies. And, it is in these countries that the largest areas of wetlands have already been filled-in or destroyed. It is in these countries that the greatest contamination of air and waterways has already taken place. The populations that live near these existing transport corridors and nodes can perhaps least afford the consequences of continued development to meet this increased transport demand. It will be critical to the long-term environmental, and thereby economic, health of these regions for any further development to be sustainable development.

A cautionary tale for the over-zealous

In the early 1990s the Peruvian Authorities stopped chlorinating their water supplies because of environmentalists' claims that the chlorine was carcinogenic. Cholera then flourished in the chlorine-free water, infecting over a million people and killing 10,000.

THE CAUSES OF PORT ENVIRONMENTAL POLLUTION

See also Chapter Five.

(1) Pollution from port maintenance.
  (a) Maintenance dredging. In 1997 New York had to delay important channel dredging until it could find a suitable dumping place for the toxic dredged material.
  (b) Maintenance of superstructure and equipment.
(2) Pollution from developing infrastructure.
  (a) Deepening access channels.
  (b) New construction—both the above may unsettle the local marine ecosystem.
(3) Pollution from maintenance and repairs to ships and port industrialisation.
(4) Pollution from cargo handling and storage. With dry bulk cargo there appears to be a widely accepted principle that 1% of cargo is "lost" in the process of transportation and most of this will be in ports. Enclosed handling systems for dry bulk materials were first introduced in 1967. An example is the Eurosilo concept manufactured by ESI Engineers and Contractors in the Netherlands. See *ICHCA Cargo Today*, October 1996.
(5) Pollution due to sea-based activities
  (a) Tanker accidents.
  (b) Discharges from ships.
  (c) Discharge of "clean" ballast water may cause unwanted effects due to the presence of pathogens and foreign

organisms. An article in *The Times*, 18 October 1998, indicated that in a survey of 111 ports, that 79% of these ports had no policy or regulations concerning dumping of ballast water. In fact only three ports had any idea that ballast water posed an environmental risk.

12 billion tonnes of ballast water are transferred each year. 4,500 species of plants and animals transported round the world each day (IMO estimate).

Email for information on ballast water news: *dpughiuc@imo.org*

    (d) IMO seeks total ban on tributyltin and other toxic anti-fouling paints by 2008.

 (6) Pollution from shore based transport operations—the port/city interface

    (a) Visual and noise pollution.

    (b) Traffic congestion.

    (c) Accidents involving dangerous substances.

Top 10 port environmental Issues—Lloyd's List, *26 October 1999*

Air quality, dredging, dust, energy use, habitat loss, health and safety, noise, soil contamination, waste management and water quality.

PORT AND HARBOUR RELATED POLLUTION TYPES, SOURCES AND ENVIRONMENTAL EFFECTS

Type of Pollution	Sources	Environmental effects
Oil and Hydrocarbons	Municipal and industrial effluent. Urban run-off and riverine input. Accidental spillage. Bilge waters, fuel oil and ballast water. Marine terminals and refinery input. Dry docking/repair operations. Atmospheric input.	Very common pollutant in harbours. Large slick spills impact on marine wildlife. The social impact of tar ball formation. Tainting of fish and shellfish tissue can occur.
Oxygen demanding wastes	Sewage outfalls within the port and from ships. Gull colonies. Fishing related waste. Process industry waste (organic). Agricultural and Industrial riverine input.	Organic decay giving rise to smelly and toxic hydrogen sulphide, ammonia and methane. Migratory salmonids will not travel through low oxygen water. Seagull droppings reduce oxygen and introduce viruses and bacteria (such as salmonella).
Litter and garbage	Discharges from marine transport. Recreational areas and all harbour areas. Construction work and riverine input.	Unsightly and a health risk as it encourages rats and gulls. Danger to wildlife and harbour activities.
Heavy metals	Riverine input, municipal and industrial effluents. Anti-fouling paints, chemical spillage, dredging disturbance	The metals can be toxic and cause abnormalities in those organisms, which accumulate them. Shellfish and algae are important bioaccumulators.
Solid inorganic	Capital and maintenance dredging, ship propeller disturbance, construction work, riverine input.	Water clarity is affected and increased suspended solids have smothering implications for sessile marine flora and fauna.
Persistent pollutants	Persistent halogenated organic compounds such as PCBs are components of a variety of materials and effluents. The drins are used as pesticides.	Effects are little understood but may be toxic or carcinogenic or harmless depending on compound. May affect some organisms more than others and in different ways.
Nutrients (nitrates and phosphates)	Agricultural runoff. Domestic and industrial effluents.	Nutrients contained in riverine and coastal runoff can in certain climatic conditions, lead to algal blooms and low oxygen conditions resulting from the decay of algal matter and europhication.
Atmospheric pollutants	Transport exhaust emissions. Volatile organic carbon compounds. Cargo spills, construction work, reefer units.	Poor air quality, greenhouse effect. The oxides of nitrogen and sulphur cause acidification by wet and dry deposition. Harmful organic nitrate compounds may also be formed.

Type of Pollution	Sources	Environmental effects
Noise	Virtually all activity but especially repair, maintenance and construction work.	Health threat and nuisance. Disturbance to local wildlife.
Odours	Cargo/materials storage, leakage, disposal.	Local nuisance with possible toxic consequences.

Level of risk

Level of Risk = Frequency x Magnitude of Damage

The frequency can be calculated from past experience at the port and the experience of other ports with similar activities and geographical characteristics. *Lloyd's List* tabulates most incidents that occur in ports world-wide.

The effect will vary greatly from port to port according to the particular physical features and situation of the port. Thus each port will have to make its own assessment.

Examples: Major claims to large P&I Club		
Pollution claims	*Percentage 1993*	*Average value ($ million)*
Grounding	23	1.6
Bunkering	12	1.5
Collision	12	0.9
Valve failure	12	0.3
Shell plate failure	11	1.1
Wrong valve	8	0.6
Pipe failure	5	0.2
Fire/Sinking	4	5.0
Other	13	1.3

Source: UK P & I Club—Analysis of Major Claims 1993.

Costs

Direct costs = personnel (recruiting and training), infrastructure, equipment, operating and maintenance, creation of laws and regulations, etc.

Development costs—in 1999 a large UK port developing a large new terminal found that current environmental factors added 10% to development costs, not to mention many additional delays.

Indirect costs = protective measures which cause delays in port activities, and in traffic and port productivity zones.

The "polluter pays" principle states that the polluter should in principle bear the costs of pollution, prevention and clean up as determined by the public authorities (Rio Declaration—Principle 16).

Cost Examples 1992—One European port made an investment of one USD million in specific devices to control water pollution while a major Australian port spent almost two million dollars on harbour cleaning and beach cleaning vehicles. The harbour vehicle alone costs 0.2 million USD a year to operate. Zero pollution is not possible and the more one strives for it the more expensive it becomes. Therefore, for every pollution situation, there is an optimum point for corrective measures to be taken. In each country/ port the authority should define such an "acceptable degree" of pollution.

Consider the implication of the above as regards the ports pricing policy.

Note: In 2001 700 tons of styrene, a colourless and toxic liquid, was spilt into the Shanghai delta following a collision involving a small chemical tanker—but no conventions or funds exist to deal with this problem

A POLICY FOR SUSTAINABLE DEVELOPMENT IN A PORT

Objectives

In terms of action an environmentally sensitive port development objective must involve a balance between the exploitation of resources, the direction of investments and the orientation of technological development and institutional change. The objective must achieve harmony between the viable commercial sustainability of the port's performance and the sustainability of the port's total environment.

Within the port authority and other bodies working in the port area, there should be specific and quantitative sub-objectives or targets assigned to each organisation or unit.

Environmental impact assessment

(a) What changes will be caused in coastal ecology by the proposed physical development?
(b) What effect will ships' operations have on the environment?

(c) What effect will the various emissions have on the environment?

(d) How will dredged material be disposed of?

Environmental audit

The EC Directive 85/337 advocates that all major industries carry out an environmental audit. In the UK this is implemented by the 1990 Environmental Protection Act. This applies to every port, including those on inland waterways, which accepts vessels of over 1,350 tons. A comprehensive audit should detail in tabulated and map forms the handling and storage areas of prescribed materials, waste emissions, spoil disposal areas, dust and noise zones and all other sources of pollution. It should detail areas of fishing, wetlands, zones of specific scientific or cultural interest, recreational areas, urban and industrial areas, and so on. It will show the impact of port activities on the environment as a whole and the way in which the port is dealing with these. Such an audit must be available for public scrutiny.

The purposes of an audit will include provision of a proper basis for identification of priorities in environmental protection, where and how regulations such as MARPOL and the Dangerous Goods Code are being applied, and indicate degrees of conflict between uses and interests involved.

In the UK environmental audits are not yet mandatory but port management's can be and have been found liable for environmental damage with consequent punitive damages.

Control

It is obviously necessary that the policy be initiated and controlled from a central point which might be the Port Authority or a branch of the Transport Ministry. An important part of this policy must involve *waste management strategy*. This will include the classification of wastes and sources, setting standards and controlling permits/licences for transporters, operators and facilities.

International conventions require ports to provide *adequate reception facilities* to meet the needs of ships without causing undue delay. One very important decision that has to be made by the appropriate authority concerns the cost recovery mechanism (CRM). Points to consider are:

1. Will the CRM reduce or prevent illegal discharges?
2. Does the measure stimulate waste-reducing measures on board?
3. Is the CRM environmentally acceptable?
4. Does the CRM interfere with free competition?
5. Does the CRM obstruct the "polluter pays" principle?
6. Does the CRM provide an incentive for reception and treatment facilities to apply innovative technologies?
7. Is the CRM enforceable?

Port waste facilities (UK)

In the UK the Department of the Environment, Transport and the Regions (DETR) has produced a requirement for port waste management plans. Detailed requirements are given in the Merchant Shipping Notice MSN 1709. See also Statutory Instrument 1997/3018, Port Waste Reception Facilities Regulations 1997. Under these regulations every harbour authority in the UK must prepare a waste management plan with respect to the provision and use of facilities. Such plans had to be submitted to the Marine Safety Agency by 30 September 1998 and a revised plan must be submitted at two-yearly intervals following formal approval of the plan.

The European Commission has proposed a directive setting tight rules on ship-generated waste and cargo residues in all ports in the European Union. This requires all ports and marinas to provide adequate reception facilities and to have an approved waste-management plan. The pricing system must be such to encourage vessels to use the facilities and it will oblige all visiting vessels to

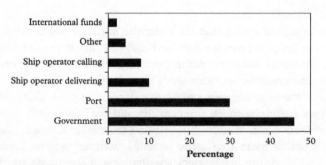

Source: Survey of international port managers.

Figure 43: Who arranges for reception facilities.

deliver all wastes and residues to the reception facilities unless the Master can prove that the vessel has sufficient storage space for the proposed voyage.

Communication and consultation

Ideally these objectives would be arrived at by consultation and agreement rather than by being imposed, and above all everyone should know what they are. For instance the British Ports Federation has adopted an "Environmental Code of Practice" in the hope that it will create a greater awareness of the environment on the part of both port employees and users. Such a Policy Statement should include sections on:

— Environmental management systems.
— Monitoring the environment.
— Preparedness plan.
— Compliance with legislation.
— Consultations.
— List of current legislation.
— List of environmental consultants.

The establishment of a legal framework

See "The Organisations Concerned and their Involvement", on page 223.

Example: NLS Certificate—International Certificate for Prevention of Pollution by Noxious Liquid Substances in Bulk.

Enforcement and control

This is the essence of the problem. An excellent policy which lacks this element is obviously useless. Note the usefulness of civil liability as a means of allocating responsibility for the costs of environmental damage. Note also the difficulties and problems that arose in the early days of Port State Control.

ISO 14001 environmental management system (EMS) is focused on environmental impacts. The idea is to identify significant impacts and, if negative, to reduce or remove them.

Tankers trading to USA must have a letter (renewed each year) from USGC before loading and discharging. The purpose of the letter is to indicate that the vessel is essentially safe and environmentally sound.

Green Award Ships

An award established in Rotterdam in 1994. In 2000 143 tankers sailed under the Green Award flag. Forty ports in the world give some 6% discount on all port dues for ships under the Green Award flag. Sullom Voe gives a 5% reduction in dues to ships accredited by the Green Award scheme.

EMERGENCY PLANS, PERSONNEL AND TRAINING

Seaport oil pollution emergency plans (IMO Contingency Plans 1995)

An analysis of oil spill incidents between 1974 and 1990 indicates that over 70% occurred in port during loading and discharging operations, and a further 12% were from ships in port that were engaged in bunkering operations. The majority of these spills were of less than 7 tonnes; therefore it is important that port authorities and terminal operators develop plans designed to respond to the most likely spill scenarios.

In the year 2000 it was estimated that 12% of all maritime pollution came from shipping activities. Further, of all the maritime pollution caused by shipping, a greater percentage came from non-tankers rather than tankers.

In preparing a port plan due consideration should be given to all emergency incidents which could occur such as collisions, grounding, fire, personnel casualties. Based on the foregoing, priorities may be defined and response mechanisms established.

An On-Scene Commander should be designated and personnel should be trained in the use and deployment of available equipment. Such a port plan will of course be integrated into and be a sub-group of a *national emergency response plan*.

Maritime Environmental Risk Management System—MERMS

This should comprise the following:

1. Identification of sources of environmental risk – such as cargo handling and storage areas, tank cleaning facilities, etc.
2. Establishment of objectives and targets for MERMS.

3. Compliance with Laws and Regulations on Environment, Health, and Safety.
4. Compliance with all the relevant IMO Conventions and Codes of Practice.
5. Compliance with all the relevant ISGOTT, OCIMF, ICS, SIGTTO, INTERTANKO, and IAPH Guides.
6. Organisation of and responsibility for the implementation and maintenance of the MERMS.

Organisation and responsibilities for environmental risk management

— Appointment of a MERMS Manager.
— Appointment of Environmental/Safety Officers who are responsible for the carrying out of site audits using the predefined checklists, and carrying out spot checks.
— Establishing standard operating procedures for each main area of identified environmental risk.
— Setting up emergency response procedures which should be practised under realistic conditions.
— System maintenance and review.
— Establishing a marine environmental forum where complaints or suggestions from interested parties or the public can be aired.
— Training managerial staff to be able to cope with media and pressure groups on environmental sensitive matters.

EXAMPLES

Rotterdam

Rotterdam is a municipal port. The Rotterdam Municipal Port Management (RMPM) is the landlord of the port industry within the legal limits of the port. RMPM provides the port infrastructure and leases the site ready to terminal operator who provides his own superstructure.

RMPM is divided into three directorates:

1. Directorate of Shipping, which regulates the shipping traffic, enforces by-laws and national laws concerning dangerous goods and the environment.

2. Directorate of Commercial Development, which leases out sites, acquires new business and is responsible for port dues.
3. Directorate of Planning which is responsible for long term development, strategic planning and research.

Each directorate has its own safety and environment department. Their activities are co-ordinated by a group which answers to the management board.

The environmental standards are set by the national government but RMPM has its own policy on water quality and quality of silt.

Each year 23 million cubic metres are dredged of which 10 million are contaminated to such an extent that they cannot be dumped at sea or deposited on land except in the Slufter, a 150- million cubic metre hole that has been specially lined. RMPM hopes this level of pollution will decrease and is taking legal action against the industrial polluters upstream. Pollution from ships (of which bunkering has been one of the worst offenders) is being continually reduced by the operation of better procedures.

The port has reception facilities for oily and chemical waste and garbage.

Spills of hazardous materials must be reported immediately and equipment is available within RMPM control to allow for speedy clean-up, the cost of which is borne by the polluter. Computer models are available to calculate the possible extent of the potential damage and danger area.

Polluted industrial sites are being encouraged to clean up their operations. The goal is to make all sites clean within one generation (30 years).

The State has strict noise levels, necessitating the research into quieter cranes, for example.

RMPM is advocating a common European Ports Policy on the environment so that this aspect of cost could no longer feature as an aspect of competitive advantage.

RMPM employ some 20 staff directly responsible for environmental protection and this does not include those engaged on research projects. Some 700 operational personnel are also involved in the process of enforcing RMPM policy.

Sea Empress (23 February 1996)

In July 1997 the UK Environment Agency commenced criminal prosecutions following the grounding of the *Sea Empress* against:

1. Milford Haven Port Authority.
2. Milford Haven Harbour Master.

The charges were:

(i) that the Port Authority caused a nuisance to the public by the discharge of crude and bunker oil into the harbour area and the neighbouring coastline by failing to properly regulate navigation within the harbour and by also failing to take adequate steps to prevent or reduce the discharge of oil after the incident occurred;

(ii) that the Port Authority failed to provide a proper pilotage service in that they permitted an insufficiently trained and qualified pilot to perform an act of pilotage alone on the *Sea Empress*.

The Harbour Master was also charged with failing to safely control and regulate shipping at the entrance and within the port.

The Marine Accident Investigation Report found that the immediate cause was pilot error caused by inadequate training and experience. The Report also suggests that the standards of training and examination in the port are unsatisfactory and in need of improvement.

Following the incident, the initial salvage response by the ship's crew, the port authority, the Marine Pollution Control Unit and the salvage consortium was, say the inspectors, prompt and efficient, but as the situation progressed lack of information, poor communication between the parties concerned and worsening weather meant that all the possible options were not fully explored and mistakes were made. A problem also seems to have been caused by key personnel having to be diverted to answer media briefings at critical periods. A further criticism also suggested that the onshore management team became too large and unwieldy to cope with the rapidly changing incident.

In January 1999 the port was fined £4 million sterling arising out of these charges, however this was reduced to £750,000 on Appeal in March 2000.

INDEX

Added value activities. See Value-added
    activities
Administration. See Port management
Age of cargo-carrying ships, 51
Agency costs, 215
Agent. See Forwarding agent; Ship's
    agent
Air freight, 90
Albert Dock, 137
Algeciras (Spain), 9
Amsterdam (Netherlands), 23
    competition with Rotterdam, 127
Angle of repose, 150
Antwerp (Belgium), 13, 23, 24, 25
    competition with Rotterdam, 127
    economic impact of port on the
        region, 107
    investment, 210
APELL (Awareness and Preparedness
    for Emergencies at Local Level), 77
Armstrong, William, 157, 159
"Arrived" ship, 82
Artificial harbours, 13
Asia
    terminal charges, 217–218
Associated British Ports (ABP), 93
Australia
    terminal charges, 217–218

Bad weather
    damage to ports, 23
    delays to shipping and cargo-handling,
        198–199
Bahrain
    floating terminal, 145
Ballasting
    changes affecting port requirements,
        60

Ballasting—*continued*
    water quality, 60, 116, 228–229
Barges, 35, 81, 145, 146
    Rhine, 88
Barrel, 43, 157
Bay of Fundy (Newfoundland)
    tidal range, 85
Benchmarks
    cargo-handling and storage stan-
        dards, 162
    port productivity, 203, 206–207
Berth occupancy ratio, 133, 204
Berth utilisation, 133
    peaking factor, 135
    port productivity, 204
Berths, 131–148
    container ships. See Container terminals
    costs, 131–132
    cruise ships, 140
    dry bulk carriers, 141
        ship/shore liaison, 141–142
    legal definition, 8
    logistics, 147–148
    maintenance, 145
    optimum number required in a port,
        131–135
    passenger ships, 140
    Ro/Ro ships, 140
    size and layout, 136–145
    tankers, 142–143
    terminal productivity definitions, 133
    types, 140–141, 142–143
    utilisation, 133
BIMCO (Baltic and International
    Maritime Conference) on causes
    of port congestion, 200–203
Bird, J., 26
Blue Book, 73

Boards governing a port, 98–99
Boatmen, 80–81
    charges, 215
BOT (Build, Operate and Transfer),
    94
Breakbulk cargo. *See* General cargo
Breakwater, 7
Bremen (Germany), 18
    competition with Rotterdam, 127
Bremerhaven
    Co-operation with Hamburg, 109
Bristol (UK), 13
British Ports Federation, 125, 126–127
    Environmental Code of Practice, 235
Broken stowage, 58, 151–152
Bruges (Belgium), 23
Build, Operate and Transfer (BOT), 94
Bulk cargoes
    containerisation, 55–56
    handling, 161–162
        mechanisation, 157–158, 159
        speed, 193–195
    proportion of total, 24
    terminals, 41
Bulk carrier terminals, 41
    league table, 142
    ship/shore liaison, 141–142
Bulk carriers
    development, 3
    IMO safety recommendations, 142
Bunker supply regulation, 82–83
Bunkering
    changes affecting port requirements,
        59–60
    port facilities, 82–83

Cabotage, 119
Callao (Peru)
    economic impact of port on the
        region, 107
Canals. *See* Inland waterways
Cargo
    claims, 173, 207
    consolidation, 148
    dangerous, 73–74
    drug control, 174
    pre-shipment planning, 152
    safety, 171–173, 207
        causes of cargo claims, 207
    port productivity, 207
    security, 173–174
    specialised ship type, 48–51
    theft, 173–174

Cargo—*continued*
    tonnage, 35, 44
    warehouse technology, 174
    weight limits, 151–152
Cargo-handling, 149–174
    automated, 161
    barges/barge-carriers, 81, 145, 146
    benchmarking quality standards, 162
    cargo-positioning and stowage on the
        terminal, 152–153
    containers, 162–165. *See also* Con-
        tainer terminals, Containers
    costs, 210–212, 216–218, 220
    developments, 156–162, 169
    discharge costs, 216–218
    discharge using barges, 144, 145–146
    equipment, 166–171
    floating terminals, 145–147
    heavy-lift barges, 145
    impact of technology, 174, 193–194
    manual, 160, 176
    mechanisation, 157–162, 176, 177
    offshore terminals, 146, 147
    operational delays, 196
    positioning of cargo on terminal,
        152–153
    purchase, maintenance and control
        of equipment, 170–171
    safety, 171–173
    ship/shore liaison at bulk terminals,
        141–142
    ship stresses and stability, 153–156
    speed, 190–196. *See also* Port time;
        Speed of cargo-handling
    technological change, 23
Centre port, 6, 9–12
Chain Register, 173
Chain Testers' Association, 173
Charges
    boatmen, 215
    canal, 214
    cargo-handling, 210–212, 216–218,
        220
        container terminals, 216–218
    non-cargo handling, 215–216
    pilotage, 215, 219
    port, 212–215. *See also* Port charges
        State aid and tariffs, 126
    ship-handling, 215
    towage, 219
    see also Costs
Charterparty disputes on safe ports/
    berths, 74–75

China
  growth in economy, 20
Chrzanowski, I., 117
Claims
  cargo, 173, 207
  pollution, 231
Clearance procedures
  port congestion, 200, 202
Co-operation between ports, 109
Coal
  export ports , 12–13, 30, 142
  handling, 157–158
  world trade, 19
Coastal submergence port,   13
Colombo (Sri Lanka), 22
Colquhoun, P., 173
Commodity export port, 12–13
Commodity stowage factors, 150–151
Common Transport Policy (EU), 122
Communications
  effects of computerisation, 58, 111–113.
      See also Information technology
Comparisons
  port development, 23–25
  port ownership, 95–96
  transport costs, 89
  transport modes, 88
Compensation for port delay (demur-
      rage), 203
Competent Harbour Authority, 80
Competition
  advantages of scheme ports, 180
  complaints of unfairness, 127
  distortion through State aid, 125–127
  inter-port, 10, 107–110
    and co-operation, 109
    criteria, 108
  pricing, 218–219
Computerisation. *See* Information
      technology
Conrad, Joseph, 149
Consolidation of cargoes, 148
Container Freight Stations,(CFS), 148
Container Security Initiative (CSI) 71
Container ships
  development, 35, 36,
  sector classification, 53–54
  size increase, 36, 53
    consequences, 54
    reduction of unit costs, 55–56
Container terminals
  cargo positioning and stowage, 152–153
  container shuffling, 139

Container terminals—*continued*
  cranes, 167, 170
  development, 37–40, 161
  estimating land required for stacking
    area, 139
  global operators, 109
  handling charges compared, 216–217
  land productivity, 135–136
  layout, 137–139
    traffic paths, 138
  planning and control of operations,
    152–153
  ship size, 53–56
  top ten, 37
  water depth, 84
Container traffic, 35–37
  growth in the Hamburg-Le Havre
    range, 104
  growth in world tonnage, 35
  trans-shipment traffic, 9–10
Containerisation, 19
  bulk cargoes, 55–56
  growth, 35, 36, 161, 162–163
  problems for port operators, 36
Containerisation International, 26
Containers, 36, 162–165
  CSC (Container Safety Convention),
    163–164
  dangerous goods in, 74
  ISO definition, 163
  labour requirements, effect on,
    185–186
  leasing, 164
  loading/discharge speed, 192–193
  port charges, 130
  speed of handling, 192–193
  stuffing, 163
  trailers and trucks, 169–170
Corruption, 119–120
Cost Recovery Mechanism (CRM),
    233–234
Costs
  cargo-handling, 210–212, 216–218,
    290
  centre v. feeder ports, 10
  charges on ship, 219–220
  comparison of transport modes, 87–89
  cost centres, 219–220
  cranes, 169
  management goal to reduce, 105
  non-cargo-handling disbursements,
    210–211, 215–216
  pollution control, 231–232

Costs—*continued*
  port, 127–130, 209–221. *See also*
    Port charges
  sale and development of port, 209–210
Cranes, 166–167, 169
  costs, 169
  development, 30, 157
  features and parts, 167
  port requirements, 166, 168
  safety, 77, 171, 172
  types, 167
Crew
  ITF action on wages and conditions,
    183
Crude oil
  world trade, 19
Cruise ship terminals, 26, 140
Customs, 81–82
  anti-drug smuggling measures, 174
  Customs and Border Protection
    (CBP) (US), 71
    initiatives against terrorism, 71–72
  Customs-Trade Partnership against
    Terrorism (C-TPAT) (US), 71
  free ports, 12, 104–105, 148
  history of change in procedures, 29
  24-Hour Rule (US), 71

Dampier (Australia), 13
Dangerous cargoes, 73–74
Dangerous Goods Note, 74
Deadweight cargoes, 151
Deadweight tonnage, 45
Dedicated carriers, 35, 48–48. *See also*
    Specialised ship type
Demurrage, 203
Department of the Environment, Trans-
    port and the Regions (DETR)
  waste management strategy, 234
Derricks/derricking, 166, 167
Developing countries
  compliance with ISPS Code, 72
  energy needs, 20
Devlin Inquiry/Report, 178, 180
Direct-call port, 10
Discharging. See Cargo-handling
Distribution centres, 148
Dock Regulations 1988, 77–78, 172–173
Dockers, 8
  Dockers' Union, 177. See also
    Unionisation
  employment patterns, 179–181
  health and safety, 171–173

Dockers—*continued*
  International Labour Organisation,
    183
  National Dock Labour Board, 180
  numbers employed, 177–178
  pay and conditions, 177, 178,
    181–184.
  see also Labour
Docks, 7
  enclosed, 85, 176
Documentation
  port congestion, 202
  role of ship's agent, 66
Dolphin, 8
Domestic port, 12
Douglas, R.P.A., 80
Dover Harbour (UK), 13
Draft, 46–47, 51–52, 54, 55
  correlation with tonnage, 46–47
Dredging, 51, 78–79
  costs, 219
  Rotterdam, 78–79, 238
  toxic material, 78, 228
Drewry (H.P.)
  Report, 1997, 9-10
  review of terminal operators, 2003,
    110
Drug control, 174
Dry bulk carrier berth, 141–142
  league table, 142
Dubai (UAE), 27, 29
Dunnage, 150
Dwell time, 133
  port productivity, 204

Economic Impact Studies, 5
  ports, 105–107
EDI (Electronic Data Interchange),
    111–113
Efficiency of ports, 113–114
Emergency plans, 236–237
  APELL (Awareness and
    Preparedness for Emergencies
    at Local Level), 77
  Principles for Emergency
    Preparedness and Response, 76
Employment
  dockers, 79–181
  employers' liability, 172
  regional economic impact of,
    106–107
  see also Labour
Enclosed docks, 85, 176

Energy
 world demand, 20–21
Entrepot port, 12
Entry procedures, 81–82
Environment Agency
 charges following the *Sea Empress*
  grounding, 239
Environmental audit, 233
Environmental Management System
 (EMS), ISO 14001, 235
Environmental Officer, 237
Environmental pollution in ports,
 228–232
 ballast water, 116
 causes, 228–231
 claims to P & I clubs, 231
 costs, 231–232
 effects, 230–231
 oil spill emergency plans, 236
 risk levels, 231
 Sea Empress incident, 239
 see also Environmental protection;
  Sustainable development policy
Environmental protection, 223–239
 ballast water regulations, 60
 cost recovery mechanism (CRM),
  233–234
 costs to ports, 231–232
 enforcement, 235
 international organisations, 223–224
 Maritime Environmental Risk
  Management System
  (MERMS), 236–237
 MARPOL, 223
 policy for sustainable development,
  232–236. *See also* Sustainable
  development policy
 provision by port, 76–77
 Rotterdam, 237–238
 UK legislation, 233
 waste management, 233–234
Environmental Protection Act 1990,
 233
Environmental safety, 116. *See also*
 Environmental protection
Equipment
 cargo-handling, 166–171
 purchase, maintenance and control,
  170–171
 quantity needed for efficiency, 136
 see also Cranes
ESCAP, 224
Estivage, 149

Estuarial port, 13
 dredging, 78
Eurogate terminal joint venture, 109
European Harbour Masters'
 Association (EHMA), 66
European Investment Bank (EIB), 122
European Sea Ports Organisation
 (ESPO), 123, 224
European Union/Commission
 Green Paper on Sea Ports, 13
 Maastricht Treaty plans for industry,
  123
 port and transport policy, 122–123
 inter-port dialogue, 123
 main proposals, 122–123
 research and development, 123
 over-supply of ports, 121–122
 shipping policy, 122–123
 shipping traffic, 122
 Trans-European Network, 122
 waste management proposals, 234–235
Evergreen-dedicated terminal, 210
Expenditure of ports, 218

Facilities provided by ports, 6–7
Fairplay World Shipping Encyclopaedia, 13
Falmouth (UK), 9, 13
FastShips, 57
Federation of European Port Operators
 (FEPORT), 123
Feeder port, 9, 10, 12
Felixstowe (UK), 18, 180
 privatisation, 93
Finance
 and profitability, 220–221
 port development, 29
 State aid, 125–127
Fishing port, 12
Flag State control of ship safety, 72
Floating terminals, 145–147
 FSOs, 147
 legal considerations, 147
Forwarding agent, 68
Frankel, Ernst, 3, 104, 118
Free ports, 12, 104–105, 148
Free Trade Areas, 104, 120–121
Freeport (Bahamas), 9

Gang size, 165, 184–185
Geen, G.K., 80
General/breakbulk cargo
 alternative handling methods,
  145–146

General/breakbulk cargo—*continued*
  speed of handling, 190–192
  world trade, 20
General Lighthouse Authority, 80
Geographic types of port, 13
Gioia Tauro hub port (Italy), 12
Global Integrated Shipping
  Information System (GISIS), 70
Global terminal operators, 109–110
GM (metacentric height), 154–160
Goss, Richard, 98–99
Government assistance. *See* State aid
Grain
  world trade, 19
  see also Bulk cargoes
Green Award scheme, 236
Gross tonnage, 4, 45
  growth, 47–48
Guide to Port Entry, 15

Hamburg (Germany), 24, 33
  co-operation with London and
    Bremerhaven, 109
  economic impact on region, 107
  free port, 105
  investment, 29
  State aid, 126, 219
Harbour, 7
  artificial, 13
  dues, 215
Harbour authorities
  management boards, 98–99. *See also*
    Port management
  pilotage, 76, 79–80
Harbour master, 61, 63–64
  functions, 61, 63
Harbour patrol service, 78
Hatch size, 56
Hatchless vessels, 56
Hay Point (Australia), 12–13
Health and safety, 171–173
  accidents, 172
  Docks Regulations 1988, 172–173
  Ports Safety Organisation, 172
Health officials, 82
Heel. *See* Ship stability
History of port development, 23–25.
  See also Port development
Hogging, 153
Hong Kong
  barges designed for containers, 81
  economic impact on region,
    106–107

Hong Kong—*continued*
  effect of political changes on, 21
Hub ports, 9–12
  hub and spoke operations, 9, 10
  interchange ports, 9
  pendulum routes, 9, 11
Hull Dock Company, 30, 176
Hydrographic surveying, 79

ICDs (Inland Clearance Depots), 148
ILO (International Labour
  Organisation), 183
IMDG Code, 73–74, 238
Immigration departments, 82
IMO. *See* International Maritime
  Organisation
Industrial zones, 12
Infestation of cargo, 74
Information on ports, 13, 15
Information technology (IT)
  analysis of berth occupancy, 132–133
  effects on communications, 58,
    111–113
  Electronic Data Interchange, 111
  impact on ports, 111–113
  logistics, 110–113
  management information systems, 111
  in ports, 111
  on ships, 110
Infrastructure
  changes in, 17–18
Inland Clearance Depots (ICDs), 148
Inland transport, 86–90
  alternative to sea transport, 86–87
  comparison of modes, 87–90
  logistics, 87
  shoreside distribution, 86
  see also Railways; Road transport
Inland waterways, 88, 89
  traffic in EU, 89, 90
Inspection of ships by ports, 71, 72–73,
  123
Insurance
  demurrage, 203
  liability, 102
  P&I claims, 173, 207
    pollution, 231
  weather damage to ports, 23
Intermodal transport, 5, 9, 87–90
  environmental issues, 226–227
International Association of Ports and
  Harbours (IAPH), 66, 98, 223
  environmental policy, 223, 237

International Chamber of Shipping
(ICS), 224, 237
International Federation of Ship, Dock
and River Workers, 183
International Harbour Masters'
Association (IHMA), 61, 66
International Labour Organisation
(ILO), 183
International Marine Pilots'
Association (IMPA), 66
International Maritime Organisation
(IMO)
chemical spill contingency plans, 223
Container Safety Convention (CSC),
163–164
conventions on oil pollution, 223
Dangerous Goods Code (IMDG
Code), 73–74, 233
International Maritime Security
Trust (IMST) Fund, 72
London Dumping Convention, 223
port safety measures, 69, 114–115
port security measures, 69, 115
Principles for Emergency
Preparedness and Response, 77
recommendations on bulk carrier
handling, 142
International Maritime Security Trust
(IMST) Fund, 72
International Ship Security Certificate,
70–71
International Standards Organisation
(ISO)
containers, 163
ISO 9000 (Quality Assurance), 59, 105
ISO 14001(Environmental
Management Systems) 235
Internet, 112–113
Maritime e-Commerce Association,
113
INTERTANKO (International
Association of Independent Tanker
Owners), 224, 237
Iron ore export ports, 13, 142
ISGOTT (International Safety Guide
for Oil Tankers and Terminals),
224, 237
*ISL Shipping Statistics and Market
Review*, 24–25
ISO. *See* International Standards
Organisation
ISPS (International Ship and Port
Facility Security) Code, 68–71

ISPS Code—*continued*
defence against terrorism, 69
International Ship Security
Certificate, 70
requirements, 69–70
risk management, 69
role of IMO, 68
security levels, 70
IT. *See* Information Technology
ITF (International Transport Workers'
Federation), 183

Jackson, Gordon, 30–31
Japan
major ports, 4
Jetty, 7
Just In Time (JIT) requirements, 59, 87

Kanban (JIT), 87
Keiyo Sea Berth, 147
Kobe, 4

Labour, 175–188
cargo transfer, 59, 165, 184–186
casual, 176, 178, 179-180, 181, 188
conditions, 177
ITF action, 183
development, 175-178
disputes, 178. *See also* Unionisation
"dockers' tanner" strike 1889, 175,
177, 182
effect of containerisation, 185–186
gang size, 165, 177, 184–185
government report (1888) on sweated
labour, 32, 160, 177
labour split, 184
management, 187–188
numbers employed, 177–178,
184–186
decrease due to mechanisation,
185–186
pay, 177, 178, 181–182, 183
piecework, 181
rates, 182
port congestion, 201
porters, 176, 179
productivity
in general cargo operations, 33
in privatised ABP ports, 93
strikes. *See under* Unionisation
technology, impact of, 186–187
training, 188
unions. *See* Unionisation

Labour—*continued*
  unrest, effect of, 22
  working hours, 177, 183–184
  working practices, 177–178
  see also Dockers
Land bridges, 86
Land productivity
  container terminals, 135–136
Landlord port, 93
LASH (lighter aboard ship) barges, 35, 146
Laytime
  demurrage, 203
Layout of terminals, 136–144
Le Havre (France)
  economic impact on region, 106
  lock, 86
Length overall (LOA), 46
Less than Container Load (LCL) shippers, 148, 152
Liability insurance, 102
Licensing
  pilots, 79–80
  river works and dredging, 78
Lifting-plant, 166–169
  purchase, maintenance and control, 170–171
  safety regulations, 77, 171, 172
  see also Cranes
Lighter, 81
  LASH (lighter aboard ship) system, 35, 146
Liner industry
  ship's agents, 67–68
Linesmen, 80–81
Linkspan, 140
List. *See* Ship stability
Liverpool (UK), 18
  development, 33
  labour, 176
Load centre port, 9
Loading. *See* Cargo-handling
Location. *See* Port location
Locks, 7, 85–86
Logistics, 18, 87, 147–148
  approach to transport, 87
  structural changes, 21
  use of information technology, 110–113
London, City of
  maritime commercial centre, 25
  see also Port of London
Louisiana Offshore Oil Port (LOOP), 146

Ma, Shuo, 10
McLellan, R.G., 54
Maintenance
  berths, 145
  inadequate, cause of port congestion, 202
Malta
  hub port, 9
Management. *See* Port management
Management information systems, 111
Manufacturing Resource Planning (MRP), 87
Marine Accident Investigation Report
  Sea Empress, 76, 239
Marine Safety Agency, 234
MARIS maritime information highway, 123
Maritime e-Commerce Association, 113
Maritime Environmental Risk Management System (MERMS), 236–237
Maritime Industrial Development Area (MIDAS), 12
Maritime information highway (MARIS), 123
Maritime transport
  environmental issues, 224–239
Maritime Transportation Security Act 2002 (US), 71
MARPOL, 223
Marsaxlokk (Malta), 9
Measurement cargoes, 151
Mechanisation of cargo-handling. *See under* Cargo-handling
Medway ports, 13
Mega port/megahub, 9. *See also* Hub ports
MERMS (Maritime Environmental Risk Management System), 236–237
Metacentric height (GM). *See* ship stability
Miami (US), 26
MIDAS (Maritime Industrial Development Area), 12
Milford Haven (UK), 145
  Sea Empress grounding, 76, 239
  tanker berths, 142
Modal transport split
  comparison over time, 89–90
Mole, 7
Montreal (Canada), 13

Mooring time, 198
Moorsom, George, 44
Multiport, 67–68

NAFTA (North American Free Trade
    Agreement), 120
Narvik (Norway), 13
National Dock Labour Board, 180
National port planning, 121–122
National Ports Council, 125, 129, 213,
    219, 220
Naval port, 12
Net tonnage, 44, 45
New York (US), 13
    port development, 24, 25, 33
Non-tidal river ports, 13
NVOCCs (Non Vessel Owning
    Common Carriers), 68

Offshore terminals, 145–147
    legal considerations, 147
Oil
    cargoes. *See* Tankers
    world consumption and trade, 19–20
Oil Companies International Marine
    Forum (OCIMF), 224
    safety guidelines, 143, 237
Oil pollution
    emergency plans, 236
    Oil Pollution Preparedness,
        Response and Co-operation
        (OPRC) Convention 1990, 223
    Sea Empress grounding, 76, 239
Oil ports, 12, 146–147
    offshore terminals, 146–147
    see also Tankers
On-board stowage, 152
Ownership. *See* Port ownership

P & I clubs
    cargo claims, 173, 207
    origins, 172
    pollution claims, 231
    ship claims, 231
Paris Memorandum on Port State
    Control, 72
Passenger berth, 140
Pendulum routes, 9, 11
Permanent International Association of
    Navigation Congress (PIANC), 224
Pier, 7
Pilotage
    charges, 215, 219

Pilotage—*continued*
    mooring time, 207
    review after *Sea Empress* Marine
        Accident Investigation, 76, 239
    training and licensing of pilots, 79–80
Pipelines for oil and gas
    alternative to sea transport, 86
Pivot port, 9
Planning
    emergency/contingency plans, 223,
        236–237
    inadequate, cause of port congestion,
        200–201
    national strategies, 121–122
Policy
    port, 117–130. *See also* Port policy
    port environmental issues, 232–236
Politics
    effect on trade and ports, 21–22
Pollution. *See* Environmental pollution
Port administration, 91–116
    types, 92–95
    see also Port management
Port approaches, 61–90
    air transport, 90
    inland transport, 86–90
    sea, 61–86
    Vessel Traffic Services (VTS), 64–66
Port Authority, 94
    governing boards, 98–99
    responsibilities, 94
Port captain. *See* Harbour master
Port charges, 212–215
    comparisons between ports, 212–215
    standardisation, 220
    subsidies, 213
Port congestion, 199–203
Port delays, 197
    causes, 196, 198–199
    congestion, 199–203
    demurrage, 203
Port development, 17–41
    changes in growth patterns, 25–29
    container traffic, 35–40
    factors constraining, 17–25
    factors in success, 23
    financing, 29
    increase in ship size, 51–57
    increase in world fleet, 47–48
    influence of ship developments,
        47–57
    land management, 29
    location, 27–29

Port development—*continued*
  measurement of growth, 23–25
  physical stages in, 26–27
  political factors affecting, 21–22
  specialised ship types, 48–51
  terminal operation, 29–41
  value-added activities, 18
  world trade and, 19–25
Port entry procedures, 81, 202
Port facility security plan/officer, 69–71
  security levels, 70
Port Hedland (Australia), 13
Port Klang (Malaysia)
  privatisation, 97
Port location, 5, 27, 29
  congestion, 203
  effect of port speed/ship size, 58
Port management, 91–116
  constraining influences, 124, 125
  development, 99–101
  efficiency 113–114
  labour relations, 187–188
  liability insurance, 102
  management boards, 98–99
  objectives, 105
  ownership of port, 92–98, 125–126
  policy. *See* Port policy
  reduction of costs, 105
  risk management, 69, 102, 236–237
  role in congestion, 210
  Rotterdam, 237–238
  types of ownership and administra-
      tion, 92–98
Port Marine Safety Code (UK), 114–115
Port of London (UK), 13, 14, 23, 25
  co-operation with Hamburg, 109
  development, 23, 24, 26, 27, 33, 176
  growth, 17, 23, 24, 25, 32
  history of port operations, 30–33
  labour relations, 177–178, 179–182
  lighterage, 81
  location, 27, 28
  river police, 29, 173
Port of London Authority
  establishment, 93
Port of Virginia (USA), 13
Port ownership, 92–98, 125
  autonomous, 92
  landlord port, 93
  municipal, 92
  privatisation, 93, 95–98
    Build, Operate and Transfer (BOT),
        94

Port ownership—*continued*
  Build, Operate and Transfer—
      continued
    labour productivity, 93
  public (in UK), 92, 93
  survey of who owns what, 96
  types, 92–96
Port policy, 117–130
  emergency plans, 236–237
  environmental issues, 232–236
  EU. *See under* European Union
  hidden agendas, 119
  maritime policy issues, 118
  maritime subsidies, 119
  national port planning, 121–122
  objectives, 124–125
  perceived corruption, 120
  pricing, 127–130, 218–220. *See also*
      Pricing
  State involvement, 123–125
    State aid, 125–126
Port productivity. *See* Port productivity
Port safety
  dangerous goods, 73–74
  Dock Regulations 1988, 77–78
  IMO codes, etc., 114
  Marine Operations Code, 76
  Port Marine Safety Code (UK),
      114–115
  Sea Empress report, 76
  see also Safe ports
Port security
  ISPS Code 68–71
  port facility security plan/officer,
      69–70
  security levels, 70
Port State control, 71, 72–73, 123
Port time, 189–207
  berth occupancy ratio, 133, 204
  compensation for delay (demurrage),
      203
  other than berth time, 198–199
  pilotage and mooring, 198
  port congestion, 199–203. *See also*
      Port congestion
  port productivity, 133, 203–207. *See*
      also Productivity of port
  relationship to ship size and speed,
      57–58, 190–191
  ship casualty, 198
  speed of cargo-handling, 190–196.
      See also Speed of cargo-handling
  strikes, 196–197

Port time—*continued*
  weather delays, 198–199
Port Vulnerability Assessment, 115
Porters, 176, 179
Ports
  administrative function, 6
  as business, 91–92
  as cargo interface, 9-12
  characteristics, 2–7
  civil engineering features, 6
  competition, 107–110
  containerisation
    early problems for port operators,
      36–37
    see also Container terminals
  co-operation, 109
  definitions, 2
    legal, 8
    operational, 7–8
  distribution centres, 148
  as economic multiplier, 105–107
  efficiency, 113–114
  evolution through four generations
      of port, 99–101
    differences summarised, 101
  expenditure, 218
  functions, 2, 4, 6–7
  geographic type, 13
  importance, 2–4
  information sources, 13, 15
  investment costs, 210
  labour, 175–188. *See also* Labour
  league tables, 102–104
  numbers, 2
  operational functions, 7–8
  planning. *See* Planning
  pricing, 127–130, 218, 229. *See also*
      Pricing
  provision of environmental protec-
      tion, 76–77
  relative status of major ports, 23–25
  safety. *See* Port safety; Safe ports
  sale price, 209
  security. *See* Port security
  technical developments, 58–60
  types
    by function, 9–13
    geographic, 13
  worldwide growth, 104
Ports Safety Organisation (PSO), 172
Pre-shipment planning, 152
Pricing, 127–130, 218–220
  competition, 218–219

Pricing—*continued*
  differing approaches to, 128
  methodology, 128–129
  responsibility for, 218–219
  tariff structures, 128–130
Private sector involvement, 93–98
  arguments for, 97
  motives, 95
  privatisation, 93, 94, 95, 97–98, 180
  survey of who owns what, 96
Productivity of port, 131–133,
      203–207
  benchmarks, 203, 206–207
  berth occupancy/utilisation ratio,
      133, 204
  cargo claims, 173, 207
  data needed, 205
  increases, 206–207
Profitability of ports, 220–221
PSO (Ports Safety Organisation), 172
Pudney, John, 30, 176

Qinhuangdao, 12
Quality Assurance, ISO 9000, 59, 105
Quality standards
  cargo-handling and storage, 162
  see also International Standards
      Organisation

Railways, 88–89
  block trains, 88
  effect on port development, 17, 30,
      31, 32, 33
  ports with rail connections, 88–89
  Trans-Siberian Railway (TSR), 86
Ras Tanura (Saudi Arabia)
  oil port costs, 214
Register of Dock Workers, 180
Revenue and expenditure
  ports of Singapore and Rotterdam,
      218
Richards Bay (South Africa), 12, 195
Rio de Janeiro, 13
Risk management, 102
  ISPS Code 69–71
  Maritime Environmental Risk
      Management System (MERMS),
      236–237
River police (Thames), 29, 173
Road transport
  comparison of transport modes,
      88–90
  costs, 88

Road transport—*continued*
  effect on port development, 17–18, 33
  EU transport network (TEN) policy, 122
Rochdale Report on British ports, 218–219
Rolling. *See* Ship stability
Ro/Ro berth, 140
Rostock (Germany), 21–22
Rotterdam (Netherlands), 13, 18, 25, 237–238
  barge access, 81
  bunker supply, 82–83
  changing water depth, 52, 83–84
  competition with nearby foreign ports, 127
  dangerous cargoes, 73
  development, 23, 24
  dredging, 78–79, 238
  economic impact on region, 107
  environmental policy, 237–238
  growth, 23, 24, 25, 33
  revenue and expenditure, 218
  specialised facilities, 49
  State aid, 126–127
Ryas port, 13

Safe berths, 73–75
  charterparty disputes, 74–75
  legal definition, 8
Safe ports, 70, 74–79
  characteristics, 75
  charterparty disputes, 74–75
  definition, 8, 74–75
  conclusions of *Sea Empress* report, 76
  Dock Regulations 1988, 77
  dredging, 78–79
  elements of safety, 75
  environmental protection, 76–77
  harbour patrol service, 78
  hydrographic surveying, 79
  turning basins, 78
  see also Port safety
Safety
  berth maintenance, 145
  cargo/cargo operations, 171–173, 207
  environmental, 116. *See also* Environmental protection
  lifting-plant, 77, 171, 172
  ports, 68, 114–115. *See also* Port safety; Safe berths; Safe ports
  ships, 59
    Port State control, 72–73

Safety—*continued*
  workforce, 77–78, 171–173
Safety Officer, 237
Sagging, 153
Salalah (Oman), 9
Saldanha Bay (South Africa), 13
Scheme ports, 180
Sea Empress Marine Accident Investigation Report, 76, 239
Security
  cargo, 179–180
  ports, 115
    ISPS (International Ship and Port Facility Security) Code 68–71
    port facility security plan/officer, 69–70
  security levels for ports and ships, 70
  ships
    Ship Security Alert System (SSAS), 70
    Ship Security Certificate, 70
    SOLAS, 70
Select Committee on Sweating, Report of (1888), 32, 160, 177
Sepetiba (Brazil), 12
September 11, 2001
  maritime security initiatives, 71
Service port, 94
Service time (Ts), 133
  port productivity, 204
Services provided by ports, 6–7
Shanghai (China)
  port privatisation, 98
Ship casualty, 198
Ship-handling charges, 215
Ship management
  changes in attitudes and goals, 58–59
Ship safety, 59
  Port State control, 72–73
Ship size, 5, 48, 51–58
  economies of size, 55
  increase in 51–56
    container terminals and, 53–55
  port time, 57–58, 190
Ship speed
  relationship to time in port, 57–58
Ship stability, 154–156
  list and heel contrasted, 154
  metacentric height, (GM) 155
  rolling, 155–156
  slack tanks, 156
Ship stresses, 153–154

Ship technology
  impact on ports, 43–60
Ship tonnage, 43–48. *See also under*
  Tonnage
Ship types
  evolution of new, 27, 30–31, 33, 35
Ship's agent, 66–68
Shipping lines. *See* Liner industry
Shore leave for crew
  port security, 71
Shore-led cargo operations, 59, 152
Shoreside distribution, 86
  intermodal transport, 87
  logistics, 87
  see also Inland transport
SIGTTO (Society of International Gas
  Tankers and Terminal Operators),
  224, 237
Sines (Portugal)
  as hub/centre port, 10–11
Singapore, 9
  bunker supply, 82–83
  growth, 24–25
  port investment, 29
  privatisation, 94
  revenue and expenditure, 218
Slack tanks. *See* Ship stability
SOLAS (Safety of Life at Sea)
  Convention
  ship security, 70–71
Southampton (UK), 13
  development estimate, 210
Specialised ship type, 35, 48–51
  categories, 50
  history, 49
Specialised terminals, 12–13, 26, 49
Speed of cargo-handling, 190–196
  bulk cargoes, 193–195
  containers, 192–193
  general/breakbulk cargoes, 190–192
  tankers, 195–196
  see also Port time
Speed of ship
  relationship to port time, 57–58,
  190–191
Squat
  water depth, 84
State aid; 119, 213, 219
  distortions to competition, 124,
  126–127, 219
State involvement in policy, 123–125
  State aid, 125–127
  trend towards decentralisation, 125

Steamships
  development, 30–31, 48
  dock design, 30–31
Stevedore/stevedoring, 8, 149–150
  costs, 210–212
    container terminals compared,
    217–218
  see also Labour
Storage
  container-stacking, 139
Stowage, 149–152
  on-board, 152
  on terminal, 152–153
Stowage factor, 150–151
Stowage plan, 152
Strikes, 177, 178, 183, 196–197
  "dockers' tanner" strike 1889, 175,
  177
Subsidies. *See* State aid
Sub-standard ships
  ITF action, 183
  Port State control, 72–73
Sullom Voe Harbour
  ownership, 94–95
Superhub, 9. *See also* Hub ports
Sustainable development policy,
  232–236
  control, 233–234
  cost recovery mechanism (CRM),
    233–234
  enforcement, 235
  environmental audit, 233
  environmental impact assessment,
    232–233
  Green Award scheme, 236
  objectives, 232, 235
  port waste facilities, 234–235
  risk management, 236–237
Swot analysis of ports, 22

Tanjung Pelepas (Malaysia), 23
Tank containers, 164
Tanker berths, 142–143
Tankers
  moorings, 146–147
  speed of cargo-handling, 195–196
  terminals, 146, 147
Taranto (Italy)
  investment, 210
Tariff structures, 128–130
Technical changes affecting ports
  ballasting, 60
  bunkering, 59–60

Technical changes affecting ports—
    continued
    computerised communications, 58
    management attitudes, 58–59
    safety, 59
    shore-led cargo operations, 59
Technology
    impact on labour requirements, 165,
        184–187
    ship design
        impact on ports, 43–60
    warehouse, 174
    see also Information technology
Terminal Handling Charges (THC),
    216–218
Terminals, 28, 34, 38, 39, 40, 131–148
    bulk cargo, 41, 141–142
    facilities, 140–144
    FSOs, 147
    layout, 136–145
        ship to storage distance, 144
    offshore, 146–147
    operation
        history of development, 29–41. *See
            also* Port development
    productivity, 131–133
    public user v. private dedicated, 136
    tankers, 142–143
    see also Berths; Container terminals
Terrorism
    CBP initiatives against (US), 71–72
    ISPS Code, 68–71
    Port Vulnerability Assessment, 115
Thamesport (UK)
    modal transport split, 89
    sale, 209–210
Theft of cargo, 173–174
Tidal estuarial port, 13
Tides, 85–86
    locks, 7, 85–86
Tilbury Docks, 27
Time in port. *See* Port time
Ton, 43–44
Tonnage, 43–48
    cargo tonnage, 44
        increase in containers, 35
    definitions, 44–45
    history, 44–45
        Tonnage Convention, 45
    ship tonnage, 44
        deadweight, 44, 45
        gross 43–46
        increase in world fleet, 47–48

Tonnage—*continued*
    ship tonnage—*continued*
        net 43–45
            correlation with draft, 46–47
Tool port, 93
Towage charges, 219
Trade patterns
    effect on ports, 18
Traffic control centre
    port approaches, 63–66
Trailers for containers, 169
Training
    pilots, 80, 239
    port labour, 188
Trans-European Transport Network
    (TEN) Policy, 122
Transhipment cargo
    competition, 108
    containers, 9–10
Trans-Siberian Railway (TSR), 86
Transit port, 12
Transport
    comparison of modes, 87–88
    environmental issues, 224–228
    EU policy, 122–123
Trinity House, 80
Ts. *See* Service time
Tubarao Praia (Brazil), 13
Tugs, 8, 80
    charges, 219
Tun, 43, 157
24-Hour Rule, 71–72

UN Conference on Environment and
    Development, 223
UNCTAD
    Report on Port Pricing, 220
    Sustainable Development for Ports
        Report, 223
    working group on port congestion,
        200
Under Keel Clearance (UKC), 84
Unionisation, 175, 177, 182–184
    differentials, 183
    Dockers' Union, 177
    strikes, 177, 178, 181, 183, 196–197
United Kingdom ports, 18–19, 33
    infrastructure and, 17–18, 33
    stages of development, 26–27
    tariffs, 126
United States
    anti-terrorism measures, 71–72
    terminal charges, 217

Unitisation
  development, 36
  see also Container/containerisation,
    etc.

Value-added activities, 5, 18
  distribution centres at ports, 147
  economic impact of port on region,
    106
  Le Havre, 106
  role of the forwarding agent, 68
Vessel Traffic Services (VTS), 62, 64–66
Victoria Docks, 159
VLCCs (Very Large Crude Carriers), 51
Vleugels, R.L.M., 106

Wages
  crew
    action by ITF, 183
  dockers, 177, 178, 181–182
Waiting ratio, 133
Waiting time (Wq), 133
  port productivity, 133, 205
  reducing, 134–135
Warehouse/warehousing
  history, 31–32, 33
  technology, 174
Waste management strategy, 233–235
  port waste reception facilities
    DETR requirement, 234
    EU proposals, 234–235

Wasted space (broken stowage), 58, 151
Water depth, 46–47, 83–85
Watermen, 80–81
Weather delays, 198–199
Weight limits on cargo, 151–152
West India Dock, 176
Wharf, 7
Working hours of dockers, 177, 182,
    183–184
World Bank
  paper on ports/environment, 224
World fleet
  age, 51
  container ships, 54
  ship types, 50
World Ports (electronic publication), 13
World trade
  effect of trade patterns on ports, 18
  energy consumption, 20
  growth, 19–25
  political factors affecting, 21–22
World Trade Organisation, 21
  port policy agreements, 120
Wq. *See* Waiting time

Yokohama (Japan)
    charges, 224